The Story o

Ernest Gilliat-Smith

Alpha Editions

This edition published in 2024

ISBN : 9789362923981

Design and Setting By
Alpha Editions
www.alphaedis.com
Email - info@alphaedis.com

Contents

PREFACE

Probably there is no quarter of Europe more thickly studded with mediæval towns than that embraced by the Flemish provinces of Belgium—the old Duchy of Brabant and the old County of Flanders. Curious places they are, some of them, little changed from what they were at the close of the fourteen hundreds; and some of them, so modernised that hardly anything is left to prove their identity but their geographical position and their names.

All of these cities, however, have this in common, and this it is which makes them so interesting: we know something of their general history, and something too of the intimate lives of the men and the women who inhabited them, five hundred years ago—how they were lodged and clothed, what they drank and ate, the way in which their food was dressed and their tables served, something of their distractions and their business pursuits, how they loved and hated, what they thought of this world, and what of the next.

These things are set forth by three distinct classes of contemporary witnesses:—Pictures, a host of them, minutely detailed, with almost photographic accuracy; furniture of every description—ecclesiastical, domestic, personal; written documents of various kinds—chronicles, private letters, books of devotion, guild registers, town accounts. Many of these have been carefully examined, and a very considerable number of them printed; also, especially in recent years, some of the most accredited Belgian historians have busied themselves by writing monographs of their native towns, or treatises on their ancient municipal institutions: notably Pirenne, Vander Linden, Wauters, Henne, Piot, Van Even. From their works and from other sources, ancient and modern, I have gathered the material for my Story of Mediæval Brussels, in the following pages, and which necessarily includes, for the two cities were intimately connected, a considerable portion of the Story of Mediæval Louvain. To this I have added some notes on Brabant painters and pictures, and also on Brabant architecture, with descriptions of the chief mediæval monuments in Brussels and in the neighbouring towns, and such information as I have been able to obtain concerning the great masons who built them.

Constrained by the narrow limits of this volume to curtail and compress, I have been content to set down facts, clearly I hope and coherently, but for the most part without comment or criticism.

Intended as it is for the general reader, I have done my utmost, and my first care has been, to make this pocket-book readable. I cannot venture to hope that I have escaped all error; but I think that upon the whole I have been able to outline a sufficiently faithful sketch, which I trust may be of some service to those into whose hands it may fall.

E. G.-S.

BRUGES, *February 1906*.

CHAPTER I
In the Days before Brussels was Built

The beginning of the story of Brussels, like the beginning of the stories of most of the mediæval towns of Northern Europe, is shrouded in mystery. Set at the time of its origin in a land of marsh and wood, it probably takes its name, like so many German cities, from the natural configuration of its site and the nature of the settlement from which it was gradually evolved— Bruk Sel, the manor in the marsh. So, too, the neighbouring towns:— Antwerp, at wharf; Tervueren, by the river Vuer; Schaerbeek, by the heath stream; Aerschot, the home by the water; and the sister city, the city whose history is so intricately woven with the history of the capital of Belgium that it is impossible to disentangle them, Looven, the wooded hill alongside the fen; and the province in which all these places are situated: Brabant, from Brac, uncultivated, barren, wild, and Bant, the frontier land.

The fierce tribes whom Cæsar found in this part of Gaul gloried in the tradition of their German origin, but it is not to them that the towns and villages and hamlets of Brabant owe their German names. The Nervii and the Treveri, like the despised and hated Celts who surrounded them, were compelled at last to submit to Rome's legions and to learn the Roman tongue; they learnt it so well that when later on a whirlwind of barbarism swept Latin civilisation from Northern Europe they had altogether forgotten their own. Driven for the most part south into those provinces which we now call Liége and Hainault and Namur, to this day their descendants speak the time-honoured language of Rome, and to this day German is the tongue of the offspring of the men who ousted them. It was the Salic Franks, then, who, for the most part, were the builders of the cities of Brabant, and they it was who gave them their rough German names.

In the dark, troublous times which witnessed the birth of the new civilisation and the making of the new towns, two figures stand out pre-eminent—the figure of the hero, of whom later on, and the figure of the saint. The bishop in his embroidered cope, who never failed to throw the mantle of his protection about the downtrodden and the oppressed, nor to vindicate the sacredness of the marriage vow and the sacredness of human life: at his menace of retribution the half-tamed German chief quailed as at the threat of a sorcerer, if he dared violate this man's domain maybe he would stumble on the threshold and break his neck, or perchance a worse thing might happen to him; the monk in his tattered cowl, who going forth day by day from his hovel in the wilderness gradually brought the land once more under tillage, or patiently sitting at home in his cell, little by little gathered up what fragments remained of human knowledge, and so saved what could be saved of human culture; the consecrated virgin whose whole life proclaimed to a people, who knew nothing of these things, the beauty of chastity and the beauty of humility and the sweetness of self-denial; the layman whose heart had been touched by the fire of Divine love, sometimes a son of the people, sometimes the scion of a noble house, and who, attaching himself, often in a menial capacity, to some church or religious establishment, had one object in life—to serve God and His poor. Such were the women and such were the men who in those dark and violent days poured some drops of sweetness into the bitter chalice of existence; they were the chief agents and the choicest and most perfect flowers of that great institution which we call Christianity. Incalculable were the benefits which they conferred on the human race, and the greatest of them all, even from a human point of view, was this—to a people sitting in darkness and in the shadow of death they brought back hope. In an age when, for the vast majority of mankind, the sum of human happiness was so slender, they reinspired men with the wish to live, or at all events with the courage to endure existence, conjuring up before their despairing eyes, 'a glorious pavilion of gold at the end of life's muddy lane,' a vision of eternal beatitude which the weakest and the vilest of them might one day enjoy. Thus Taine, epitomised, speaking of Europe generally.[1]

Profane and fierce were the men of Brabant, 'infinitos prædones, vulgo dictus Brabantiones, qui nec Deum diligunt nec viam veritatis cognoscere volunt,' as Aimoin has it, at the close of the ten hundreds; but for all that they had their heroes, and amongst them, too, were saints. Men like that mighty hunter, Hubert, Bishop of Liége (706-727), the apostle to whose untiring zeal Brabant in great measure owed her conversion to the Christian faith, and who, in the days of his stormy youth, before he met the stag with the cross between its horns, and turned devout, dwelt in a castle at a place called Tervueren, on the fringe of that mysterious forest of Soignes, which still overshadows Brussels, and which still, the peasant folk will tell you, he loves and protects: here he received holy orders, here he sang his first Mass, here, worn out with travail and fever, he died, with the fall of the leaf, in the year 727: no trace of his villa remains, but St. Hubert's Chapel, in the royal park of Tervueren, is said to mark its site, and on one of the walls of the parish church hard by, there still hangs an old ivory hunting horn, which once belonged, tradition says, to the huntsman's patron saint. Men like 'that impious robber Adhilck,' lord of Hesbaye, surnamed the Fierce, one of Charlemagne's ancestors, who, touched by the preaching of Saint-Amand, shaved off his beard, took a new name, Bavo, which means the mild, and changed, too, his manner of life, distributed all his goods to the poor, went and hid himself in the woods of Beyla, there did penance for seven years in the trunk of a hollow tree, which all that time was covered with leaves and flowers, and at last withdrew to the monastery which Amand had founded at Ghent, where he died in the odour of sanctity, tended in his last moments by his friend Domlinus, a hermit from the distant forest of Thor, whom, because Bavo desired to bid him farewell,

THE ABBEY CHURCH, FOREST.

an angel conducted to his bedside. Presently they built a church in his honour, and St. Bavo became the patron of Ghent. Men like Rombold, the son of an Irish chief, who left his father's court and his native land to become an evangelist, and wandering about Brabant, preaching and teaching wherever he went, at last founded, on the banks of the Dyle, a monastery, where he presently fell a victim to his zeal and won the crown of martyrdom, and around which gradually grew up the city we now call Mechlin; or women, like Pepin of Landen's daughter Gertrude, who founded the Abbey of Nivelles and the town which clusters round it; or her niece and disciple Gudila, who led the life of a recluse in the castle of Ham by Alost, and whose bones three hundred years after her death were translated to Brussels, and presently laid up in the church which now bears her name; or poor little Halene, slain by her own father, a Pagan chief, because she became a Christian, and whose tomb you may still see in the old church of Forest, hard by Brussels.

Of these heroic men and women we know hardly anything for certain save their names. They lived in that age of legend and mystery during which Paganism was making its last stand against the victorious onslaught of the new faith. If their actions were recorded by contemporary writers, the manuscripts were destroyed by the barbarian hordes who scourged the land in the course of the nine hundreds—and the biographies of later writers, compiled as they must have been from hearsay evidence, and after ample time had elapsed for the legends to grow, are little more than a fascinating texture of folklore and myth—naïve and beautiful fairy tales, of which the most that can be said of them is that, perhaps, they are founded on fact.

BY THE DYLE, AT MECHLIN.

But if there are no authentic chronicles of the lives of the early saints of Brabant, we know that their lives were not lived in vain; the bountiful harvest which was reaped by after generations bears witness to the excellence of the seed which these men had sown, and to the care and the diligence with which they and their successors had tended it; and after all the ecclesiastical seal of canonisation has been in most cases, especially in these early days, the outcome rather than the cause of popular devotion. As Taine shrewdly notes, man is too envious and too egoistical to lavish gratitude where none is due, and the estimation in which they were held by the people is sufficient proof of their sterling worth. We see them pale, shadowy, vague, like the white cloud which hovered over the battlefield of Louvain, but the victors saw in that white cloud, 'la benoite vierge Marie et Saint Lambert avec Monsieur Saint Pierre semblant de vouloir secourir le peuple Chrétien,' and so heartened were they by the vision that they put to flight the Pagan host, and no less fruitful in results are the forgotten lives and the forgotten labours of those great pioneers of civilisation who to-day are for us but as beautiful phantoms.

CHAPTER II
The Norsemen and Louvain

The victory of Louvain (Sept. 10, 891) marks an epoch in the history of Brabant. The Danes under Rolf the Ganger, who later on became first Duke of Normandy, were utterly routed, and though they succeeded in rallying their forces and for a few months continued their devastations in the Ardennes, Brabant at least was free of them, and after the storming of 'a certain stronghold newly constructed upon an exceeding high mountain whither a vast multitude of them had taken refuge,' the Pagan host was disbanded and as if by enchantment melted away.

Perhaps the peasants, descendants of men who had been driven to the font, had at first lent assistance to the invaders, and that now at last convinced that Thor was not mighty enough to withstand Christ they had withdrawn their co-operation.

For well-nigh a century the storm had raged and the brunt of its fury had fallen on the Church, for it was not greed alone which had driven forth these fierce pirates from their homes in the north, but, and in the first place perhaps, a fiery zeal for their time-honoured traditions and their time-honoured faith: they would have rebuilt their broken altars and brought back the old gods to the lands from which they had been banished.

It was toward the close of the year 880 that the Danes, who had ere this made themselves masters of Holland and Friesland, for the first time visited Brabant. Coming up the Scheldt in their long black boats, they presently ascended the Dyle as far as 'a place called Lovon,' as a contemporary writer has it, where the river ceases to be navigable. This is the first time that Louvain is mentioned in history; it was then what its name signifies—forest and fen. Here they made camp on a little island formed by two branches of the stream, and the site of the future capital of Brabant became their headquarters. From thence they issued daily, and the usual consequences followed—churches and monasteries went up in flames, altars were cast down, and those who served them tortured and slain; whilst the most cherished objects of Christian worship were profaned and trampled in the dust.

In the vast diocese of Liége, which embraced at this time the whole country between the Meuse and the Dyle, hardly a sacred building was left standing. At Mechlin, the only one of the five great towns of Brabant which had as yet begun to exist, there was not a church but was reduced to ashes. So, too, further afield at Tongres, St. Trond, Maestricht, where the Danes had another camp. In the episcopal city itself they fired the church and the monastery of St. Caprais, and cut the throats of the monks. The monks of St. Peter's fared worse: they were nailed by their heads to the walls of their cloister, and there left to die. The Cathedral of St. Lambert, too, was invaded, rifled for treasure, and then burnt to the ground; and a host of other sanctuaries shared a like fate. As for Francon, the bishop, though after events showed that he was in reality no coward, when he heard that the Danes were approaching, he packed up his relics and his treasures, and made for Huy, on the banks of the Meuse between Liége and Namur, where there was an impregnable fortress.

At first, indeed, very little resistance seems to have been made; at all events, there was no organised and concerted action, and in some cases no opposition whatever was offered. Panic laid hold of whole populations, and not only clerks and monks, but stalwart knights and sturdy burghers, turned tail and fled. Presently, Charles the Fat was summoned from Italy in order to prevent, if might be, the complete demoralisation of the people; but though in due course that weak and vacillating monarch arrived with the largest army that had ever been seen in the Pays de Liége, he showed himself utterly unable to cope with the situation, and it was not till the advent of his successor, Arnulph I., that matters began to mend. In 884, after more than one engagement, in which his troops had not been worsted, Charles had made terms with the Norsemen, and the invading host had withdrawn; but the following spring saw their long black boats once more on the Dyle, soon the marauders were again encamped 'in the place called Lovon,' and soon they were again vexing the surrounding country. But for some reason or other the natives now seem to have plucked up their courage. In the skirmishes, which were of almost daily occurrence, they were sometimes able to hold their own; and when presently the Emperor Arnulph appeared at the head of an army of Germans, so great was the enthusiasm of the urban populations that crowds of townsfolk flocked to his standard—Francon of Liége amongst the rest, and his example was followed by a host of monks and not a few of his canons. 'He was the first of our bishops to draw the sword,' notes an old Liége chronicler; but when the excitement was over and the battle had been won, Francon's conscience pricked him, and he sent messengers to Rome begging to be relieved of his episcopal functions. 'It were not meet,' he said, 'that hands stained with blood should have the administration of holy things.'

Great was the joy of the men of Lotharingia at the triumph of Louvain, and King Arnulph ordained that on the first day of October 'solemn litanies should be chanted by way of thanksgiving, and he himself and his whole army joined in the procession, singing praises to God who had given them the victory.'

Though cities had been pillaged and the country laid waste, though heaps of ashes and tottering walls were all that remained of the monuments with which Charlemagne and his successors had adorned the cradle of their race, though art and culture had been well-nigh wiped out, the Church laid low and the State shattered almost beyond hope of repair, there was one body of men in the old kingdom of Lotharingia whose interests had been singularly favoured by the coming of the Danes—the great lay proprietors. Thrifty men who for years past by purchase, by marriage, by promises of protection, by means of loans in times of stress, by hook or by crook, by fair means sometimes, and sometimes by foul, had been gradually gathering into their own hands the freehold tenements of their weaker brethren; strong men who, instead of turning tail when Hungarian or Dane threatened them, bared their breasts to the foe, and with their swords in their hands defended alike their own property and the property of their neighbours; astute men, who knew very well, from personal experience, what an exceedingly profitable pastime it sometimes is to fish in troubled waters. For them the coming of the Danes had been almost a godsend; at all events, a blessing in disguise; and their departure left them free to reap the rich harvest which these rude northerners had unwittingly sown—to obtain, that is, a vast increase of their landed estates and a no less vast increase of privileges, immunities, authority, and of political and social prestige.

In the first place they had little difficulty in making themselves masters, in fact if not in name, of the abbey lands. Many of the monks had been slain or had fled, and so fearful were the remnant that remained of further depredation that they were glad enough to hand over the administration of their estates to the only men who were strong enough to defend them. Thus, by the close of the eight hundreds almost all the monastic domains of Lotharingia had in reality become the property of laymen who, as the monks' avoués or stewards, took up their abode in their cloisters, received and expended their revenues, became participators in their rights and immunities, and exercised jurisdiction in their name over their vassals and dependants.

To obtain control of the secular clergy was a matter no less easy of accomplishment, for although the cathedral chapters still retained the right to choose their own bishops, so great was the power and influence of the landowners that they had become practically irresistible, and were almost always able to secure the election of their own nominees, and thus were enabled, through them, to rule the Church.

But this was not all, such of them as were invested with civil authority now began to exercise it in their own names, and the emperors, whose power and prestige had long ago been impaired by the fratricidal strife of the children of Louis the Mild, had been so enfeebled by the recent invasions that they were unable to offer any effectual resistance. Thus were laid on the ruins of Imperialism the foundations of that feudal system which was destined later on to play so great a part in the civilisation of Europe.

CHAPTER III
The House of Long Col

Foremost among the landowners, who at this time were laying the foundations of dynasties, was Régnier au Long Col, the great ancestor of the Counts of Hainault and of the Counts of Brussels and Louvain, the man to whom all the sovereigns of Brabant, from Lambert Longbeard to Francis II., traced their descent:[2] the son of one Count Giselbert, who, in the middle of the eight hundreds, had made his fortune by carrying off a daughter of the Emperor Lothaire, he was the owner of vast estates in Hainault, in Hesbaye, in Ardennes, and lay-abbot to boot of three great monastic domains. Of the vassals and serfs who dwelt on his lands some, then, were Teutons and some were Celts, and he himself, who spoke the language of each race, was perhaps unable to say to which stock he belonged, and herein lay his strength: he was a man whose nationality was merged in the great feudal chief.

Such a one could alone command the confidence of the mixed race which inhabited Lotharingia, and when presently the Emperor Arnulph set up a German king in the person of his illegitimate son, Zwentibold (895), and Régnier unfurled the standard of revolt, the discontented feudal lords to a man rallied round him.

A stranger in a strange land, without the means to purchase the goodwill and support of the native chiefs, since their fathers had already received in bribes the whole of the royal domains, from the first the new sovereign had to fight for his throne, and from the first the issue of the conflict was a foregone conclusion. Zwentibold fell in an obscure skirmish on August 13, 900, and Régnier became virtual ruler of Lotharingia, and though he had no legal sanction for the authority which he exercised, before his death he had so consolidated his power that when that event took place (915) his son Giselbert stepped quietly into his shoes, and presently the reigning Emperor Henry I. acknowledged him Duke and gave him the hand of his daughter Gerberge, and with it, by way of dowry, large estates, including among other tenements, the castles of Brussels and Louvain. If Henry believed that he had thereby definitely bound his redoubtable vassal to the imperial house, he little knew with whom he had to deal. A contemporary chronicler has left us his portrait, and it is not a flattering one. 'Giselbert,' he tells us, 'was small of stature but strongly built, always in movement, and with eyes so keen and so shifty that no man knew their colour. Eaten up with ambition, audacious, crafty, false, he cared not what means he took to compass his ends.' The goal that he was striving for was, in all probability, a royal crown: the darling wish of his heart was to re-establish the kingdom of Lotharingia. His whole life had hitherto been one long course of treachery and intrigue, and though after his marriage he kept faith with Henry, when that prince died he soon showed that he was still the same Giselbert as of yore; in spite of an oath of allegiance, and in spite of his imperial wife, he proved himself as false to Otho the Great, the son of his benefactor, as he had been in former days to Rodolphe of Burgundy and to Charles the Simple of France.

Of this last act of treason the outcome was death. Surprised by the imperial forces at Andernach, on the Rhine, and hemmed in on all sides, he made his horse plunge into the water, hoping to reach the further bank and so make his escape, but the current was too strong for him, and horse and rider were swept away. Thus died Duke Giselbert (939), and at his death the star of his house for a while waned. His only son, an infant whom Otho placed under ward, died shortly afterwards, and though his nephew, Régnier III. of Hainault, seized his widow's dower, he was not strong enough to grasp the reins of government, and presently the Emperor Otho conferred the duchy on Conrad the Red, a native of Franconia, who, like his predecessor, was allied by marriage to the imperial house (944). Conrad was an energetic and capable man, but rude, passionate, vindictive, and, as the issue showed, untrustworthy. At first, however, all went well: the new duke rigidly enforced order, any attempt at rebellion he crushed with an iron hand, and for some ten years the land had peace; and then, having taken it into his head that Otho had treated him badly, he himself turned rebel. Whereat Régnier of Hainault, and the rest who had experienced Conrad's lash, taking heart, banded together against him and drove him from their midst (953). If Régnier believed that the Emperor would recompense his services by restoring him to the throne of his ancestors, he was doomed to signal disappointment. Otho was in no way deceived by the specious loyalty of his Lotharingian vassals. He knew very well that, in helping him to crush Conrad, they had in reality made him the instrument of their vengeance against one whom they hated, not on account of his recent rebellion, but because of his zeal for law and order and his former loyal service, and he refused to reward these lawless men by setting over them a chief as lawless as themselves, and one too, who, by reason of his popularity, would have all the more power to work mischief; nor would he confer the duchy on another German vassal, for such would be not unlikely to follow the example of Conrad. Henceforth he would govern Lotharingia by means of the Church.

True, the Church had ceased to be the power which she had been in Charlemagne's day. Her authority was no longer enhanced by the glamour of wealth and the glamour of learning and the glamour of political prestige.

Her spiritual life had waned. She had lost much of her pristine fervour, something of her child-like faith. Her sanctuaries had been ruined; she had been robbed of her treasure; a considerable portion of her landed property had been appropriated by laymen, and it needed all her tact and all her vigilance to safeguard the rest, a task the more difficult from the fact that many bishops owed their appointment to harpies eager to despoil them. But for all that she was still a power to be reckoned with—an ally whose friendship was not to be despised. If only she could be freed from the feudal incubus which was strangling her, she might yet do yeoman service for the Crown.

This then was the task which Otho set himself to perform, and the method which he adopted to accomplish it was a bold and an effectual one: he rendered it henceforth impossible for his vassals to interfere with episcopal elections by naming the bishops himself, and at the same time he took good care to appoint none but worthy, capable and reliable men, entirely devoted to his interests. But this was not all; if the bishops were to hold their own in their perennial conflict with the barons, their hands would have to be strengthened; and henceforth it became Otho's policy, and the policy too of his successors, as opportunity offered, to gradually enlarge their boundaries, to endow them with fresh sources of revenue, to increase their temporal authority, and to shower on them all sorts of civil and political rights.

Nor was the result disproportionate to the Emperor's expectations—the bishops of Lotharingia became their most faithful and devoted servants. 'If the Emperor were to pluck out my right eye,' cried Bishop Wazon of Liége (1042-1048) in an outburst of enthusiastic loyalty, 'I would still use the left in his honour and service.'[3] That was the spirit which animated all of them, and for a hundred and fifty years they were able to keep the wolf at bay.

The man on whose head Otho now placed the ducal crown was his brother Bruno, a clerk in holy orders, on whom he also conferred the metropolitan See of Cologne, which included among its suffragans Utrecht, Liége and Cambrai, thus making him supreme alike in Church and State (953). The success of Otho's policy in Lotharingia was in great measure, if not entirely, due to the energy, the perseverance, the courage, and, above all, to the consummate tact and the marvellous administrative capacity of this great man. His work was essentially a constructive one, out of chaos he brought order, and his success as an organiser and administrator was only equalled by his success as an educator. 'His schools at Cologne,' says M. Pirenne, 'were frequented not only by clerks who aspired to ecclesiastical dignities, but also by young nobles—for many of the feudal lords confided their sons to his care—and all of them returned reconciled to the Empire and entirely subjugated by the charm of the Archbishop-Duke.'[4] In the twelve years during which he governed Lotharingia—he died in 965—he succeeded not only in pacifying that rebellious province, but, if we may trust his biographer, in working a marvellous change in the lives and morals of its inhabitants: 'he found them,' says Ruotger, 'rugged and fierce, and he left them gentle and tame'; and though the conversion of the vast majority was sufficiently short-lived—when the benign influence of Bruno was withdrawn they soon relapsed into their old blood-thirsty and lawless ways—the grandeur of his work is sufficiently appreciable when we compare such ruffians as Régnier au Long Col, for instance, or his slippery son Giselbert, with one who came immediately under Bruno's influence, whose character, indeed, he formed—his friend and disciple Ansfried, Count of Louvain, who, after having been for long years a faithful and devoted servant of the Emperor, at last took orders, became Bishop of Utrecht, and died in the odour of sanctity; or to men like Godfrey of Verdun, the most perfect type of those nobles whom Bruno had reconciled to the imperial cause, a man who had no more sympathy for feudal aspirations than had Bruno himself, and whose staunch loyalty may be gauged from the message he sent to his wife when he was a captive in a French prison, and which has been preserved for us in the Memoirs of Gerbert—who afterwards became Pope Sylvester II. (997-1003)—whom he charged to deliver it:—'Remain staunch in your fidelity to the ever august Empress and her son. Make no truce with the French; hold your forts firm against their king, and let not the hope of restoring your husband and your son to liberty diminish the energy of your resistance.'[5]

I.—Genealogical Table of the House of Long-Col

Régnier au Long-Col., *d.* 915

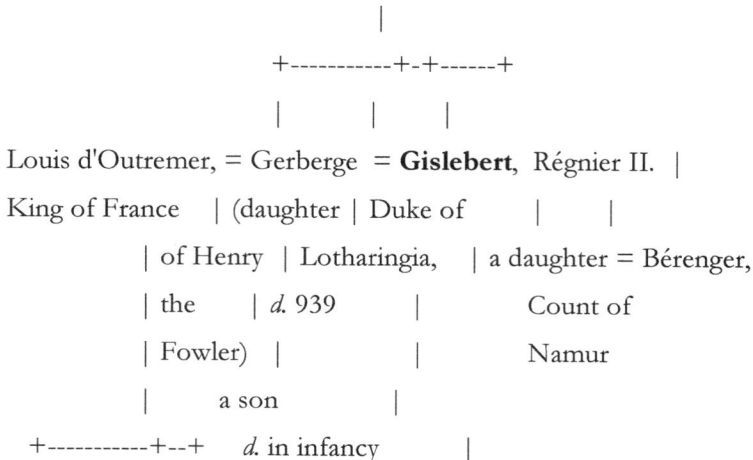

```
                        |
           +-----------+-+------+
           |           |        |
Louis d'Outremer, = Gerberge = Gislebert, Régnier II. |
King of France   | (daughter | Duke of        |      |
                 | of Henry  | Lotharingia,   | a daughter = Bérenger,
                 | the       | d. 939         |          Count of
                 | Fowler)   |                |          Namur
                 |        a son              |
      +-----------+--+    d. in infancy       |
```

```
    |         |                    |
Lothaire,  **Charles**, Duke of       Régnier III. *d.* 958
King of    Lower Lotharingia,          |    (in exile in
France,    *d.* 992                     |    Bohemia)
*d.* 987      |                         |
              |                         |
      +--------+-------+        +---------+----------+
      |         |       |        |
```

Otho, Duke of   Gerberge = **Lambert Longbeard**,   **Régnier IV.**,
Count

Lower Lotharingia,   first hereditary   of Hainault,

d. 1012   Count of Louvain,   *d.* 1013

                          d. 1015

Between Régnier of Hainault, that half-tamed leader of rebels, and the gentle scholar and polished gentleman, Saint Bruno of Cologne—men whose dispositions were so different and whose interests and ideals were so diametrically opposed, the one the incarnation of feudal chaos and feudal license, and the other the representative of imperial liberty and imperial law, each of them endowed with unflagging perseverance, and an indomitable will—no treaty of peace would have been possible, even if Régnier had not believed that the Emperor had ungratefully bestowed on Bruno the inheritance which was lawfully his, and from the first they were at daggers drawn.

As was natural, the man who had been rejected did all in his power to thwart his successful rival and to frustrate his projects of reform. For three years the conflict continued and then Bruno was able to pluck the thorn from his side. Fortune delivered his tormentor into his hands and he forthwith banished him to Bohemia and detained him there until he went the way of all flesh. But the house of Long Col was not extinguished by the death of its chief—the old count had two sons, Régnier and Lambert, who, when their father was captured and his estates confiscated, found an asylum in France at the Court of King Lothaire. The French monarchs, as direct heirs of Charlemagne, had always regarded Lotharingia as their own inheritance, and Lothaire himself and his brother Charles were the sons of

Duke Giselbert's widow Gerberge by her second husband, Louis d'Outremer.

Thus ties of kindred and a common grievance disposed the French king to befriend the children of Régnier of Hainault, and at his Court they remained for fifteen years nourishing their enmity against Bruno and the Emperor, and praying for an opportunity of vengeance. At last the day of reckoning came. The strong and gentle hand of Bruno had been removed by death in 965, and Otho the Great was gathered to his fathers in 973.

Taking advantage of the confusion incident on this last event Charles of France now claimed his mother's dowry, and Régnier and Lambert their father's estates, and presently they invaded Lotharingia to make good their demands at the sword's point.

Welcomed by the feudal chiefs and backed by the power of France, so formidable were the invaders that Otho II. deemed it prudent to treat with them and at last restored their paternal heritage to Régnier and Lambert and conferred the duchy on Charles. Two considerations made him the more ready to grant this last concession. Charles on his father's side was a descendant of Charlemagne and as such was likely to be a persona grata to the nobles, many of whom had Carolingian blood in their veins, and through his mother he was the grandson of Henry the Fowler, thus first cousin to Otho himself, and hence there was reason to believe that he would prove a loyal vassal.

Otho's hopes, however, were only partly realised. He had no reason to suspect Charles's good faith, but the feudal chiefs, with Régnier and Lambert at their head, so far from acknowledging the new duke, did all in their power to second the desperate efforts which Lothaire was making to annex Lotharingia, efforts which in despite of his allies were doomed to disappointment. True he at one time succeeded in reaching the imperial palace at Aachen, and there 'had the satisfaction of eating a dinner which had been prepared for Otho himself,' but he was forced to beat a hasty retreat, and his death, which took place shortly afterwards, followed as it was by the death of his only son, left the Emperor master of the situation (987), and Duke Charles heir to a crown which he was never able to wear. Hugh Capet, who for years past had been drawing nearer and nearer to the French throne, had himself proclaimed king at Noyon, and though Charles fought valiantly for his heritage, and there seemed every likelihood that his efforts would meet with success, he failed, almost in the hour of triumph: treacherously delivered into the hands of the usurper by the Bishop of Laon, he was cast into prison at Orléans where he shortly afterwards died (992).

This unfortunate prince is the first ruler whose name is intimately associated with Brussels. Tradition says that he was born there, and he certainly made it his chief place of abode. His palace was situated on a little island between two branches of the Senne, somewhere about the site now occupied by the Place Saint Géry, and that little island contained the whole of the settlement called Brussels, for in those days Brussels was not a town, it was little more than a castle and a cluster of huts:—the dwellings of such of the ducal servants and court officials as were not lodged in the castle itself and of those who catered for the ducal household and maybe also the homesteads of a few farmers whom a sense of greater security had induced to settle there.

Charles was succeeded in the Duchy of Lotharingia by his only son Otho, and when he died childless twenty years afterwards (1012), Lambert Long Col, who had married Charles's eldest daughter Gerberge, claimed his heritage as next-of-kin. He did not obtain the dukedom—that dignity fell to Godfrey of Ardennes, the son of Bruno's pupil, Godfrey the Captive—but he managed to make good his claim to a very considerable portion of his father-in-law's maternal heritage—the rich dowry which Henry the Fowler had bestowed on his daughter, the elder Gerberge, on her marriage with Duke Giselbert, and which later the Emperor Otho II. had granted to Duke Charles, her son by her second marriage. The castles of Louvain and Vilvorde and Brussels, and all the adjoining territory, fell to Lambert's share, and this vast and rich domain, called until the close of the century sometimes the county of Brussels, more often the county of Louvain, was the nucleus of the Duchy of Brabant.

CHAPTER IV
The Making of the Duchy of Brabant

In obtaining legal recognition of his right to the county of Louvain, Lambert I., as we must now call him, had accomplished something, but the house of Long Col had not yet realised, nor was it ever to wholly realise, the darling dream of its ambition—the establishment in Lotharingia of an independent realm, although that cherished wish did, in later days, receive some measure of fulfilment: in their long contest with the Empire the triumph of the barons was presently assured, and with the title of Duke the Counts of Louvain at last obtained practical independence.

It was on the Church, as we have seen, that the emperors mainly relied for the maintenance of their authority in Lotharingia, and by a strange irony of fate it was to the Church that the overthrow of that authority was in great measure due. Not that the bishops belied their trust: against tremendous odds they held the fortress which had been confided to their keeping for over a hundred years, and only at last surrendered when their master's breach with the papacy gave to his turbulent vassals what had before been lacking to them—a legitimate excuse for rebellion. Given the conjunction of events, no other issue was possible. The bishops had no choice: the quarrel concerning investiture broke the back of imperial rule.

Amongst the clergy the monks alone had succeeded in endearing themselves to the native population, and the power which they wielded was immense. The bishops—learned, capable, God-fearing men as most of them undoubtedly were, had never been able to gain the confidence of the people: save to the higher clergy, whom they had formed, and to a handful of the lay aristocracy who had received their education at Liége or Cologne, they were almost unknown to them. It could hardly have been otherwise, they were strangers in a strange land, they were the standard-bearers of order amid a barbarous people, whose lawlessness filled them with horror and contempt, and of whose very language they were in many cases ignorant. Well might they bewail their lot in the words of Tetdon of Cambrai, for a moment cast down at the hopelessness of the task before him, 'O wretched man that thou art, in vain didst thou quit thy native land for this land of savages!'

The lot of the regular clergy, and the conditions under which they laboured were altogether different. The strong man who by his marvellous energy, his burning zeal, his eloquence, his sweetness, his piety, and, above all, by the example of his stainless life, had made of the undisciplined rabble, who, calling themselves monks, scoffed at the Evangelical counsels, and hardly believed in the Gospel, an army of humble, hard-working men, ever ready to spend themselves and be spent in the service of Christ, was himself nurtured in the bosom of feudalism: Gerard of Brogne wore a coat of mail before he put on the monk's frock. One day out hunting in his own domain along with his master, Count Bérenger of Namur, a son-in-law of Régnier au Long Col, he had turned into a wayside chapel to pray, whilst the rest of the party were dining. Presently he fell asleep, and dreamed that St. Peter bid him build a church there and dedicate it to St. Eugène. That was the origin of the famous abbey of Brogne, and Gerard became its first abbot (923). Presently the rumour spread abroad that a band of monks who kept their rule had established themselves in the Forest of Namurois, and that their leader was a saint. Strangers flocked from far and wide to see if such things could be, and Brogne became a place of pilgrimage. Soon the fame of Gerard's holiness outstepped the borders of Namur: at the request of Duke Giselbert (915-939) he reformed the abbeys of Lotharingia; later on (965-976) summoned to Cambrai by Bishop Tetdon, and to Flanders by Arnulph the Great,[6] he accomplished a like work in their domains; before his death, towards the close of the century, there was hardly a religious house from the Meuse to the sea which he had not set in order. Nor was this all, so great was his influence with the feudal lords that many of them who held ecclesiastical appointments resigned them, and everywhere the right of free election was restored; a host of new monasteries were founded, some due to the munificence of the feudal aristocracy, others to that of their political opponents, the bishops; and so great was the religious enthusiasm of the people that they gave their time and labour freely for the erection of these buildings. Gerard was crowned with the aureole of sanctity—that was the secret of his success: he loved God with his whole heart and his neighbour as himself; he was inspired by 'that wisdom which proceedeth from the mouth of the Most High, and reacheth from end to end, and mightily and sweetly setteth all things in order.'

The great reformer's interpretation of the rule of St. Benedict, a rule which leaves much to the discretion of local superiors, was large, mild, tolerant, without exaggerated asceticism. His disciples, like their master, in touch with baron and bishop, were careful not to compromise their good relations with the Episcopate by any expression of sympathy with the ideals of feudalism. Indeed, St. Gerard's anonymous biographer, who most likely was a monk of his own abbey at Brogne, does not even spare Duke Giselbert, his master's chief benefactor, averring that his untimely end was a just punishment for his rebellion:—'Sicque completur vaticinium psalmigraphi qui dicit *Homo cum in honore esset, non intellexit.* Ob ambitionem quipe regni circa eos istud obvenit.'

Such was the monasticism of Gerard of Brogne and such was the spirit which for half a century after his death inspired his disciples. The work which they accomplished was immense. The influence which they exercised is almost incredible. The Low Countries became for the time more devout than any other region of Europe; in the eyes of the people the monk alone was the true servant of God, the incarnation in his own person of the mystical body of Christ. A wave of religious enthusiasm swept over the land, and it prepared men's minds to receive later on a more drastic reform of which the consequences were momentous.

Lavish in alms-deeds, given to hospitality, a loyal friend to the poor and oppressed, upright, virtuous, dogged, keen, ever ready to do battle for justice sake, contemned and worshipped, beloved and loathed, such was the monk of Cluny. Uncompromising in his championship of the rights of the clergy and of the rights of the apostolic See, clerical laxity and lay interference alike stank in his nostrils, for him the bishop whom the Emperor had named was a Simonist, and the married clerk an adulterer. Gentle to others sometimes, always stern to himself, strait was the gate and narrow the way by which he went to Paradise. To fast, to labour, to keep silence, to submit, these things were to him meat and drink; his one earthly consolation was in the sweetness of his psalmody and the splendour of his ritual, and in magnifying the glory of the priesthood collectively he perhaps found some compensation for his complete abasement of self. His manner of life, he averred, was in strict accord with the spirit of the old Benedictine rule, he alone of the monks of his day had discovered its true meaning, but for better or worse the reform of Cluny constituted in fact a new order, for one essential feature of Benedictine life, the family tie, was all but blotted out: wherever Cluniac discipline prevailed the local abbot ceased to be his own master, he obeyed the Abbot of Cluny, and the monk no longer regarded his own monastery as his only home—he was a member of a vast international community, and in each of the hundred homes of his Order he was sure of a welcome as a son of the house.

Inaugurated at the beginning of the nine hundreds by William of Aquitaine, who had exchanged a ducal coronet for a monk's cowl, perfected by a series of capable rulers, who were possessed of that faith which removes mountains and whose consistency of life inspired respect, the new order rapidly spread from province to province and realm to realm till at length it became a power in Christendom.

Early in the ten hundreds 'the sweet savour of its good report' began to fascinate the monks of the Netherlands, and though some of the elder brethren who remembered St. Gerard or had been trained by his immediate disciples had little liking for these new-fangled French ways, monastery after monastery adopted them. A wave of enthusiasm swept the land and bore down all opposition. The people from honest conviction were heart and soul with the movement, the lay lords who saw in Clunyism a weapon to further their own ends favoured it with no less zeal; the bishops, in spite of their imperialism, were carried along with the stream, and by the close of the century there was hardly a religious house in the Netherlands which had not adopted the new rule.

Notwithstanding their conversion to Clunyism the bishops were still at heart true to their old political creed, or may be their ingrained loyalty to the Empire was stronger than their religious belief, certain it is that they did not at first translate their new theories into action. When the investiture quarrel broke out, they were among the staunchest of the Emperor's adherents, but as the relations between their master and the Holy See became more and more strained they began to falter, uncertain which road to take, and at last the time came when no further choice was left them—in spite of themselves they were constrained to separate their cause from his: the lay aristocracy were in open rebellion, the people aroused by the preaching of the monks were raging against the married clergy and 'those Simonists the bishops,' with a violence past belief; Godfrey the Hunchback, the one man who might perhaps have quelled the storm, had been struck down by the hand of an assassin.

If that rickety, misshapen dwarf had lived, the course of events might have been different. Duke Godfrey was a man of marvellous enterprise, undaunted courage and indomitable will; a man, too, of infinite tact— shrewd, long-headed, keen, and withal a convinced believer in the justice of the imperial cause. Through good report and evil report he had been true to Henry; he was his intimate counsellor and devoted friend, and the only man who had any influence over him for good. He always showed himself a staunch supporter of the bishops, and during the six years of his government of Lotharingia (1070-1076), with their aid he had kept the feudal lords at bay. If he had lived out his days he might perhaps have been able to curb alike the violence of Henry and of his vassals, and thus have averted the terrible chastisement which afterwards overtook his master's misdeeds. He was the last Duke of Lotharingia who exercised, as such, any real power in the land, and his death was the deathblow of imperialism in this quarter of Europe, but the agony was not a short one: it was prolonged for thirty years, and then came the funeral.

Though circumstances had compelled the bishops to withdraw their support from the Emperor, there was one amongst them, Otbert of Liége, who clung to him to the bitter end. Cut off from the society of Christian men, deserted by his wife, a fugitive from his own son, it was in Otbert's episcopal city that the old Emperor found a refuge during the closing months of his chequered career. Inspired by their bishop, the men of Liége banded together to defend him, and with such success that they drove young Henry from the town. Nor was this all. So great was their pity for the misfortunes of the fallen Emperor that they altogether forgot the follies and the crimes which had produced them. In their eyes, the sinner had become a saint; and when he died they pressed round his coffin to touch his poor lifeless body as though it were some holy thing, and strewed over it their seed-corn, firmly convinced that by so doing they would insure a bountiful harvest. Henry was excommunicate, and as such it was impossible to give him Christian burial. They laid him to rest in a small unconsecrated chapel beyond the city walls, without dirge or requiem, and his mournful funeral, to quote the words of Pirenne, was the funeral of imperial rule in Lotharingia.

When Duke Godfrey the Hunchback died in 1076, Henry IV., perhaps because at that time he mistrusted Godfrey of Bouillon, the late Duke's nephew, and the next in the line of succession, had conferred the Duchy of Lotharingia on his own son Conrad, a child of two years old, thus, to all intents and purposes, leaving the throne vacant—a false move, which Henry himself recognised too late: when, in 1089, he set the crown on the head of the rightful heir, the feudal lords, who for thirteen years had been accustomed to the sweets of anarchy, refused to acknowledge him, Godfrey, who lacked what had always been the mainstay of his predecessors—episcopal co-operation, was not strong enough to coerce them, and the old imperial dukedom became little more than an empty title. The man who held it was almost a nonentity in his own dominions; and when, in 1096, he set out on that eastern expedition which gave him a name, and from which he never returned, the barons were left to their own devices for over five years, and then at last Henry set over them his namesake, Henry of Limbourg, almost the only one of his Lotharingian vassals who kept faith with him to the end. This man, when Henry V. put on his father's crown, refused to acknowledge the usurper, who in consequence deprived him of his duchy and conferred it on the fallen Emperor's direst foe, Count Godfrey of Louvain—this was only a few weeks before the elder Henry's death—and, at the same time, he gave him the March of Antwerp, 'the land of Ryen,' as it was then called, an imperial fief which had been held by the Dukes of Lotharingia since the days of Godfrey the Hunchback certainly, and most likely since the days of his grandfather, Gothelon I., and which brought the territory of the Counts of Louvain right up to the banks of the Scheldt. Henceforth that territory was known as the Duchy of Brabant, and the man who owned it styled himself Duke of Brabant and Lotharingia. Thus at last did the house of Long Col obtain the title its chiefs had so long coveted, and for which throughout so many generations they had intrigued and fought. It was nothing more than an empty title now—a mere name, which, perhaps from old-time associations, added something to Godfrey's prestige, but gave him no increase of territory, and in no way augmented his power. He was the most redoubtable prince in the Netherlands, but he owed his strength to his mighty hand and his outstretched arm, not to his phantom duchy. Presently the Emperor deprived him of it in favour of the rival house of Limbourg (1128). Matter of little moment to either dynasty: in Louvain the imperial mandate was ignored, and in Limbourg it had long ago been anticipated, and for more than a hundred and fifty years the chiefs of each house continued to use the illusory title. Then, at last, the fortunes of war gave Limbourg to John the Victorious, and henceforth the Dukes of Brabant were the only Dukes of Lotharingia (1288).

II.—Genealogical Table of the Counts of Louvain

Lambert Longbeard

d. 1015. (See Table I.)

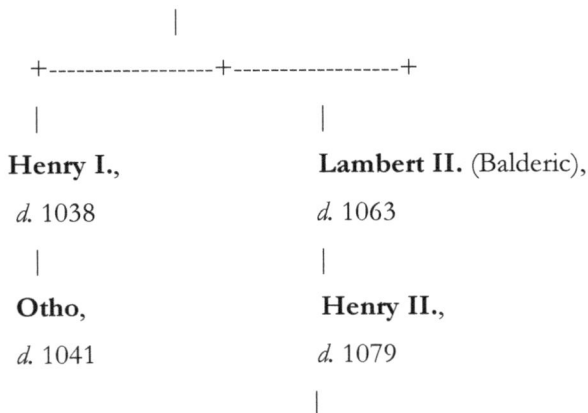

```
                  |
    +------------------+-----------------+
    |                          |
Henry I.,                 Lambert II. (Balderic),
d. 1038                   d. 1063
    |                          |
Otho,                     Henry II.,
d. 1041                   d. 1079
                               |
```

Henry III.,

d. 1095

|

Godfrey Longbeard,

Count of Louvain from 1095,

Duke of Brabant from 1106,

d. January 15th, 1140

CHAPTER V
The Rise of Brussels and Louvain

The cities of Belgium, unlike the cities of Italy or of the Rhine-land, or of France, which often go back to Roman times, and trace their descent to great administrative centres, date nearly all of them from the Middle Age, and are the children of industry and commerce. Bruges, Ypres, Ghent, the three bonnes villes of Flanders, were not towns in the modern sense of the word until the beginning of the ten hundreds, and it was almost a century later before the farmers of Brussels and Mechlin and Louvain became manufacturers and merchants.

Its geographical position between France and Germany, its long coast line, its nearness to England, its numerous navigable streams—all these things rendered the Low Country a region peculiarly adapted to mercantile pursuits; nor was it less favourably situated with regard to that industry which afterwards became, and for centuries remained, the staple trade of the country: the herbage of the seaboard was naturally suited to sheep, from time immemorial vast flocks of them grazed on the polders, and their wool was of the finest quality; thus there was at hand the raw material for the fabrication of cloth.

When the Danish incursion ceased and the land became comparatively tranquil, men soon began to consider how best they might turn these natural advantages to account, and presently along the waterways came bands of wandering traders with rich cargoes from foreign parts: wine from France and from the Rhine-land, silk and spices from Italy, furs from the North—all kinds of merchandise destined to supply the growing needs of the country, or to be exported to England or Denmark, or the regions round the Baltic; and when they had disposed of their wares they would return to the lands from whence they hailed with their barges laden with woollen goods—product of the looms of Flanders. Coming and going, they broke the journey at such places along stream as were best suited to afford accommodation for themselves, their servants, and their draught cattle, and where they would be likely to find a market for what they had to sell: by some castle or abbey or collegiate church, around which clustered the houses of clerks or Court officials, and the homesteads and the hovels of yeomen and serfs. In these settlements, too, they took up their winter quarters, and they often found wives among the daughters of their hosts. When this was so, the place of sojourning became a home—the permanent abode of their little ones and of their women folk, the spot where they purposed to end their days when they had made their fortunes, or, perchance, had been worn out by the hardships of their calling.

Amongst these early traders, the first merchants and the first commercial travellers who gained a livelihood in the Low Country, foreigners there were no doubt, but by far the greater number of them were natives of the soil, and they seem to have been recruited from all ranks of society. Some were knights, who hoped to find the business of buying and selling more profitable than the trade of war; some were Karls from the seaboard, men who had lost their land, if they ever had any to lose, but still retained their freedom, and some were runaway slaves. Matter of little moment, they were birds of passage; no man knew their condition or whence they came, or what lord, if any, claimed their allegiance, and they were all of them treated wherever they went as their own masters. The freedom which they enjoyed compelled association, for since they were no man's vassals no man was bound to protect them; what rights and privileges they possessed were necessarily in their own keeping; hence the great merchant guilds famous in the story of the Netherlands. Meeting together at night to discuss over their liquor their own personal transactions, the guild brethren soon began to consider the public affairs of the settlements in which they dwelt or which they frequented, and little by little to busy themselves with municipal administration, and presently they obtained the charters which gave them a legal standing. Nor were they without funds: their coffers were filled by self-imposed rates, and by fines levied by their elected chiefs for infringements of their rules of association. The money thus raised served for the erection of guild halls and belfries, the building of town walls, the maintenance of waterways, and the making of roads and bridges.

Another element was soon to be added to the population of these river-side settlements of agriculturists and tradesmen: hard on the heels of the merchant came the manufacturer. Thanks to the greater security which the land at this time enjoyed and the consequent increase in the number of its inhabitants, the fens were being drained rapidly, and vast areas which had been lakes were already under pasture; this meant an increase of flocks, and a wool crop so abundant that the shepherds unaided were no longer able to convert the whole of it into cloth. Hence the professional weaver, and the new commercial activity made weaving a profitable profession. The men who adopted it—and their name was legion—naturally flocked to the towns, where, in touch with merchant and trader, they would be likely to find a more ready market for their wares. Like them, and from like motives, they found it expedient to band together, and soon the 'Draperie,' or Cloth Guild, became an institution of mark in the Netherlands.

As for the original settlers—the serfs attached to the soil, the yeoman bound by less stringent ties to the Church or the chief under whose protection they dwelt, the ministeriales who collected manorial fines and dues, administered justice in their lord's name, and managed generally his estate, and who were practically free men—living alongside of the new-comers, often united to them by marriage ties, they gradually adopted their manner of life, and themselves became merchants and manufacturers. For a time they seem to have been submitted to the old manorial régime, but they soon began to agitate for emancipation, and presently they obtained the parchments which gave them complete freedom.

The making of the great commercial and manufacturing centres of mediæval Belgium was for the most part and generally speaking in this wise, but they did not all of them come into being at the same time—not even in the course of the same century. As a rule the towns of Brabant are less ancient than the towns of Flanders, and most of them owe their development less to the river than to the road. It was so with Brussels and Louvain, and, to a certain extent also with Mechlin. Off the main waterways, on the banks of tributary streams, navigable only by light craft, what business they at first did was more or less of a local character. It was not till the opening of the eleven hundreds, when the great high road was made from Bruges to Cologne, passing through Louvain and Brussels, and within easy reach of Mechlin, that these little towns at last became places of importance.

The commercial movement reached Brussels earlier than it reached Louvain. If we may trust St. Guy's anonymous biographer, who lived most probably in the second half of the ten hundreds, there was a settlement of merchants established there at the commencement of the century. He tells us a curious story concerning one of them, a friend of Guy's, who seems to have done a thriving trade.

But first a word as to Guy himself, the poor man of Anderlecht, as people called him—a picturesque and interesting figure from several points of view. To this man—the earliest private inhabitant of Brussels whose name we know, the first of whose doings we have any record, the only one who has ever attained the honours of the altar, the most ancient sanctuary in the town, the crypt of Anderlecht, is dedicated. In this church when he died they laid his body to rest; here his tomb may still be seen, and his bones are still treasured; and strangely enough it was in this same building that in his childhood he used to pray. Then it was the Church of St. Peter; a hundred and fifty years afterwards the dedication was changed, and henceforth men called it the Church of St. Peter and St. Guy. Of this beautiful remnant of a forgotten age we shall have much to say presently. Guy was born somewhere about the middle of the nine hundreds. His parents were very humble folk, probably serfs attached to the soil of Anderlecht. He himself began life as a farm labourer, and his employer's holding seems to have been hard by the Castle of Brussels. A beautiful legend has come down to us concerning him at this time. It was his master's custom to provide the labourers with a mid-day meal, served to them in the fields, and Guy's to carry a portion of his each day to his parents at Anderlecht. One of his comrades, a cross-grained, ill-conditioned fellow, took umbrage at this, and accused him to their master of wasting his time. Next day, during the dinner-hour, the farmer betook himself to the field which Guy was tilling, determined, if his man had played truant, to rate him soundly on his return, but though Guy, as usual, had gone to Anderlecht, when presently he came hurrying back, with no harsh words was he greeted, for during his absence an angel had taken his place at the plough. This story is the subject of an ancient and very beautiful wall painting in the upper church at Anderlecht.

And how many other fairy tales, some of them no less touching, have been woven about the name of this popular hero, the only man of his day whose memory is still green in the city of Brussels! And yet throughout his whole career no deeds which the world calls great are recorded of him. His life for the most part seems to have been an even and uneventful one. He soon gave up farm labour, and for many years he was sacristan to the little church at Laeken, now a populous suburb of Brussels, then a hamlet just outside the town. The last ten years of his life he spent in making two pilgrimages to Jerusalem and in travelling over Europe to visit famous shrines. All these journeys were made on foot, and doubtless they were not devoid of adventure, but his earliest biographer, who wrote nearly a hundred years after his death, has little to tell us on this head. In the fall of the year 1012 he returned to his native village, and in pitiable plight, worn out with want and fever and the wear and tear of the road. The canons of Anderlecht received him into their hospice, where he was tenderly cared for, for nine days, and then at last, on the 12th of September,

Subterranean Church of St. Guy at Anderlecht

he set out for Jerusalem the Golden. He loved God with his whole heart, of his penury he ministered to those who were poorer than himself, and he did what he could in his small way to sweeten and soften the hard lot of his neighbours. Even during his lifetime he was regarded as a saint: his anonymous biographer informs us that when Dean Wonedulph of Anderlecht and a company of pilgrims on their way to Jerusalem encountered him unexpectedly at Rome 'they fell down on their faces and adored him,' and when he lay dying in the hospice of the canons of Anderlecht, Heaven itself, so runs the legend, miraculously proclaimed his sancity. A heavenly light filled the room in which he lay, a white dove hovered over his head, and a voice was heard saying: 'Veniat dilectus meus ad percipiendam æternæ jocunditatis coronam.'

Strangely enough 'the poor man of Anderlecht' at one time seriously thought of embarking in trade. Satan, in the guise of a rich Brussels merchant, would fain have persuaded the saint, then sexton of Laeken, to enter into partnership with him, cunningly representing that by so doing he would soon make a fortune, and thus be the better able to help the poor, and Guy fell into the trap; but it was not God's will that His servant should imperil his soul in so hazardous a calling, and hardly had he started on his first journey down Senne, when his craft grounded on a sandbank in mid stream, and, notwithstanding all their efforts, the boatmen were unable to float it; and, worse still, when the saint himself vainly seized the barge-pole it miraculously adhered to his fingers, nor could he unclasp them until he had made a solemn vow to utterly eschew commerce.

'Mercatura raro aut nunquam ab aliquo diu sine crimine exerceri potuit,' shrewdly notes his biographer, who was most likely a clerk of Anderlecht, and that seems to have been the general opinion of the ecclesiastical authorities of the day. The Church looked askance at trade, the methods of the merchant were too nearly allied to the methods of the usurer, as she knew very well to her cost. When she wanted a loan she sometimes had to pay him fifty or sixty per cent. Yet, strangely enough, it was on Church land, and under the auspices of a collegiate chapter, that the most flourishing of the great commercial centres of Brabant gradually grew up: it was not by Lambert Longbeard's castle, but higher up stream, alongside the Church of St. Peter, that the wandering merchants who frequented Louvain first pitched camp.

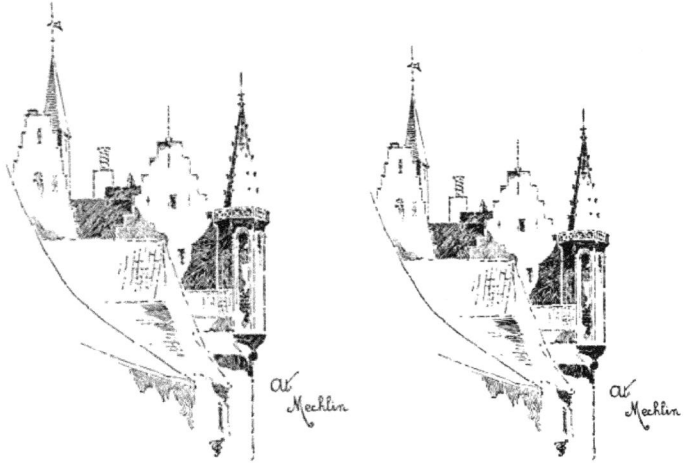

At Mechlin

CHAPTER VI
The Serfs of St. Peter

Though Lambert Longbeard was the first hereditary Count of Louvain, he was certainly not the founder of the city of Louvain, or even of the Castle and its dependencies—the 'Old Bourg of Louvain,' as it was called in later days—which he made his capital.

The city dates from a much later period than Lambert's day, and there is a tradition that some Merovingian noble had built himself a home on the site of the Old Bourg soon after the Frankish invasion. Certainly since Arnulph's victory over the Danes there had been a fortress there, which, until Lambert's day, was held in the Emperor's name by a series of provincial governors, one of whom was Bruno's friend St. Ansfried. This building, which has long ago disappeared, and of the site of which even we are ignorant, is said to have stood on an island formed by two branches of the Dyle, and there is little doubt that it was for a time at least the home of Lambert I., but the Counts of Louvain did not long continue to dwell there. Most likely, on account of the frequent floods and the dampness of the situation, they soon migrated to a new castle, built on the height now called Cæsar's Hill—some vestiges of it still remain—and which, in all probability, was built by Lambert II.—Lambert Longbeard's younger son, Lambert surnamed Balderick. A name to be remembered this, for the man who bore it was the real founder of Louvain: it was Lambert Balderick who built and munificently endowed the great Collegiate Church of St. Peter, the church around which, as we have already seen, the city grew up, and which in its early days was its nursing mother. The collegiate chapter was invested with all the rights and privileges of a great monastic corporation, and the yeomen and serfs who dwelt on their lands, and who formed what was called St. Peter's family, participated in their immunities, and were submitted only to their jurisdiction—no small boon, for the conditions of life on an ecclesiastical estate were far more conducive to liberty and progress than were those on lay domains. There was no taille, nor droit de gite, nor forced labour for the maintenance of ramparts; Church land was universally held to be the patrimony of the saint to whom it was dedicated, to violate it was sacrilege, a crime which the greediest feudal robber was generally loth to commit, and thus, amid the turmoil and warfare with which the surrounding country was so often vexed, its inhabitants for the most part enjoyed the blessing of peace. Further, justice was administered by themselves, and they were altogether free from State exactions. Indeed, so jealous was the Provost of Louvain of this privilege that he would suffer no civil officer to sojourn within his borders.

Though the landed estate of the collegiate chapter was not a large one, the 'Petermen' or lay members of St. Peter's family seem to have been sufficiently numerous. The Provost had the right to admit outsiders, his conditions were not onerous—a trifling entrance fee, generally two deniers and an undertaking in the event of marriage to pay a small tribute, and upon these terms a host of free men and liberated serfs were glad enough to barter their liberty, to quote the characteristic phrase of the charters of the day, 'for a servitude freer than freedom itself.'

Saint Peter's Louvain

The privileges and immunities of the Church of St. Peter were not peculiar to that foundation, almost all the great ecclesiastical establishments of the Low Countries were similarly favoured; but whereas in other towns which had grown up on Church land the laymen affiliated to the religious community which originally owned the soil—the Martinmen at Utrecht, for example, the men of St. Rombold at Mechlin, the men of St. Bavo at Ghent, when at last they obtained rights of citizenship, lost the ecclesiastical privileges and immunities which hitherto they had enjoyed, at Louvain this was not the case: the privileges of the Petermen survived long after their obligations to the institution which conferred them had become a dead letter, and for centuries too after they had obtained full civil rights. Indeed, by the opening of the thirteen hundreds, perhaps even earlier, their connection with the Chapter of St. Peter's had ceased to be anything but a nominal one: they remained exempt from taxation and were amenable only to their own court, but the Mayor of Louvain had taken the place of the

Provost in all that appertained to their government. They were still a class apart, but these men who owed their distinction to servile descent had now become a rich, influential and aristocratic caste, the cream of the burgher nobility, and thus they continued until the close of the seventeen hundreds, and then, at last, 'the men of St. Peter' were ruthlessly swept away, along with so many other interesting and time-honoured abuses.

Such was the famous collegiate church which Lambert Balderick founded at 'the place called Looven,' and whose rights and privileges every successive sovereign of Brabant swore to maintain at his 'Joyous Entry,' until the days of Albert and Isabel.

So completely identified was it with the town which grew up around its walls that a likeness of the material fabric was graven on the city seal, its steeple was the city belfry, the gold and silver pieces coined at the city mint were called 'Peters,' and proof that a man was a 'Peterman' was held to be sufficient proof that he was a burgher and a patrician of Louvain. Without any further investigation he was at once admitted to all the rights of citizenship.

CHAPTER VII
The greater and the lesser Folk

The municipal organisation of the towns of Brabant was at first of a very simple character. It consisted in every case of an unpaid magistracy—a college of schepen or aldermen appointed by the Duke for life from among the chief freeholders of the city, of which they were held to be its representatives—presided over by a paid officer, who bore the title of Mayor or Ecoutête or Amman—from town to town the title differed—was the sovereign's direct delegate, and in all things the representative of his authority. He was not necessarily or even usually a burgher of the city over which he presided. The Duke was free to choose whom he would, and to revoke the appointment at will; and though this officer held the first place in the civic hierarchy, he was in reality nothing more than his master's hired servant.

Alongside of the College of Aldermen was the Merchants' Guild. Whether this corporation had any legal existence prior to the institution of the magistracy is a problem which has yet to be solved; but it is certain that by the end of the eleven hundreds the guild was firmly established in most of the towns of Brabant; that, including as it did all the commercial and industrial capitalists of the city, it had exercised from the first no little influence on public affairs, and that it contributed in great measure to the full expansion of municipal self-rule.

The next century saw the birth of another institution, the Council of Jurors, and there can be no doubt that it was to the Merchants' Guild that the Jury owed its origin.

With the increase of the population, outcome of the commercial development which signalised the opening of the twelve hundreds, the old machinery no longer sufficed for the maintenance of public peace and the regulation of trade. It became necessary to devise some new means to check the growing disorder, and the burghers, united as they were in the powerful organisation of their guild, were strong enough to take the matter into their own hands. Hence the Council of Jurors, a subsidiary body, annually elected by the people for policing the city and the management of municipal affairs, and which also participated with the College of Aldermen in the administration of justice.

So far from offering opposition, the sovereigns of Brabant from the first showed themselves favourable to this development. Not that they had any particular liking for democratic institutions, but because they were sufficiently clear-sighted to see that, in the interest of their revenue, it was incumbent on them to do so: they were well aware that the towns of Brabant depended wholly on trade, and that this delicate plant can only thrive in an atmosphere of freedom.

There is no record of the Jury at Brussels prior to 1229, at Antwerp till 1232, at Louvain till 1234, and at Tirlemont till 1249, but it is most likely that in all of these towns it dates from an earlier period, and by the close of the first half of the century it had been granted to almost all the communes of Brabant.

Its existence, however, as a body distinct from the higher magistracy was nowhere, save at Louvain, of long duration. As early as 1274 the Jury had disappeared at Brussels, and in hardly any of the great towns did it outlive the century. From the first the relations between the two corporations had almost everywhere been strained: they were the embodiment of hostile ideals—oligarchy and popular rule. Presently the burghers obtained a voice in the election of aldermen, and their term of office was limited to one year. The Council of Jurors thus ceased to be the sole expression of the will of the people; the higher magistracy had become, not only in theory, as it had always been, but in fact, representative of the city, and had risen proportionately in public esteem. Thus protected by the mantle of popularity, it was able, seemingly without opposition, little by little to itself assume the functions of its rival, and thus, little by little, to absorb it into its own bosom.

At Louvain, however, the case was different. In that city the aristocratic element was all-powerful, and the jury was recruited from the same families which furnished the College of Aldermen; from the first the two corporations had worked together in harmony, and until the end of the Middle Age they continued to exist as two distinct bodies.

For a long period after the municipal organisation of the cities of Brabant had been definitely determined, all administrative and legislative power remained in the hands of a narrow oligarchy of great capitalists, headed by the old patrician families, which from time immemorial had furnished the magistracy.

One was the source of their title to distinction—the ownership of land; but the means by which the first patricians had acquired their title-deeds were not in every case the same, nor were they all of like origin. Some of them were the descendants of ministeriales who, when the township was a feudal domain, had levied their lords' dues for him, and generally managed his affairs; others of yeomen of the same period, whom thrift or good fortune had enabled to purchase the freehold of the soil they tilled; others, again, were successful traders, or the sons of successful traders, who, retiring from business, had invested the wealth which commerce had given them in real property.

Together they formed a class apart, distinct alike from the feudal nobility and from the general body of townsmen. They were divided into groups in each city, which bore the characteristic title of lignages or clans; but it is certain that many patricians were not the direct lineal descendants of the houses whose names and arms they bore: the status of patrician was transmissible in the female line, and patrician daughters were not unfrequently given in marriage to prosperous plebeians; moreover, some of the sons of the house were only sons by adoption—the wealthy merchant of alien blood was not always refused admission to the charmed circle, though as a rule the door of matrimony was the only door open to him; and occasionally we find whole families, sometimes sections of families, forsaking their original clan to enroll themselves in another. Indeed, the great lignages of Brabant, which play so large a part in the stories of her towns, were, to a certain extent, voluntary associations of aristocratic families banded together for the sake of mutual protection and help, and with a view to securing the election of their own nominees to the magistracy; and though, no doubt, a considerable number of the members of each clan traced their descent to one stock, it is certain that the ties by which they were most strongly knit together were not those of blood, but of kindred pursuits, and kindred associations and kindred political interests. It is a significant fact, as Pirenne observes, that the number of lignages in each town corresponded to the number of their aldermen, and that each lignage had obtained a prescriptive right of representation in the magistracy.

Though the patricians as a body were a wealthy class, all of them were not rich men; some, indeed, were so poor that they were glad to earn a livelihood by hiring themselves as servants to their more fortunate kinsmen; others, on account of their poverty, renounced their privileges, and sank back into the general body of the people. On the other hand, the wealth of the patricianate was being constantly augmented by the new men who found admission into its borders, and with the increasing prosperity of the town, their land was becoming daily more valuable for building purposes. Many of them were thus able to live in luxury on the rents produced by their property, others increased their revenue by farming the State taxes, others were engaged in banking operations, others again in commerce. In that case they became members of the Merchants' Guild, for the Guild, whose members were constantly being enrolled in the lignages was always ready to open its doors to the son of the aristocratic house who wished to resume the calling by which, most likely, his ancestors had attained wealth. Thus it was growing daily more and more aristocratic, and at last nearly all its members were patricians by birth or by adoption. Embracing as it did at first traders of every kind, it now became an exceedingly close corporation, and only admitted to its membership the sellers of cloth and the sellers of wool, the cream of the commercial world.

Such were the men who owned the soil of the cities of Brabant, who had endowed them, often at their own cost, with magnificent public buildings,[7] who had won for themselves free institutions, and who for the best part of two hundred years tyrannised over everyone else.

Mightier than the feudal chiefs, whose fathers' swords had made the evolution of the city possible, they had absorbed them into their own ranks, or driven them forth from their borders, and now adopted their dress and speech and manner of living. In time of war they wore coats of mail like knights, and they

Cloth Hall Louvain

alone of the civic army were mounted. They lived in great houses of stone, whose turrets and battlements towered above the thatched hovels of the helots who did their bidding:—weavers who starved when work was slack, and in good times just managed to keep body and soul together, the poorest and the most numerous of them all were they, the most turbulent, too, and the worst organised, always snarling at their hard lot and their impotence to better it, ready to break out into rebellion on the slightest provocation, and never content with their wages; dyers with blue nails— outward and visible sign of moral degradation, for though it was owing to their skill that the cloth of Brabant was more beautiful than that of any other land, and sometimes, though not often, they obtained wealth, they could never hope for the rights of citizenship until time had wiped out those fatal stains; men of a hundred other callings, degraded creatures all of them, who earned their bread by the sweat of their brow, mere human chattels without heart and without soul, whom an honest burgher might cuff at will, aye, and, if he would, carry off their daughters without fear of incurring any legal penalty.

It was not always so. Before the year 1200 class distinctions were far less marked. In the early days the weaver could sell his own cloth, and even petty traders were admitted to the Merchants' Guild. The advent of the middleman had changed all this, and as time went on the patricians, the majores et potentiores, as an ancient chronicler calls them, grew more and more exclusive and more and more overbearing. But though they looked down on the 'lesser folk,' the bowels of their compassion were not shut up against them: they built and lavishly endowed hospitals where they might be tended when they were sick, refuges to which they could retire when hard work and old age had worn them out, orphanages for such of their children as had been deprived by death of their natural protectors, and above all, churches, glorious without and within—palaces of the people, where Lazarus and Dives knelt side by side. Nor is the stream of their charity yet dried up: the rich endowments of the Bureaux de bienfaisance throughout Belgium are in great measure due to the munificence of these merchant princes of the Middle Age, who in turn cuffed and caressed the turbulent folk on whose hardships they fattened, and whose poverty rendered their riches possible.

No less inconsequent was the patrician burgher in his dealings with the Church—with one hand he smote her in the mouth and with the other he loaded her with benefits. And yet, after all, perhaps he was not so inconsistent, for the soul of this man who possessed the faith, in his way a devout Christian, was consumed by pride and the lust of power. He would share his authority with no man, he would be master in his own house, and so he ousted the noble, ground down the toiler, flouted the clerk and set his heel on his neck. A firm believer in the rights of the laity, he would never suffer priest or monk to meddle with his affairs, but he did not hesitate, whenever it suited his purpose, to busy himself with theirs. Thus, from time immemorial most city livings had been in the gift of one or other of the religious houses which dotted the countryside, but he quietly ignored their abbots' pretensions, and named his parish priests himself, and never rested until he had obtained a legal right to do so. So, too, in the matter of education: the management of schools had been always recognised as the especial province of the clergy, but he was not happy until he had succeeded in placing them under municipal control, or, in other words, until he had undertaken their management himself. Nor would he always recognise the clerk's right to justice in his own courts, though when he himself was technically a churchman, he never scrupled to make use of them if he thought it would be an advantage to him to do so. Thus at

Louvain, where almost all the patricians were *Hommes de Saint Pierre*, the old ecclesiastical courts, officered indeed by laymen, were maintained intact for his behoof till the Revolution.

The peculiar circumstances of the Church in Brabant favoured these pretensions. The one great ecclesiastical power in that province, where no bishop had his See, was monasticism, and when the burgher was in the heyday of his magnificence monasticism was spiritually and temporally at a low ebb. The fiery zeal which characterised the days of the Cluniac revival had long ago flickered out. Discipline had become sadly relaxed, the monk had ceased to be the saint and the popular hero he had been in days of yore, and the alms of the faithful no longer flowed into his coffers. Another source of revenue, too, had all but dried up. Owing to the fall in the purchasing power of money, the produce of his manorial dues, which he had no power to raise, had diminished almost to vanishing point. Thus was the abbot, at his wits' end how to keep order amongst his rebellious family and make both ends meet, sadly handicapped in his contests with his all-powerful foe, from whom, indeed, he was not unfrequently constrained to borrow at usurious rates of interest. But although the burgher looked askance at the old religious orders, for some reason or other his antipathy to the monk did not extend itself to the friar. He never quarrelled with the 'watch dogs of the Lord,' and with the disciples of 'the poor man of Assisi' his relations were most cordial. Perhaps as a practical business man the object of their mission appealed more to his sympathies; perhaps he thought he had nothing to fear from the children of the gentle saint who had taken for his bride the Lady Poverty. But by a strange irony of fate it was not the monk but the friar who hurled the first blow at his dominion. It was from the lips of the friar who toiled among the poverty-stricken masses that these poor folk learned, for the first time, the dignity of man, and no teacher was needed to awaken in their souls the consciousness of their degradation. They experienced it every day: when they lounged about the market-place on Monday morning waiting, often in vain, for the supply of labour generally exceeded the demand, for someone to hire them at wages fixed by the town magistrates, men who themselves were employers of labour and in whose appointment the people had no voice; when, working at home at their looms, they received the visit of the guild inspector, who had the right to ransack their hovels at all hours, with a view to assuring himself of the excellence of their work, and who received as his salary a portion of the fine imposed for any fraud detected. This was their normal lot in times of prosperity, and when work was slack, or when there was no work at all, as was sometimes the case when wool was not forthcoming from England, the wounds inflicted on their self-respect went deeper and smarted more: then were they constrained to choose between two evils—either they must starve, and, worse still, see their wives and their little ones starve; or they must band together and parade the streets whining for that bread which they could no longer win. Well might the friar preach to men set in such straits the beauty of Christian humility and of Christian resignation, and bid them despise as dross that gold which they could not obtain. The weavers and dyers who hung on his lips possessed, of earthly goods, very often only the rags they stood up in; and the wealth which they saw around them, and which they could never hope to enjoy, they knew very well was in many cases the fruit of their underpaid toil, and that the holders of it, of like origin with themselves, were not only their rulers and taskmasters, but corrupt stewards of the common-weal—the men who managed the city, and managed it in their own interests.

What wonder, then, that they soon began to confound contempt for riches with contempt for the rich, and that presently contempt engendered hatred. Were not the oppressors of the poor the enemies of Jesus Christ? Was it not easier for a camel to go through the eye of a needle than for a rich man to enter the kingdom of God? Had not one of their preachers[8] told them that the rich man, even if he were righteous, was less worthy of esteem than the woman of the street?

CHAPTER VIII
The Coelveren and the Blankarden

Strangely enough it was the patricians themselves who placed in the hands of the lesser folk the weapon with which they presently won independence. For years past it had been cause of just complaint that municipal affairs were managed in the interest of one class only, and before the middle of the twelve hundreds things had come to this pass: the men in office considered alone their own advantage and the advantage of their kinsfolk and their friends. Hence heartburning, jealousy, strife without end, the upper classes split into factions, and sometimes the fire thus enkindled burnt so fiercely that it could only be extinguished by the shedding of blood. This was so all over Brabant, and in the year 1260 there broke out a conflict which brought forth unlooked-for results.

The Coelveren and the Blankarden were two of the mightiest families of Louvain; for generations past they had been rivals, and they hated one another with 'a perfect hatred.' Whatever may have been the first cause of their mutual hostility, the quarrel was of ancient date; it had been handed down from father to son, and had become in each case a family tradition.

The times were favourable to disorder. Duke Henry III. had just died (February 6, 1260); his eldest son had not yet reached man's estate; his widow, Adelaide of Burgundy, harassed by ambitious kinsmen, who claimed a share in the administration of the realm, was holding the reins of government with faltering hands. For years past the rival families had been only waiting for an opportunity to settle their long dispute, and hardly had Duke Henry been laid in the grave than they flew to arms. What was the immediate cause of the conflict is unknown, but it is always easy to find a pretext when men are determined to fight, and the war in this case was probably the outcome of some very trifling affair.

Be this as it may, opinion was sharply divided at Louvain as to which side was in the right, and men took such interest in the quarrel, and party feeling ran so high, that by the end of the year 1262 there was not a patrician in the city who had not taken up arms on behalf of one or other of the belligerents.

Nor was this all: the Blankarden had sought and obtained the support of Duchess Adelaide, and the Coelveren, casting about for some pillar of strength to counterbalance this advantage, presently found a more dangerous ally—the mob. They appealed, and not vainly, to that herd of downtrodden and plundered helots, who for years had been writhing under the sense of their wrongs, and riot and confusion reigned in the city for two years;[9] and then matters, instead of becoming better, grew worse, for Adelaide added fuel to the fire: she provided the belligerents with a fresh bone of contention. On the ground that her elder son Henry was incapable, she disinherited him, and proclaimed her younger son John heir to the Duchy of Brabant, whereat the Coelveren cried 'Shame! If Henry were indeed as poor a creature as his mother alleged, that were no excuse for trampling on the rights of primogeniture. Could he not appoint responsible ministers and rule through them?' The Blankarden, of course, were of the opposite opinion, and shouted their loudest for John, but, supported by the great mass of the people, their rivals were strong enough to silence them, and when presently Adelaide and her younger son appeared before the gates of the capital they found them shut.

Meanwhile the strife had extended to the whole of Brabant, and until 1267 the land was a prey to civil war; and though at last a reconciliation was effected, and the Coelveren consented, for a consideration, to acknowledge John, the government of the city had become completely disorganised, and the patricians, who for five years had been disporting themselves by cutting one another's throats, were not only thinned in numbers, but had lost credit.

Before the war they had been hated and despised, but until then at least they had been feared. The craftsman hitherto had only ventured to snarl and show his teeth. He was a bolder dog now. The experience of the last five years had shown him something of his own might. He had not only fought, and fought on the winning side, but it had been in great measure owing to his efforts that the victory had been won. If he could fight so well for others, why not one day fight for himself? The flame of hope was rekindled within his breast. That was something. It was probably some such thought as this which moved him to demand as guerdon for his services a boon which would place him in a position to do battle with some chance of success. The moment was a propitious one for craving favours. Duke John and a considerable number of the aristocracy were alike beholden to the men who petitioned—men flushed with victory, and still under arms. Fear, if not gratitude, then counselled compliance, and the boon was not denied. By the charter which John granted to Louvain in 1267 it was expressly ordained that the craft guilds, which, until now, had been purely industrial corporations, should henceforth be endowed with military organisation, and that each guild should march under its own banners, and be commanded by its own elected chiefs.

The result was what might have been, and what probably was, foreseen, though no doubt the situation developed sooner than the longest-headed of them had expected: before the year was out the rabble who had thus been imprudently armed turned their weapons against the men who had armed them, and though the rebellion was promptly quelled, and the ringleaders were sent into exile, it was impossible to extinguish the flame of hope which recent events had enkindled. The craftsmen were firmly convinced that the flowing tide was with them, and though the victory was not in their day, after events showed that they had accurately gauged the situation.

During the confusion incident on Duke Henry's death, the craftsmen of several other towns had likewise been able to wrest some shreds of power from their patrician taskmasters. In some places, notably at Brussels, the old Council of Jurors was re-established, but in no case was its new lease of life a long one. The young Duke had little sympathy with democratic ideas, and no sooner was he firmly established on his throne than he set to work to restore the old order of things. John the First was a strong man, and with a mighty hand and an outstretched arm he accomplished his purpose, but it was only a putting off of the evil day. The plebeians were for a moment cowed, but their spirit was not crushed. Confident in the justice of their cause, they bent their heads to the storm, and possessed their souls in patience.

Presently (1302) the victory of Courtrai sent a thrill through Europe, for what a triumph it had been. 'On the one side was Philippe le Bel, the mightiest prince of his day, with all the chivalry of Navarre and all the chivalry of France, and a host of mercenary forces from all parts of Europe; on the other were the weavers of Bruges and a troop of Flemish boors, half naked, bare-headed, and with no other weapon but the rude scharmsax of their forebears—and these puny folk had conquered: the tyrants who would have enslaved them lay humbled in the dust.' When the news of the victory was noised abroad the downtrodden on all sides took heart, and in the cities of Brabant a general uprising was the immediate outcome. But the day of their triumph was not yet: other was the social and political situation in Brabant to that in the neighbouring county. The rulers of Brussels and Mechlin and Louvain were of a different stamp to the men who had tyrannised over Bruges and Ypres and Ghent. The latter were an effete and decrepit aristocracy—a herd of ledigoers, as working men contemptuously called them—mere loafers who despised that trade which had enriched their fathers, and who knew of no other means of increasing their dwindling income than by bribery and corruption; the former were for the most part practical business men actively engaged in commercial pursuits, and shrewd enough to reap a large profit from their several avocations. Nor were they, like the patricians of Flanders, at loggerheads with their sovereign. On the contrary, they regarded him as their natural protector, and were on the best of terms with him. In their eyes the Duke of Brabant was a highly respectable and most efficient officer of police, who, as such, deserved their confidence and esteem, and though the wages they paid him were certainly high, they considered on the whole that he was well worth his price. And the Duke on his part regarded them as men peculiarly worthy of his affection, for his expenses were heavy, and he was often short of cash, and they were always ready to make him presents with other people's money, or even to advance him their own when he could give them reasonable security and they were assured of a fair rate of interest.

In a word, these two forces were necessary to one another, and they were wise enough to know it. Thus united they were irresistible, and the plebeians hurled themselves in vain against the bedrock of their omnipotence. As long as this state of things lasted there was but one issue to their most strenuous efforts—defeat.

Once, indeed, by rare good fortune the craftsmen of Brussels almost achieved success, but the cup of triumph was dashed from their hands as they were carrying it to their lips. It happened thus. During the reign of Duke John II. and his wife Marguerite, a daughter of King Edward I. of England, there arose at Brussels, on the vigil of Candlemas 1306, a quarrel between two citizens, in the course of which one of them received a sword thrust. The wounded man does not seem to have been seriously injured, but the outrage had been committed in a public place; the assailant was an aristocrat, the victim a son of the people. That was enough. Riot ensued. The Duke was out of town. The patricians, left to their own resources, were powerless in face of the mob, and before daybreak riot had become revolution. Throughout the hours of darkness the city was a prey to the wildest disorder. Property of all kinds was vowed to destruction; strongholds, in which patricians were hiding, were taken by storm and wrecked; the mansions of the richest and most hated merchants presently went up in flames. The Duchess in vain left the shelter of her palace on the Coudenberg, and, with her life in her hands, confronted the mob. The rioters hailed her with shouts of derision, and though they offered her no personal violence, they laughed her authority to scorn. The people were drunk with their own excesses, and Brussels that night was a pandemonium. The storm was a fearful one whilst it lasted, but its fury was soon spent, and at the meeting of craftsmen, which was held next morning to deliberate on the future government of the city, the men who had been rioting in the streets all night showed singular moderation.

They decided that the magistracy should consist as heretofore of seven aldermen, but that henceforth the people should name them; that two financial assessors should be added to the city council, and that the Jury should be once more re-established. And when the time came to elect a new magistracy they gave further proof of their conciliatory dispositions, for whilst they took care to safeguard their own interests, they were not unmindful of the class prejudice of their vanquished opponents: the new aldermen were all of them members of the old ruling class chosen from among the little band of patricians whose sympathies were known to be with the popular cause.

The new order of things, however, did not last six months. John II., deeply wounded at the scant civility shown to his wife, refused to acknowledge the new constitution: the patricians' quarrel, he said, was his own, and, worse still, he swore to make no terms of peace without their consent, and until they had been fully indemnified for the losses they had sustained. This was in the middle of February 1306. Some attempt at negotiation seems to have been made, but without success, and early in May the patricians in a body left the town for Vilvorde, whither John had shortly before arrived along with what knights he had been able to muster, and whither also presently came the craftsmen in battle array, determined to exact at the sword's point the privileges denied them. When the knights at Vilvorde saw the crowd drawing nearer and nearer to camp, some of them suggested that 'the curs meant submission'; when the howling pack was at their throats, they knew better. During the first shock of battle the Duke himself was unhorsed, some said slain, and for a moment the craftsmen thought they had won, but it was only for a moment, they soon found to their cost that their enemy was again in the saddle and in the forefront of the fray, whereat they lost heart, and unable to bear up any longer against the charge of the cavalry frantically made for home. The patricians followed at full speed. It was a wild, fierce race for Brussels. On its issue hung their fate. The people knew it, and fear and hope gave to their feet wings. If only they could outstrip those cursed horsemen, were it but by a hair's-breadth, they would slam the town gates in their noses, and thus at the last moment turn defeat into victory. Vain hope. The hour of the craftsman's salvation had not sounded yet: the outcome of the contest was a dead heat, and once more the iron entered into his soul.

Seventy craftsmen had been slain at Vilvorde or in the mad rush home, the old constitution was re-established with all its odious privileges and all its time-honoured abuses, and there was a heavy bill of costs to pay, wherein note this item, 'a hundred livres to Willem Moll for burying weavers and fullers alive.'

At Mechlin, at Léau, at Tirlemont, at Louvain, all of which towns were about this time the scene of insurrection, the result was the same: in every case the patrician triumph was accomplished with less difficulty than at Brussels, and everywhere the lot of the plebeians became harder than it had been before.

The most stringent precautions were taken to guard against further disorder, craftsmen of all kinds were disarmed, their guild meetings strictly prohibited, and at Brussels at least it was death for a weaver or fuller to pass the night within the town.[10] These turbulent folk were enjoined to remain after dusk in their own wretched suburbs or pay the price of their temerity.

Nor was this all. On the 12th of June, 1306, Duke John authorised the magistrates of Brussels to crush any further outbreak by any means they thought fit. In the following September he granted like faculties to the magistrates of Louvain, and presently all the cities of Brabant agreed together that the craftsman banished from any one of them should, ipso facto, be an outcast from all the rest.

What could they do, these small tradesmen and artisans, with their wrists handcuffed and irons on their feet, but bewail their hard lot and the evil days on which they had fallen, and weary Heaven for a deliverer. Presently a deliverer was sent them, but the days of their expectation filled three score years, and during all that time their adversaries were at peace. Not only was their will law in the cities where they dwelt, but they gradually extended their dominion far into the open country, and, continually encroaching on the prerogatives of their Duke, at last succeeded in reducing his sovereignty to little more than a name, and themselves, to all intents and purposes, directed the helm of State.

The patricians of Brabant had at length ascended the mountain of their ambition, but for no long time were they able to hold the high place which their gold had conquered.

III.—Genealogical Table of the Dukes of Brabant from Godfrey I. to John III.

Godfrey I. (Longbeard),

Count of Louvain from 1095,

Duke of Brabant from May 13, 1106,

d. Jan. 15, 1140

|

|

Godfrey II., *d.* 1142

|

```
        |

Godfrey III., d. Aug. 10, 1190

        |

        |

Henry I. (The Warrior), d. Sept. 5, 1235

        |

        |

Henry II., d. Feb. 1, 1248

        |

        |

Henry III., = Adelaide
d. Feb. 6, 1260 | of Burgundy

              |

  +----------------------+----+
  |                      |

 Henry,               John I.
retired into a       (The Victorious),
monastery, 1267,      d. May 3, 1294
renouncing his right        |
to the duchy to             |
his younger brother  John II., = Marguerite,
John                 d. Oct. 17, | daughter of
                     1312      | Edward I. of
                               | England.
                                    |
                               John III.
```

CHAPTER IX
Peter Coutherele

Amongst the tangle of intricate causes which at last brought about, not, indeed, the complete discomfiture of the patricians, for to the end they were able to share in the duties and spoils of municipal government, but the shrinkage of their prestige and the loss of much of their power, three stand out pre-eminent:—the gradual diminution of their wealth after 1350, outcome of English competition in the cloth trade; the conduct of their chief officer of police, who presently, for his own ends, made it his business to foment rebellion; and the growing conviction in their own ranks that, after all, the stately edifice which they had reared was not founded on justice.

At a very early date there was a popular party among the patricians of Brussels, which little by little seems to have gained sufficient influence to modify the policy of the municipal government, for in 1306 we find Duke John II. giving discretionary powers to the College of Aldermen to admit craftsmen to the freedom of the city, and though no doubt the primary object of this grant was to enable the ruling class to purchase the goodwill of leading plebeians, the patricians would hardly have requested the right to confer such a boon, even by way of corruption, if they had been seriously opposed to the admission of commoners to the franchise.

As it was at Brussels so was it in the other towns of Brabant, and notably at Louvain, the city, above all, where the aristocracy was the proudest and the most hated, and the proletariat the most turbulent and the most oppressed. In this hotbed of storm and suspicion, where class feeling ran the highest and class distinctions were the most sharply defined, it was in the ranks of the patricians that the people at last found a leader whom they trusted, and one who showed himself worthy of their trust. That leader was Peter Coutherele, Mayor of Louvain, and, as such, the first citizen of the first city of Brabant.

Though on the paternal side he does not seem to have been a man of ancient lineage—his father, Godfrey, who was a member of the Council of Jurors in 1328, and again in 1339, is the first of the family of whom we have any record—Peter Coutherele was enrolled in the great landlord clan of Van Redinghem, and claimed kinship, probably through his mother or his grandmother, or through both, with the oldest and noblest houses of the Commune. His enemies said of him that his love of the people was born of hatred of his own class, outcome of private spleen, and that in making himself the champion of plebeian claims his first care was to feather his own nest; but whatever may have been the motives which inspired his action, there is this much to Peter's credit: to the end he was true to the cause he had espoused and to the principles he professed, and if he received large rewards, he at least did his work well. There can be no doubt that the ultimate triumph of democracy at Louvain was in the main due to his efforts. For four hundred years the constitution which he gave to his native city was the guarantee of the rights and liberties of all sorts and conditions of men. He was no wanton shedder of blood, he was very zealous for law and order, he always showed himself a just, a merciful, and a moderate man, and at last he died poor and forgotten.

We first hear of Peter Coutherele in 1348, when, no doubt owing to the influence of his high connections, he was appointed by Duke John III. to the important office of Mayor of Louvain, a position which must not be confounded with that of a modern English or French mayor. The Mayor of Louvain was the immediate representative of the Sovereign. His office corresponded in some sense to that of the high sheriff of an English county. He was also chief constable and commander-in-chief of the civic militia, and he took precedence of all other ducal officers. At this epoch, then, Coutherele was still on friendly terms with the ruling class, for John, who was always very tender with his patricians, would never have chosen for his representative a man who was not a *persona grata* to them, but the break soon came. The new Mayor was no respecter of persons, and before his first year of office was out he denounced certain measures which the aldermen had taken as infringements of the ducal prerogative. The magistrates, indeed, succeeded in justifying their conduct, but from that moment between them and Coutherele there was war to the knife. Presently in their turn they denounced him: he was hatching a plot with the plebeians to overthrow their power. But they were able to furnish no proof, and Duke John maintained him in office.

Though it was common knowledge that the Mayor sympathised with the aspirations of the lesser folk, it is not probable that at this period he had translated his sentiments into action. He was shrewd enough to know that any uprising of the masses against their oppressors could have no hope of success unless it were backed at least by the tacit consent of the Sovereign, and he had already had experience of Duke John's friendliness to the patricians. Four years later, in 1359, the Mayor of Louvain was again at loggerheads with the magistracy, and this time the consequences were far reaching. The quarrel arose out of a very small matter. De Dynter thus relates the story of its origin:[11]—

'It came to pass at this time that as a certain fishmonger was on his way to Louvain, there to dispose of his wares, as was his wont, the barrow on which his fish was charged stuck fast in a deep hole full of mud, whereat he was beginning to have grave doubts whether by reason of the bad road he would be able to reach the city in time for market, when haply he espied, in a field close by, some horses grazing, one of which he caught and harnessed to his truck, and when by this means he had extricated himself from his trouble he led him back again to the pasture whence he had taken him.

'Now it so happened that a certain wicked, false ribald, who had seen all that had taken place, at once made report thereof to Myn Here Coutherele, Mayor of Louvain, and affirmed upon oath that the fishmonger had stolen the horse; and thus it came to pass that no sooner had the said fishmonger set foot in Louvain than he was arrested for a thief and cast into gaol. At last the matter was brought before the Court of Aldermen, who adjudged the accused not guilty and directed that he should be set free; whereat the Mayor refused to comply, and the magistrates were cut to the quick. In flouting their sentence Coutherele had infringed one of those very privileges which, upon taking office, he had solemnly sworn to maintain. He was no longer worthy to be their Mayor. Henceforth they would cease to regard him as such.'

In refusing to carry out the sentence of the aldermen Coutherele had no doubt acted illegally, and the magistrates, in retaliating as they did, were strictly within their rights, but if they had not been blinded by passion they would have surely held their peace. They knew very well that the Mayor of Louvain would be certain to represent the course they had pursued as a flagrant violation of the ducal prerogative; and they knew too that the man who now sat on the throne of Brabant was of other blood and of other complexion to those friends and fosterers of freedom—the princes of the House of Louvain. The last of them was John III., and when (December 5, 1355) he was gathered to his fathers the mantle of their policy did not fall on the shoulders of his son-in-law and successor. Winceslaus of Luxembourg, the new Duke, knew nothing of civic institutions. How should he? There were no great towns in the land in which he had been reared. And though it was to the burgher-nobles of Brabant that he owed his recently acquired domains, he deemed the influence and pretensions of these tradesmen a standing affront to his dignity, of which from the first he was determined to be rid. Moreover, he was aggrieved with most of them personally, for had they not welcomed Louis of Maele when that sycophant of patrician pride, under pretext of recovering his wife's portion, had invaded his domains, and was it not by their counsel that he had afterwards styled himself Duke of Brabant? Added to this, it was the lesser folk who had at last driven out the usurper, and when others of his order had deserted their prince Coutherele had stood by him manfully.

Such was the complexion of affairs at the moment when the patricians of Louvain defied their enemy, and such was the man into whose jaundiced ears that aggrieved individual now poured the story of their aggressions.

Nor was Coutherele without allies in the ducal council—amongst them Reynold, Lord of Schoonvorst, a personal friend who shared his own opinions anent the plebeian question, and one of his Sovereign's most trusted advisers. This man plainly told the Duke that if he would be master in Louvain he must find some means of raising the people and of abasing their proud taskmasters. As for Winceslaus, he made no sign, and promptly withdrew to Luxembourg, as though unwilling to interfere in the quarrel; but when Coutherele returned to his native city, men noted that he was in nowise cast down—he had no doubt received some private assurance that he was free to act as he would.

For a little while there was calm at Louvain, calm before the storm, and the patricians had almost begun to hope that their trouble with Coutherele was over, when presently it was rumoured abroad that his nephews were tampering with the weavers. Employers of labour, comparing notes, called to mind that of late their men had shown themselves idle beyond wont, sullen, fractious, insolent; they had wondered what this meant, now they knew the reason. When the days grew longer, and honest merchants came forth after supper to cool themselves with the evening breeze, they noted that the loungers, muttering together in market-place and at street corner, leered at them as they passed with evil eyes, and scarce vouchsafed to lift their hats.

Mischief, it was clear, was brewing. At last the plot was discovered, and then the crisis came. Edmund De Dynter tells us how it all happened.

On the evening, he says, of the Feast of St. Mary Magdalen (July 21), in the year of Our Lord 1360, it came to pass that a certain meschine in the service of one of our magistrates, having been sent by him to a certain tavern to fetch a flask of wine, fell in with her sweetheart, who in confidence told her that the people, egged on by Peter Coutherele, intended to rise that night against the patricians, take possession of the Town Hall, and make a pretty piece of mischief (*faire aulcune mauvaise oevre*). Of course she divulged the secret to her master, and he without delay imparted the same to his brother aldermen, who forthwith betook themselves to the Town Hall, and arrived there amazed and confounded at the manifest evidence of commotion which they had witnessed on the way, for by this time the night was restless with the tumult of a gathering mob: men were hurrying from all sides to the great market behind the Cloth Hall, where the Mayor of Louvain was already addressing a crowd of weavers, 'with arms in their hands and anger in their brains.'

And what had Myn Here Coutherele to say for himself? If we may trust De Dynter, who wrote indeed more than fifty years afterwards, he began by enlarging on the misery of the people, and on the pride, the wealth, the corruption, of those who held them in bondage, and who fattened on their toil and on their tears. Was it not the people who paid the taxes, and the patricians who had the spending of them? Did not the poor man have to bear the heat and the burthen of the day whilst the rich were growing richer on the spoils of administration? And what right had these men to lord it over them? Were they not their fellow-citizens, of like birth and of like origin with themselves? And when he saw that he had enkindled their ire, he said that now was the time to strike; their oppressors were at their mercy, they had mortally offended the Duke, he would close his eyes and close his ears to aught which might be attempted against them. It were madness to lose so favourable an opportunity, let them then take up arms for dear liberty's sake.

It chanced that a certain great feudal lord, one Gerard of Vorsselaer, was in town that day along with a band of retainers. This man seems to have been esteemed in Louvain, and having no personal interest in city affairs, he was on friendly terms with the leaders of each party. Having vainly endeavoured to dissuade Coutherele from his purpose, he made his way, as best he could, to the Town Hall and offered his services to the patricians. 'Let them come forth like men and face the mob, and he and his followers would help them de bon coer et de bon courage. For,' said he, 'the people have not yet had time to muster; if we go forth now, I doubt not that with God's help we shall put to shame the handful that are already in the market-place, and when the rest behold their discomfiture they will run to cover like poulets that have spied a hawk.'

Sound advice probably, 'but those hommes de loy were men of such frail and meagre courage' that they deemed it too hazardous. Whereat Vorsselaer, disgusted, incontinently leapt into his saddle and made for Brussels, where we shall presently meet him. Meanwhile the mob was increasing each moment in fury and in numbers, and the patricians, thus left to their own devices, very soon came to the conclusion that no other course was open to them but to treat with Myn Here Coutherele. They did so, and with this result. To their envoy he made reply that the people would fain be assured that the city accounts were in order. Let the doors of the Town Hall be opened, and he and his friends would enter and examine their books, and, when they had done so, withdraw. The patricians complied, and Coutherele kept faith to the letter, nay, he went even beyond his bond, for not only did he examine the account books, he made a bonfire of them, and added thereto the charters of patrician privileges and all other parchments he could set hands on; and when at last he and his friends withdrew, they took care to bring their opponents with them disarmed and under arrest.

Thus did the old régime at Louvain come to an inglorious end. The patricians had not struck a blow in defence of their privileges, and the fact that the revolution was accomplished without bloodshed bears witness not only to the humanity and moderation of Coutherele, but to the marvellous influence which he must have had over the mob. Next morning Coutherele himself, who was now practically dictator, named a new magistracy, consisting of four patricians, men who were known to favour the people, and three plebeians. It was the first time that a commoner had been named alderman in any town of Brabant.

Meanwhile the men who had been captured in the Town Hall were still in prison, and presently their friends made private appeal to Duchess Jeanne, who opened communications with Coutherele with a view to their liberation. Perhaps it was the policy of neither party to come to an understanding; in any case, after several weeks had elapsed and nothing had been effected the negotiations were broken off. Whereat the prisoners, fearing for their lives, which after all hung by a thread, proceeded themselves to treat with the all-powerful dictator, and with better results, for after some haggling they purchased their freedom upon undertaking to quit the city as soon as they should be set at liberty.

The ransom which each man paid was assessed in proportion to his means, but the sum-total thus realised amounted to a very large figure, and his enemies said that, by this transaction, Coutherele had made himself one of the richest men in Brabant, but in reality he expended the whole of this fund, or, at all events, the greater portion of it, in the purchase of the new charter which Duke Winceslaus granted to the city of Louvain in the month of September 1360.

In this remarkable document, which was no doubt drawn up by Coutherele himself, the Duke gave legal sanction to the changes accomplished in July. He fully recognised the claim of the plebeians to participate in the government of the city; he decreed that henceforth three aldermen and eleven jurors should be chosen from among their ranks, and that all other municipal functions should be equally divided between the two classes. The elections were to take place annually, the plebeian members being named by the patricians and the patrician members by the plebeians—a very prudent regulation, calculated to secure in each case the return of moderate men.

The action of Coutherele in this matter must not be judged by the standard of to-day. In permitting his prisoners to purchase their freedom he was only following the usage of the age in which he lived. But that Winceslaus should have exacted a heavy fine or loan or gratuity—call it what you will—from the man who had realised for him his heart's desire was conduct more questionable. The only excuse that can be made for him is this: his expenses were heavy and his purse was light. The men of Louvain, however, were too well satisfied at the success of their enterprise to grumble at the bill of costs, more especially as the cash with which it was paid had been extracted from their enemies' pockets, and so elated were they at Coutherele's management of the whole affair that the magistrates voted him, from the public funds, a large annuity for life.

If the patricians had been wise enough to recognise accomplished facts, and had accepted the new constitution, which, after all, gave them the lion's share in the government, all might yet have gone well, and the city of Louvain would have been saved many years of strife and bloodshed; but their privileges had been so large and so profitable, and the good things which accrue to holders of office had been theirs for so long, that they would have been more than human if they had been willing at once to forego all thought of regaining their former position, and these substantial men of commerce were neither heroes nor saints. Most of them left the city in which they had once been supreme, and where now their claims were mocked at; where their very lives were, perhaps, in danger, and certainly were made a burthen to them by reason of domiciliary visits and all kinds of vexatious precautions. For the men in power were by no means sure of the stability of the new régime—they lived in constant dread of a counter revolution. What wonder, then, that their opponents, who, if the truth must be told, were not famous for courage, found it more comfortable to plot in their country homes than amid the turmoil of their town mansions, even though their voluntary exile meant confiscation of property?

As for Duke Winceslaus, though his capital was a prey to disorder and in imminent danger of commercial ruin, it was not his policy at present to interfere. He knew very well that these purse-proud traders, who in the day of their prosperity had given themselves the airs of princes, would presently grovel at his feet, and with their caps in their hands humbly beg his assistance; for, like their brethren at Brussels and elsewhere, though it amused them sometimes to play at soldiering, they would never do battle themselves if they could find someone else to fight for them, and this was what actually occurred. When their town property had been all confiscated, and commercial ruin was staring them in the face, having vainly invoked the aid of Brussels, of Mechlin, of Liége, they humbled themselves before their Sovereign, and, about the middle of October 1361, with a great army he sat down before the city of Louvain.

But though Winceslaus made great show of helping the patricians, he had not the slightest intention of breaking with the people, and the details of the farce which followed had no doubt been previously arranged with Coutherele. Certain it is that no sooner had Winceslaus encamped before Louvain than that worthy, in the name of the city, professed submission. His friends, he said, were ready to accept any conditions that the Duke might dictate. Whereat Winceslaus, to save appearances, ordained that they should come forth from the city to meet him, unarmed, unhatted and unshod, and, when they had reached his presence, fall down on their knees and humbly ask forgiveness. His instructions were carried out to the letter, and when the farce had been duly performed he presented them with a new charter, a masterpiece of duplicity, in which may be clearly seen the hand of Coutherele. It restored to the patricians the whole of their confiscated property; ordained that the ransoms paid by the prisoners of 1360, the greater part of which, it will be remembered, the Duke had pocketed himself, should be refunded from the public purse; and further, and most important of all, deprived Coutherele of his mayoralty. This was probably as much, or more, than the most sanguine of them had looked for, but in reality, as the patricians soon learned to their cost, Peter Coutherele and his mob were still masters of the situation; nay, so far as they were concerned, things were worse than they had been before, for the charter of 1360 gave them a majority in the College of Aldermen, and though that body was still to contain four patricians and three plebeians, Winceslaus had now reserved to himself the right of appointment, and first among the patricians whom he presently named was 'the renegade Peter Coutherele.' When the reactionists knew that in spite of his specious promises, the Duke had played them false, they at once declined to take any part in municipal affairs; and sooner than be compelled to do so—for the new charter made refusal to accept office, when named thereto, a crime punishable by imprisonment—shook the dust of Louvain off their feet, and again withdrew to their country strongholds.

The great tribune was now at the height of his power: his will was law in Louvain; he himself was first burgomaster; in his friend Jan Hanneman, the richest cloth merchant of the city, and one of the few patricians who favoured the popular cause, he had an able and willing lieutenant; another friend, the plebeian Gedulphe Rogge, one of his most devoted adherents, was second burgomaster; Paul Herengolys, a clerk in holy orders, was mayor, and every other municipal office was held by one or other of his creatures. Nor was this all. As a reward for his 'manifold good and faithful services' Winceslaus invested him with the ducal fief of Asten, in Limbourg, and all the rights and privileges appertaining thereto. In addition, then, to his hereditary rank of patrician, he was now a member of the feudal nobility—an anomalous position, maybe, for the leader of a democratic revolution, but presently Peter gave thanks to Heaven that the Castle of Asten was his. About the same time, too, he made a brilliant marriage for his daughter Gertrude, whom he gave to Henri de Cuyck, a brother of the powerful Lord of Hoogstraeten—a useful alliance this, and one which stood him in good stead, as we shall presently see.

Meanwhile the city finances were in sorry plight. For years past the patrician oligarchy had not only mismanaged public funds, but had systematically enriched themselves at the public cost, and though their corruption had been one of the chief causes of complaint against them on the part of the plebeians, now that they themselves were in office they deviated no whit in this matter from the traditions of their predecessors; for years past, too, the profits arising from cloth had gradually been diminishing, and since the Revolution of 1360 all business had been practically at a standstill. Added to this, Duke Winceslaus had been paid, and paid handsomely, for the charter of 1362. Indeed the quarrels of the men of Louvain were a fruitful source of wealth to their Sovereign. His method of extorting cash seems to have been this: he first fomented disturbances, then sold his support to the highest bidder, and finally, when he was called in to arbitrate, charged a heavy fee for expenses. In this manner he succeeded in amassing vast wealth, and it was currently reported in Brabant that during the year 1361 he received more money from the men of Louvain than would have been realised had the whole city been sold with all its outlying territory. Be this as it may, the city treasury was empty, and to obtain the funds necessary to meet current expenses, Coutherele had recourse to an expedient still resorted to by communities in like straits: he invoked the aid of foreign capitalists. Jan Hanneman was dispatched to Germany to sell life annuities, and so good was the credit of Louvain, or so great, perhaps, were his powers of persuasion, that in a very short time he returned laden with treasure. Of course Peter's enemies said, judging of him by what they themselves would have done under similar circumstances, that no small portion of it found its way into his own coffers:—This were surely the fund with which he had dowered his daughter. The charge of peculation which he had hurled at them they now flung back in his teeth, and again made appeal to Winceslaus and promised him gold. Whereat he once more assumed the rôle of arbitrator, confirmed the 'Peace of 1361,' adjured the belligerents to forgive and forget, and, as surety for their future good behaviour, demanded from each party hostages and, by way of compensation for the expenses he had incurred, a further cash payment. This was in February 1363, and shortly afterwards Coutherele himself conducted the plebeian hostages to the ducal castle at Tervueren.

The Lord of Asten went forth from Louvain exulting in the glory of his might, he was accompanied by a train of seventy horsemen, the cavalcade was a brilliant one, the people cheered him as he passed; his popularity had not one whit abated, he was still their idol, the saviour of the city, the valiant champion who had broken the yoke of slavery from off their necks; but in reality his sun had set: the triumphant ride to Tervueren was but the aftermath. He knew it when he had seen Winceslaus, and he knew too that lurid storm clouds were rolling up with the night. He was as sure that the Duke had joined the enemy as if he had learned it from his own lips. For him Louvain had ceased to be a safe abode: if haply he escaped the headsman's axe, he would sooner or later be stabbed in the back by a muffled ruffian lying in wait for him at the corner of some dark street; and if his lamp were put out, the cause for which he had so long suffered would at the same time die, for who could take the place of Peter Coutherele? Prudence and duty, then, counselled flight, and he fled to his manor at Asten, where he was presently joined by Hanneman and Herengolys.

If Peter had been content to lie low for a while, the natural course of events must have presently restored him to his former position: he had powerful friends at Court, he was still in possession of his barony, Winceslaus, satisfied at his voluntary exile, seems at the present juncture to have had no intention of wholly breaking with him. The Duke's policy was a policy of expedience: at Louvain the name of Coutherele was still one to conjure with, and the force of circumstances must have presently compelled him to fall back on his former ally, for, as after events showed, the patrician reaction was only a passing phase; in reality the flowing tide was still with the people.

But it was impossible for a man of Peter's temperament to sit with folded hands whilst vandals were wrecking his 'house Beautiful' and threatening to pull it down. That this was the case there was, unfortunately, no room for doubt. He was in constant communication with Louvain, and each day his envoys returned with tidings which lashed him to fury. They told him how these men of Belial, not content with corrupting the Duke, had corrupted also some of his own followers—plebeians, in whose integrity he had placed implicit confidence; how Winceslaus, whilst cynically confirming their charter of rights, had twisted it into an instrument of torture, by naming these renegades representatives of the people in the city council; how the patricians, thus free to act as they would, had not only compensated themselves largely from the public purse for property of which they had been most righteously deprived in 1360, but had deemed it no shame to draw from the same source the huge sum they had promised Winceslaus, and this at a time when the city was honeycombed with debt, when all business was at a standstill, when thousands of men were out of work, and their wives and little ones starving. Nor did even this complete the sum of their iniquity: foreseeing that the victims of their evil deeds would at last be goaded to turn on them, they had meanly deprived them of the power to do so by taking away their weapons.

That was the last straw. Coutherele was beside himself. He would hesitate no longer. Not one of these men should escape the sword of his vengeance. His plan was to advance on Louvain under cover of night with what men and arms he could muster, enter through one of the city gates, which, at a given signal, friends within would open, join forces with the craftsmen, stealthily break into the Town Hall, where he knew there were weapons, and then, when each man had armed himself, fall on their adversaries unawares, and slay them in their beds. The plot was doubtless suggested by the Bloody Matins of Bruges, and if it had been possible to carry it out a like result might have followed; but at Bruges the craftsmen were true to one another, at Louvain there was a traitor in the camp, and on the appointed night, when Coutherele and his little band were nearing the Castle of Heverlé,[12] on the outskirts of the city, they found themselves confronted by Winceslaus and an army of knights and burghers; a desperate encounter followed, and the rebels were put to flight.

Even now Winceslaus seems to have been loath to resort to extreme measures against his former friends and accomplices. Coutherele had fled the country, and was beyond his reach, Hanneman and Herengolys had also disappeared, and if he had been left to his own devices he would most likely have found it convenient to follow the advice of his friend Schoonvorst and take no further action in the matter, but the patricians, as was natural, objected.—As long as these murderous ruffians lived they were not safe in their beds; let a price be set on the head of each one of them, and warrants issued for their arrest. And they used another argument, one which experience told them would prove convincing: they jingled their moneybags. And Winceslaus signed the required edict and pocketed 300 florins d'or. This transaction had notable results. Herengolys was presently captured, condemned to death by the city magistrates, and in due course brought to the block; but the aldermen had reckoned without their host, the ex-mayor of Louvain was a clerk, and, as such, not amenable to their jurisdiction, and John of Arkel, who at this time ruled the Church of Liége, no sooner heard of his fate than he set Louvain under interdict. He would never suffer the rights of his clergy to be trampled on with impunity, and moreover he seems to have shared, at all events to a certain extent, Herengolys's political opinions. In his own principality he consistently favoured the aspirations of democracy, and in the struggle at Louvain he more than once intervened, and always on behalf of the people. Perhaps his action in the Herengolys affair was inspired by Peter Coutherele, who, immediately after the disaster of Heverlé, had fled to Liége.

Nothing daunted by the fate of his friend, Coutherele at once set to work to concoct new measures for the deliverance of his beloved city. Having ingratiated himself with Albert of Holland, he now took up his abode in that country, where presently a great conference was held of outlaws from every town in Brabant, during which was planned another attack on Louvain; but this scheme, like the last, was betrayed, and failed miserably.

For years the great agitator led a restless and vagabond life, sometimes in Holland, sometimes in Germany, sometimes in France, never long in one place, always intriguing wherever he went, and making plans which he could never carry out, and hatching plots which, for some reason or other, he could never bring to maturity. At last, at the intercession of his son-in-law, Henri de Cuyck, Winceslaus granted him a free pardon, and permitted him to return to his native city (March 1369), but he was a broken-down, worn-out old man, and he came back to Louvain to die. The few months he had to live he passed in strict retirement in his house in the Rue de la Fontaine, where he died the following year, poor and forgotten.

CHAPTER X
The Peace of 1383

The flight of Coutherele and the failure of his subsequent efforts left the reactionary party a free hand, and by 1375 they had so consolidated their position that they were able to compel Winceslaus to cancel the charter of 1361 and grant in its place a new charter, which gave back to the old ruling class its former monopoly of political power. The result may be surmised: mismanagement and corruption were the order of the day; no accounts were published, and justice had to be bought; any manifestation of discontent was put down with cruel vigour, and even the right of sanctuary was not always respected. Once, after some abortive rising, when a score of trembling wretches, who had taken refuge in the cloister of Notre Dame, were dragged forth by order of the magistrates and put to death, the Bishop of Liége interfered and imposed a heavy fine; and no doubt the patricians laughed in their sleeves when presently the account was settled, for it was not they, but the people, who bore the brunt of the imposts.

Though taxation had never before been so high, the treasury was empty; loan had been added to loan, and private individuals travelling abroad were on all sides being arrested for public debts. Thus export trade had become impossible, and as for industry, there was nothing doing, for sooner than submit to the exactions of their taskmasters, a third of the working population had emigrated.

At last, when Louvain was on the verge of ruin, the patricians themselves began to suspect that there was something wrong with their methods of government, and, at their wits' end what to do, presently consulted Winceslaus, who, wise man, suggested a great conference of all the cities of Brabant to consider the situation. This was early in the year 1378. The patricians agreed, and in due course a conference was summoned. Towards the close of March the deputies met in the Town Hall of Louvain; the Duke himself presided, and almost every town in the duchy was represented.

It is not certain whether the craftsmen of Louvain took any part in the proceedings, but they were able to make their influence felt. Whilst the conference was sitting they sent in a petition to Winceslaus, humbly requesting, among other things, that a statement should be published of the town accounts from the time of Coutherele's administration to date; that such patricians as had been awarded annuities by way of indemnity for losses incurred during Coutherele's term of office should cease to receive them as soon as the sum justly due to them had been repaid, and that those who had already received more than their due should be compelled to refund the surplus; and, most important of all, that the town seal should be confided to the joint care of the patrician clans, the guild and the trade companies, so that henceforth no new loan could be negotiated without the unanimous consent of the burghers.

It is significant of the trend of public opinion that the deputies made these requests their own, and further, named a committee of eight patricians and eight plebeians to study the question of the town debt and the financial situation generally. By Pentecost they had sent in their report, and Duchess Jeanne—Winceslaus being absent in Luxembourg—at once laid it before the conference, which was now sitting in St. Gertrude's Abbey. It embodied many wise and prudent suggestions, some of which sound strangely modern, but they touched too nearly the rights of property to be acceptable to most of the patricians. It would have been surprising, indeed, if many of them had welcomed an income tax and death duties, or a tax on Church lands, or an all round reduction of official salaries, and these proposals, and others of a like kind, aroused such a storm of opposition that Jeanne suggested that perhaps it might be as well to leave it to the Duke and his council to solve the financial problem, but to this, naturally enough, everyone objected, and when presently Winceslaus himself returned he could only reiterate his wife's proposal, promising that he would take no step without first consulting his bonnes villes and his brother-in-law of Flanders—Louis of Maele, whose tenderness to his own patricians was notorious throughout the Low Countries; but he might just as well have held his breath, the patricians refused to hearken and things came to a standstill. Whereat the people grew restive. Difficulties, they alleged, were being purposely raised to stave off reform, they themselves would settle the matter in their own fashion; and on the 22nd of July the mob was out, battering at the doors of the Town Hall, and clamouring to Burgomaster Van Nethen to bring forth the great seal and the town charters. To do so, he said, was impossible, he had not got the keys, and, even if he had, it were contrary to law to unlock the rolls coffer save in the presence of the whole council. Needless to say, the rioters were not convinced, and at nightfall a host of them, with arms and banners, headed by the weaver, Wouter Vander Leyden, filed into the Grand' Place, took possession of the Hôtel de Ville, arrested the aldermen they found there, and, without much difficulty, made themselves masters of the town.

The victory was all the more easily won from the fact that a large number of patricians—all who had the welfare of the city at heart, were in reality not opposed to the rioters, perhaps even secretly leagued with them. These men were under the leadership of Alderman Jan De Swertere, a patrician of note who loved the people, his enemies said, because he hated Alderman

Vanden Calstere, the chief of the ultra-reactionists. It was the time when the famous 'White Hoods' of Ghent were disporting themselves in Flanders, and the revolutionists of Louvain, patricians and plebeians alike, adopted their headgear. Wouter Vander Leyden and Hendrick Portman were chosen captains of the city, there was an exodus of reactionists, and a deputation was sent to Winceslaus, now at Brussels, begging him to come at once and legalise what had been done. It was not, however, until nearly two months had been consumed in negotiation, and until he had received from the men of Louvain more than 6000 peters, that he at last consented to give them a new and acceptable charter.

The constitution with which the city was now endowed, so far as concerned the composition of the magistracy, was identical with Coutherele's constitution—the College of Aldermen and the Council of Jurors were still to contain respectively four and eleven patricians, and three and ten plebeians; but the method of appointing these officers was considerably modified: henceforth the aldermen were to be named by the Sovereign from a triple list presented to him jointly by the patrician and non-patrician members of the Merchants' Guild; the non-patrician members alone were to name the patrician jurors; and the plebeian jurors were to be chosen by the trade companies, now grouped together in ten corporations called nations, each nation electing a juror. Further, there were to be two burgomasters—the first chosen by the plebeians from among the patricians, the second by the patricians from among the plebeians—and four treasurers, all plebeians:—two craftsmen and two members of the Merchants' Guild. They were to have the entire management of the finances of the town, hold office for one year, and give an account of their stewardship to the College of Aldermen, the Council of Jurors and the Merchants' Guild, assembled in solemn council, every quarter-day. Satisfaction was also given to the people in the matter of the government of the guild: henceforth there were to be eight deans—four plebeians named by the patricians, and four patricians chosen by the nations; and, for the rest, all minor offices were to be equally divided among the two classes of the bourgeoisie.

Such, in its main outlines, was the constitution with which Louvain was endowed by the Great Charter—the Peace, as it was called—of 1378, and which, with some slight modification, continued to be the constitution of the city until the close of the eighteen hundreds. Never before had the people enjoyed so large a share in the government. The patricians, indeed, still retained a considerable place in the magistracy, but their voice was almost stifled in the matter of elections, though, mark this, what they had lost was not given to the proletariat, but to the middle class, as represented by the non-patrician members of the guild—rising merchants and manufacturers, men, for the most part, of moderate means and moderate opinions, in touch on the one side with the working-class, from which most frequently they had sprung, and on the other with the aristocracy, which already included some of their kinsmen, and within whose charmed circle it was not beyond the dreams of several of them, if trade went well, to one day find admittance.

Nobody supposed that Vanden Calstere and his friends would be grateful to Duke Winceslaus for the 'Peace' of 1378, but it was probably matter of surprise to everyone that their resentment took the form it did: they remained without the city walls, not in their own strongholds, but at Aerschot, Vilvorde, Hal, in one or other of the little towns hard by Louvain, and, sallying forth from these places with what ruffians they could hire, lay in wait for stray burghers, and with such of them as fell into their clutches it went hardly—sometimes they held them to ransom, and sometimes they cut their throats. At last things came to this pass:—no foreign trader would come within measurable distance of the city, and no burgher who valued his life would venture beyond the ramparts, but it was not till Wouter Vander Leyden had been murdered that the people lost patience. This man, who was now burgomaster, had been charged by the magistrates to make complaint to Duke Winceslaus of the conduct of the reactionists, and as he was journeying to Brussels to execute the commission, or, as some say, as he was returning home at night, he was surprised in a lonely spot by Vanden Calstere himself and Willem Wilre, his henchman, and literally hacked to pieces.

Hardly had the news reached Louvain than the craftsmen flew to arms, the city gates were shut, and all patricians suspected of being hostile to the new régime were arrested and imprisoned in an upper chamber of the Town Hall. This seems to have been done by order of the magistrates, perhaps by way of precaution, for the people were at the end of their patience. Presently they got out of hand; a rush was made for the Town Hall, the doors were forced and the prisoners thrown out of window, one by one as their names were called by the mob outside. Sixteen or seventeen persons perished in this manner (December 15, 1378)—innocent or guilty who shall say: they had not been placed on trial. Amongst them Jan Platvoet, a patrician of fourscore years whose only crime seems to have been that he was a kinsman of one of the murderers; and an archer of the guard, name unknown, who had formerly been his servant. This man, when the doors were forced, made his former master crawl under a bench placed against the wall, and had then seated himself on it, and perhaps old Jan might have escaped if it had not been for the sharp eyes of a weaver's inquisitive 'kint,' who said he saw something shining between the archer's legs. It was the gold-embroidered ends of poor Platvoet's necktie. They dragged him forth, and, in spite of his prayers, cast him headlong into the market; but the traitor who would have saved a patrician's life was pitched out of window first. Hitherto the craftsmen of Louvain had contented themselves with banishing or imprisoning their enemies; it was the first time in the course of their long struggle that they had stained their souls with blood.

For weeks after the murder of the patricians the rioters remained in the streets, and for months after order had been re-established men lived in a fever of anticipation, each side looking for some fresh outrage which would be sure to result in yet crueller acts of reprisal. But though Winceslaus knew all this, and seems to have been early appealed to, it was not till the close of May that he made any serious effort to restore public confidence by punishing the delinquents. Then he published an edict in which he enjoined twelve of the principal rioters to make a pilgrimage to Cyprus, sentenced to exile nine patricians who had been mixed up in the murder of Vander Leyden, and imposed on the city a fine of 4000 peters.

But things were in too parlous a plight to be righted by proclamation: the White Hoods, indeed, for the moment were quiet, but the reactionists refused to submit, and forthwith proceeded to harry the country estates of the rallied patricians, whom, rightly or wrongly, they suspected of having instigated the murder of their relatives. Of course De Swetere and his folk retaliated in like fashion, and in all that they attempted and in all that they did, of course they were aided and abetted by their very good friends, the plebeians: homestead after homestead was razed to the ground, castle after castle fired, and soon the whole country round Louvain became the scene of guerilla warfare.

Meanwhile Vanden Calstere, or some of his friends, had again taken to the road. Burgomaster Oorbeke, returning from Brussels, was arrested and held to ransom; so, too, several jurors; and worse still was the fate of a notable private citizen—Myn Here Van Grave, a merchant of vast wealth: they cut off his hands and his feet, and sent him home in a waggon, bidding him tell his fellow-burghers that any one of them whom they chanced to take would be treated in like fashion.

Again and again the bonnes villes tendered their good offices. Again and again the Duke did his utmost to arrange matters. Negotiations were often begun, but, for some reason or other, they always fell through. It was not till the beginning of the year 1383, after Winceslaus had been compelled to lay siege to Louvain, that the Bishop of Liége was at last able to reconcile the belligerents.

Of course, as in all such cases, the settlement was a compromise; but though it banished nineteen craftsmen for a year and a day, opened the gates of the city to Vanden Calstere and his friends, and guaranteed them complete immunity for all their past offences, it was not these men, but their opponents, who in reality had the best of the bargain: the constitution of 1378 remained intact; the people surrendered no jot or tittle of their political rights and privileges.

Peace then was at last established; the terms of agreement were on each side loyally adhered to, and the reconciliation endured. Mutual confidence had taken the place of universal suspicion, and the craftsmen nourished no rancour against those who had formerly been their bitterest foes: when presently, in the month of June, the time arrived for the annual renewal of the magistracy, Henry Pynnock, Godfrey Utten Liemingen and Goswin Vanden Calstere were elected aldermen, and that, in spite of the fact that they had all of them been reactionists; nor, it is pleasant to note, did they belie the people's trust.

CHAPTER XI
Reform versus *Revolution*

When the revolution of 1360 broke out the city of Louvain was, in name and in fact, the first city of Brabant. The cluster of cottages around the church which Lambert Balderic had founded on the banks of the Dyle three centuries before had grown into a great industrial and commercial centre, with a population of something like 70,000 souls. In the number of its inhabitants, in the extent of its trade, in political influence, in social prestige, in the splendour of its public and private buildings, it eclipsed at this time every town in the duchy. Among the burgher nobles of Brabant none were so rich and so powerful as the Petermen of Louvain: not only did they enjoy the dignities and privileges common to all patricians, but they participated, as we have seen, in the immunities of the Church, and that, without being irked by correlative duties. Also, they shone alone, there were no brighter stars in their firmament: the Sovereign had long ago left Louvain, and there were no Court nobles to rival their glory or to dispute their right to pre-eminence. As they were human, of course they were puffed up—proud of their wealth, proud of their race, proud of their solitary grandeur and of the consideration which these things gave them; exceedingly jealous of their privileges, very swift to resent any attempt at aggression, whether it came from above or from below; and of course they contemned the seething mass of shame and misery beneath them—a mutinous army of workers, many thousands strong, as eager and determined to obtain liberty as their masters were to keep them in bondage.

Such was the social complexion of Louvain during the fifty years which preceded the revolution of 1360. Paint the picture on a smaller scale and in less glaring colours, and you will have some idea of the social complexion of Brussels during the same period.

Brussels, like Louvain, was at this time divided into two hostile camps; here, too, patricians and plebeians were biting their thumbs at one another; but neither side was so strong or so violent as in the sister city. The patricians were not so rich, and perhaps in consequence not so selfish, and the plebeians were less numerous, and probably on this account less exacting; and too, though they were not born on a bed of rose leaves, they had less cause for complaint. High and mighty as were the merchant princes of Brussels, they were not so high and mighty as the descendants of Saint Peter's serfs. Their splendour was not enhanced by a semi-ecclesiastical aureole; they had no title to distinction but that which their money gave;

and though, like the patricians of Louvain, they owned the freehold of the town which they administered and governed, they were not alone in their glory. When the Duke was not at the Coudenberg he was at his hunting-lodge at Tervueren, just outside the city gates, and the burghers were in frequent contact with the nobles of the Court, who, though often poor and often in their debt, were, for all that, socially their superiors. For these or for some other reasons the local aristocracy at Brussels was less overbearing than at Louvain, class distinctions were less sharply defined, and the plebeians were treated with more consideration.

On the whole, then, Brussels was a less turbulent town than the capital, and the road to reform, as might be expected, led through smoother ways. The great struggle began about the same time as at Louvain, and, as at Louvain, the Duke's action precipitated events. In the year 1356 Winceslaus, in order to reward the plebeians for driving the Flemings out of Brussels, and also to mark his displeasure at the disloyal conduct of the patricians, who had welcomed them with open arms, granted to the trade companies by charter an equal share with the patrician clans in the government of the city; but this boon, which the people had so long coveted, and which at last they had obtained, was theirs only for a day: the ink of the new charter was hardly dry when Winceslaus revoked it.

No record has come down to us of the motives which inspired his action, nor do we even know the exact date of the cancelling of the charter. This event, however, can hardly have taken place earlier than 1357 nor later than 1360, and most likely the reactionary party in the patrician camp by means of bribes or promises had purchased the Duke.

Naturally the people were profoundly irritated. Secret meetings were held, and presently matters came to a crisis. It was just at this time that Coutherele was meditating his coup d'état, and perhaps there was some understanding between the craftsmen of the two cities: it is significant that the rebellion at Louvain began on the 21st of July, and that at Brussels the mob was out on the night of the 23rd. The craftsmen's plan of action was to surprise the patricians in their beds, and if they had been able to keep it close perhaps they might have accomplished something, but at the last moment they were betrayed, and thus it came about that whilst they were seeking their banners their opponents took possession of the market-place.

Strangely enough Gerard of Vorsselaer, the same who two nights before had been busying himself with the affairs of Louvain, first essaying to calm the mob, and when that failed, advising the patricians as to the best means of quelling them, had now arrived at Brussels, and finding the town in a similar predicament, he did what he could to set matters straight. By his advice the senior alderman essayed negotiations: he invited the dean of the butchers, who were assembled under arms in their guild house, to a conference in the Town Hall; and presently the messenger returned trembling—he had been treated with threats and curses, and the dean had bade him say that 'the butchers would come in a body soon enough.' Hardly had he finished speaking when word was brought that the weavers were attacking the Steenporte (the city prison).[13] In an instant the patricians were in their saddles. If only they could intercept the butchers the situation might yet be saved, and with Vorsselaer at their head, they made for the meat market, and en route fell in with the men they were seeking. A skirmish followed, but the patricians, who were well armed and on horseback, had little difficulty in overcoming a handful of footmen with no weapons but pole-axes: they were soon disarmed and driven home to their own squalid quarters. Meanwhile the men of the spindle had been vainly hurling themselves against the doors of the Steenporte, and now, with the assistance of fullers and dyers, they were preparing to burn it down. Why not repay the curs in their own coin by setting fire to their kennels? The suggestion came from Myn Here Van Vorsselaer; it was forthwith carried out, and the issue showed that honest Gerard was a man whose judgment was to be relied on.

When the rioters saw the redness in the sky they knew what had happened, and with a mad rush made for home, only to fall into the arms of their enemies, who barring the way in a narrow street halfway down the hill, mowed them down like grass and trampled the life out of them beneath their horses' feet; and that was the end of the rising of 1360. It does not seem, after all, to have been a very serious affair—butchers and clothworkers alone had taken part in it, but if the magistrates had followed the example set them by the magistrates of Louvain two nights before, there is little doubt that by morning things would have assumed a very different complexion.

Thanks to the energy and determination of the patricians, revolution had been nipped in the bud, but the city was seething with discontent, the plebeian triumph at Louvain had inflamed the people with an unquenchable thirst for liberty, and they were only awaiting a favourable moment to try their luck again. Of this the patricians were well aware, and since most of them were not yet prepared to relinquish a shred of their authority, only one policy was open to them—a policy of stern repression applied with energy and vigilance. Of these qualities they gave ample proof, but they do not seem to have been guilty of wanton cruelty or even, bearing in mind the object they had in view, of unnecessary harshness.

The number of weavers who perished on the night of the insurrection was indeed very considerable, but when once order had been restored they refrained from further bloodshed. Their main object was to rid the town of agitators, and all who were suspected of being such were condemned to banishment. Nor were these men suffered to unduly defer the date of their departure by taking refuge in churches: the right of sanctuary was not violated, but the proscribed were forbidden to remain in any church within the liberty of Brussels for more than a week, under penalty of a prolongation of their term of banishment by as many years as they had remained days above that period, and their fellow-citizens were forbidden to supply such persons with provisions under penalty of a heavy fine; but, on the other hand, all those who were willing to quit the city within the time prescribed were at once provided with a safe conduct.

It is impossible within the limits of this little manual to give any detailed account of the numerous penal laws with which the statute book of Brussels was at this time endowed. Suffice it to say that many of them were of an inquisitorial and vexatious character; that the dire penalties with which all of them were sanctioned—exile, long terms of imprisonment, in some cases even mutilation—were for the most part commutable for fines, thus giving to the rich an advantage over the poor, which the latter resented as a flagrant violation of right; and lastly, that they were not evenly enforced. Measures of this kind were not calculated to allay irritation, and though there was no open display of sedition, the city was seething with discontent, and the patricians knew it. Haunted by plots and rumours of plots, they were never sure when they went to bed at night that their throats would not be cut before morning, and, half blind with terror, they struck out wildly on all sides, and often the guilty escaped, and a host of harmless citizens experienced the taste of their lash.

Meanwhile the little band of patricians who from the first had favoured a conciliatory policy were steadily making converts; but it was not until they had preached for eight years, and when Brussels was on the edge of revolution, that they at last succeeded in convincing the majority that the times were ripe for reform. The first step was to restore confidence in the administration of justice, and to this end the city fathers (June 19, 1368), having first taken counsel with the leaders of the people, named a commission of four patricians and four plebeians to inquire into the numerous disputes and grievances which had arisen from the maladministration of the coercion laws, and to make report thereon to the magistrates, who, it was decreed, should be bound by oath to remedy such grievances and settle such disputes in accordance with the evidence thus laid before them, and it was further decreed that such sentence should be final. Any man who refused to accept the same, thereby lost all his rights and privileges until such time as he chose to conform: if he were a patrician he ceased to be a member of his lignage, if he were a craftsman he was expelled from his guild.

These measures proved so efficacious that before the close of the year the aldermen had sufficiently recovered from their nerve crisis to be able to consider finance, and that, though they had to face some abstruse questions—how to balance the budget without increasing taxation or having recourse to fresh loans, how to put a stop to corruption without incurring enmity or wounding the susceptibilities of friends, and, above all, how to pay off that terrible debt which was crushing the life out of Brussels, outcome of so many years of extravagance and thieving. Problems, these, not easy to solve, but again the patricians were wise enough to consult the people, representatives of the trade companies took part in their deliberations, and somehow or other between them they managed to set the affairs of the town on a sound financial basis—the following year revenue covered expenditure and the interest of the debt, the year after that they began to pay off the principal, and by 1386 the whole debt was wiped out. Matter this for congratulation, and no doubt the people rejoiced, but there was something that gladdened their hearts even more, and which they flattered themselves accounted for the fact that the loan had been repaid so quickly: for more than eighteen years their fingers had been on the purse-strings, and by the grace of God they meant to keep them there. Nor was this all, in 1368 the guild had been thoroughly reorganised, and on popular lines. About the same time it became customary to bestow a certain number of government appointments on burghers of the middle class, and though the patricians were not yet prepared to give the people any voice in the magistracy, they were determined that justice should be administered with an even hand, and that henceforth no man should be able to say that Brussels was ill governed, and to this end, in 1375, a new system had been elaborated for recruiting the College of Aldermen.

In the early days in Brussels, as in the other cities of Brabant, the Sovereign himself had named the city magistrates. Later on some form of election was adopted in which all the members of the patrician class seem to have taken part, but little by little this custom had fallen into disuse, and at the time when the reform movement set in, though the college was still annually renewed, no election had taken place for something like a hundred years—the outgoing aldermen had gradually acquired a prescriptive right to name their successors. This had opened the door to all kinds of abuses, and in order to put a stop to them and to insure that henceforth none but honest and competent men should be admitted to the magistracy, in 1375 the city fathers reverted to the old system of election, and stringent rules were drawn up to regulate the proceedings which now became exceedingly long and complicated.

In the first place, each of the outgoing aldermen drew up a list of all the members of his lineage eligible to succeed him, that is to say, of all the married members of twenty-eight years of age and upwards who had sufficient means to live without exercising any trade or profession. The next step was to summon the clans, and this, too, devolved on the outgoing aldermen, each man inviting the members of his lineage to assemble in the Town Hall on the day fixed for the election—generally the 23rd of June— and there select from the names on his list three candidates for the magistracy. 'I swear,' runs the quaint and characteristic oath which each man present was required to take at the commencement of the proceedings, 'I swear by the Saints, and on the Holy Gospels, that I am in no way bound or pledged to any man, and that no man is bound or pledged to me, directly or indirectly, nor have I purchased any man's vote, either on my own behalf or on behalf of any of my friends. I swear, on my soul, to give my suffrages to the best man, the wisest man, and in every respect the fittest man, the most devoted to Holy Church, to the Duke and Duchess of Brabant, the city of Brussels and the patrician order; consulting only my conscience and acting according to my conviction. I swear, on my soul, not to let any personal interest or private friendship move me, nor to suffer myself to be carried away by hatred or anger, or by fear of loss or hope of gain; so help me God and His Saints.'

No less curious than the preliminary oath was the process of election. Every member of the clan was bound to be present and to take the prescribed oath, under penalty of forfeiting all his rights and privileges, but never more than five, and sometimes only four, members took part in the actual voting; they were picked out from the rest by lot, and the drawing was managed in this way. A number of waxen balls, equal to the number of clansmen present, all without alike, but of which four contained within a white and one a black cipher, were placed in an urn, and, when they had been well shuffled, each member drew therefrom one of them, and presently, when the drawing was over, broke it. Whereupon the four men to whom the white-marked balls had fallen withdrew to a separate apartment to consider who was the most fitting man to represent their lineage, each man being free to propose what name he would, provided it was not his own. If they were all of one mind the man of their choice became a candidate for the magistracy, so too if three of them voted for the same individual, or, if two were agreed on one man, and each of the other two were in favour of different men. If, however, the suffrages were equally divided, that is to say, if all four electors cast their votes differently, or if two voted for one man and two for another, black ball was called in to give a casting vote. When the whole operation had been completed, it was repeated a second and again a third time, and by this means three candidates were chosen, whose names were afterwards submitted to the

Duke, and he, in due course, named one of them alderman of his clan for the ensuing year.

The College of Aldermen, it should be borne in mind, consisted of seven members, each of whom was held to represent, in a special manner, one of the seven patrician clans of Brussels.

How great had been the evil resulting from the old method of election may be inferred from the stringency of the new rules, and the dire penalties attached to any infraction of them, and also from the cumbrous and complicated machinery deemed necessary to guard against corrupt practices.

Thanks to this important measure, and to the other reforms which had been previously inaugurated, the city was now honestly and capably governed, and, in consequence, enjoyed peace. Indeed, for more than fifty years after 1368—the time of the great reconciliation—patricians and plebeians seem to have lived, if not on terms of affection, at all events without quarrelling. The latter, it is true, had not relinquished their high aspirations, but finding that the town was honestly administered, and, on the whole, equitably governed, they were wise enough to cherish their ideal in their innermost bosoms, and to take no active steps to realise it.

No doubt the greater material prosperity which the city at this time enjoyed was conducive, in no small measure, to the maintenance of peace. Brussels was not dependent on cloth to anything like the same extent as was the sister city, and, moreover, the loss which she had sustained on this head from English competition, and the competition of the country towns, was to a certain extent made good by the profit arising from trade which formerly went to Louvain, but which was now, owing to the disturbed state of that city, directed to her doors. Hundreds of merchants and thousands of mechanics went forth from the capital between 1360 and 1382, and not a few of these took up their permanent abode in Brussels. Linen, leather, tapestry and goldsmith's work were among the articles for which, about this time, Brussels became famous, and, thanks to these new industries, the loss, or rather the diminution, of her cloth trade was a matter of little concern to the people.

CHAPTER XII
Everard T'Serclaes

Chief among the giants who at this time were cleansing the Augean stables of Brussels, building up her shattered bulwarks, promoting harmony among their fellow-citizens, strangling discontent with good government, and putting off revolution by reform, towers the figure of Everard T'Serclaes, a head and shoulders above the rest of them. Everard T'Serclaes, or in plain English Everard Nicholson—politician, patriot, aristocrat, possessor of much gold and many acres, high in authority, high in his Sovereign's favour, one whom the whole town spoke well of, and, in spite of it all, an honest man. Born in the year 1315 or thereabout of an old magisterial house famous in civic annals, descended, probably in the female line, from the unknown founder of the great clan in which his family had for generations been enrolled, the clan called S'Leeuws Geslachte—that is, of the lion—so named from the magnanimous beast displayed on the S'Leeuws escutcheon, from the time when he reached man's estate Everard T'Serclaes had in all probability busied himself, after the manner of his fellows, with civic affairs; and yet for at least twenty years after this period his life is a blank to us: of his childhood, his youth, his upbringing, we know nothing; and even the date of his birth is matter of conjecture. This is all the more remarkable from the fact that T'Serclaes did more for his native town and his native land than any other man of his day, and was deservedly the most popular Brussels hero of the Middle Age. He first appears on the stage of history in 1356, when he must have already reached middle life, and his coming was in this wise.

It was the time of the Flemish invasion. On the 17th of August 1356 the Duke's forces had been utterly routed at Scheut, hard by Anderlecht; he himself had fled the country; Louis of Maele had entered Brussels almost without opposition, and his right to the duchy had been acknowledged by every town in Brabant. 'Truly it was an admirable thing to behold so sudden a metamorphosis: in two days the whole government had completely changed its face.' Thus the contemporary chronicler Butkins, but in reality the sympathies of the governing classes, had been from the first with the Count of Flanders. They knew very well that Winceslaus hated patricians, and they knew too that Louis in his own dominions was a staunch supporter of aristocratic rule. Hence they regarded his triumph as their own, and it was actually at their instigation that he had assumed the title of Duke of Brabant.

Meanwhile Winceslaus was at Maestricht collecting forces, considering invasion, and Louis's allies, Englebert de la Mark, Bishop of Liége, and William, Count of Namur, were posted on the eastern frontier of his former duchy ready to oppose him. Presently news unlooked for astounded either camp—the standard of Brabant was once more floating over Brussels, the Flemish garrison had been driven out; the feat had been accomplished by a simple burgher, Everard T'Serclaes. It was the English victory at Poitiers which made this achievement possible: the French army had been cut to pieces, King John himself was a prisoner, and the interests of Louis of Maele were one with the interests of France; hence when the news reached him at Brussels he had at once set out for Bruges, purposing from thence to proceed to Paris, where at the present juncture he deemed his presence indispensable; and thus the field was left clear for Everard's machinations. That wily burgher, now in exile at Maestricht, had trusty friends in his native town, who kept him constantly aware of all that was taking place, and by them he was at once informed of the Flemish Count's departure. The time was ripe, it seemed to him, for attempting something. A plan of action was arranged, and presently he was nearing Brussels alone, through the forest of Soignes, which at that time extended right up to the city. It was the 29th of October, and a black raw night had set in with drenching rain, which showed no sign of abatement. So much the better, there was the less chance of meeting wayfarers, and T'Serclaes was so well acquainted with the country that darkness was no hindrance to him. Making for a spot near his own dwelling,[14] where he knew the rampart was low and unprotected by water, thither he stealthily came when the night was well advanced, and without much difficulty effected an entrance. No one was stirring, there was no sign of life, no sound but the cry of the wind and the sullen drip of the rain—the city seemed wrapt in slumber; but though comfortable burghers were snoring in bed, T'Serclaes had friends expecting him, for the most part mere riff-raff who catered for the wants of the masses—the keepers of small taverns and those who helped them in their calling, tapsters, potmen, scullions, cooks, the offscum of a great city, men who feared not a reckless venture, because they had nothing to lose. Presently the signal agreed on broke the silence of the night—'Brabant for the great Duke,' and almost before the echo had died away Everard was leading a ragged army to the Groote Markt, where soon the golden lion of Brabant was to take the place of the black lion of Flanders. When the change had been duly effected and the Flemish banner spat on, shredded, dragged in the mire, the crowd, which by this time had assembled, sent up a great cheer for Everard T'Serclaes and the flag of the fatherland; whereat the Flemish guard turned out to discover the cause of the hubbub. Only half awake, deafened by fierce oaths, scared by angry faces, it seemed to them that a haunted town was peopled by a legion of furies. Like men in a dream they tried to run, but their feet were glued to the pavement, and before they had time to wonder at it they were cut down. Some by a mighty effort compelled their limbs to flight, but it availed them nothing—they were stabbed from behind. A few by rare good fortune got free of the market unobserved, and if they had kept cool these men might perhaps have escaped, but that night the town was enchanted, and fleeing from phantom pursuers they leapt on the swords of foes in the flesh, or hurled themselves over ramparts and so dashed out their lives, or trapped in a net of byways at last took some specious turning which led them back to the shambles. Death in some shape was the lot of all, and for the most part they made no resistance, but a handful stood shoulder to shoulder and sold their lives dearly. That was practically the end of Flemish domination in Brabant. Within the next few days every town in the duchy, save Mechlin, had followed the example of Brussels, and before the close of the Octave of All Saints Winceslaus was back in his domains.

Local historians are often wont to emphasise this little war, which bears witness, so they say, to the patriotism and chivalry of their forebears; but were the men who drove out the Flemings wholly inspired by love of country and loyalty to their Duke? The facts of the case, we venture to think, suggest an answer in the negative. The patricians, of course, had taken no part in ousting the Flemish garrison, but when their allies at Brussels were being cut to pieces they seem to have made no effort to help them. No doubt they deemed it a wiser, safer and more comfortable policy to remain in bed and await the issue of events. Not that they were devoid of courage: when there was anything to be gained by drawing the sword they were never loth to do battle, but as practical business men it was not their wont to embark in any undertaking likely to end in disaster, and on the night of the massacre at Brussels they knew very well that no help which they could have given would have saved their friends from destruction. As for the plebeians, their action was probably inspired by mixed motives—a little hysterical patriotism, caught perhaps from T'Serclaes, a little liking for Duke Winceslaus, due chiefly to the fact that he was the enemy of their enemies the patricians, and a very large measure of hope that somehow or other the issue would be to their advantage. Nor in this were they deceived. They presently obtained the boon they most coveted—municipal representation. And T'Serclaes, too, had his reward—a knighthood, and until the day of his death what all men love, popularity.

That the Saviour of Brussels, as he was henceforth called, should have been esteemed at Court is sufficiently comprehensible: he had re-established the Duke on his throne; that he should have been the idol of the people was natural enough: through him they had reached the goal of their ambition; but that he should presently have been able to gain the goodwill of the very men whose hopes he had shattered, and whose privileges he had taken away, is a matter past comprehension, yet such was undoubtedly the case: he was premier alderman in 1365, and again in 1372, and at this time, be it born in mind, the old order of things having been re-established, the outgoing aldermen named their successors; after the reform of 1375, when the magistracy became elective, and all kinds of precautions were taken against corruption, and with a view to securing the best possible candidates, he still retained the confidence of the patricians, who named him premier alderman in 1377, and also in 1382; in 1375 he had represented the patricians of Brussels at the National Assembly of Braine-l'Alleud, summoned at the instance of the Bishop of Liége to put an end to sundry disputes between Winceslaus and his subjects, which were threatening civil war; on September 28, 1386, in spite of his seventy years, he led the men of Brussels to the siege of Gavres, outcome of a frontier trouble with Duke Henry of Gelderland; and, notwithstanding the disastrous issue of that campaign, he still retained the confidence of the patricians, who in 1387 again named him chief magistrate. It was the last time—before his year of office was out he came to a violent end.

It happened thus. Sweder Van Apcoude, Lord of Gaesbeke, the last of the barons of Brabant who exercised sovereign sway and regarded themselves as the equals of the chiefs to whom they owed allegiance, traced his descent through his mother, Jeanne of Homes, to Godfrey first Lord of Gaesbeke, a younger son of Duke Henry the Warrior. Like many other peers of Brabant, Sweder was a citizen of Brussels, and as such, when his mother died, and his uncles disputed his succession, he had summoned them before the College of Aldermen, who, to their cost, had decided in his favour. From his father, a Dutch knight, and one of the mightiest vassals of the Bishop of Utrecht, he had inherited a large estate in Holland, which he had exchanged with his brother Giselbert for the barony of Aa, an extensive domain adjoining his own maternal heritage, and he thus became lord of a vast and undivided territory, which embraced two hundred manors, and extended from the walls of Ninove well-nigh to the gates of Brussels. Sweder was a baron of the old school, impetuous, violent, bold, within his borders his will was law, and, if need be, he could call to his flag three thousand men-at-arms.

Such was the social rank and such were the resources of the man whom the city fathers had made their near neighbour, and when it was too late they regretted it. For Sweder, not content with his own, set covetous eyes on the lordship of Rhodes, a strip of Crown land which separated their territory from his, and which, from time immemorial, had been submitted to their jurisdiction. Duchess Jeanne, who was now a widow, was heavily in his debt, and presently he approached her with offers to purchase the freehold, which she was not loath to agree to. Whereat, in Brussels, consternation and a stormy meeting in the Town Hall. 'If this iniquitous bargain were struck, trade, industry, order, right, the very existence of the city itself would be thereby threatened; nor had Jeanne any right to sell. Was she not debarred by her Blyde Incomst from alienating an inch of the Crown demesne? Even to think of such a thing was an insult to the dignity of Brussels. Let someone explain all this to the Duchess—Myn Here T'Serclaes; she would listen to him, an old and trusted friend.' He did so; Jeanne hearkened; and then it was Sweder's turn to gnash his teeth. The news reached him whilst he was at supper in the great hall of Gaesbeke Castle along with his wife, Anne of Linange, and two servants, William of Cleves, his natural son, and his chief steward, Melis Uytten-Enge; and when these men witnessed the chatelaine's wrath and heard Sweder's oath of vengeance they secretly resolved to make themselves the instruments of its fulfilment.

Soon their opportunity came. On the morning of Holy Thursday, March 26, Everard T'Serclaes rode out on his mule from Brussels to Lennick, a small village not a stone's throw from Gaesbeke Castle. The old man seemingly had no thought of danger, for he was unattended. During his stay at Lennick nothing occurred to arouse suspicion, and having transacted the business which called him there, he set out alone on the return journey early in the afternoon, riding at a foot's pace. Hardly had he left the village when two men, who had been hiding behind a hedge, suddenly sprang out at him, dragged him from his saddle, mutilated him terribly—slashed him with swords, tore out his tongue, cut off his right foot, and left him by the roadside weltering in blood, as they thought in his last agony. William of Cleves and Uytten-Enge had made their resolution good.

Some country folk had witnessed the outrage, but they were too much in awe of the tyrant of Gaesbeke to offer his victim help, and the 'Saviour of Brussels' would have been left to die like a dog in the ditch had it not been for the chance arrival of an old friend—Jan van Stalle, Dean of the great collegiate Church of Saint Mary at Hal, who happened to be driving to town that day with his secretary, Jan Coreman. These men having bound up Everard's wounds and placed him in their chariot, set out for Brussels at full speed, and arrived there about half-past three in the afternoon.

When the passers-by saw the poor mangled body they were beside themselves with grief and indignation. The news spread like wildfire, and soon reached the Duchess, who, in spite of the mob and her advanced age, at once set out for the Town Hall,[15] where T'Serclaes was now writhing under the hands of surgeons. She would fain have learned particulars, but her old friend did not even recognise her. In vain she essayed to rouse him. Deaf, blind, speechless, he was more dead than alive.

Presently she came forth into the hum and roar of the market, where an expectant crowd was awaiting her with ears itching for news and throats thundering vengeance. What could she tell these fierce men? how should she soothe their anger? The liberator was not dead, that was something. She would discover the authors of the crime and bring them to justice, they might take her word for it, but they must give her time for inquiry, they must have a little patience. Thus the Duchess. But the people refused to hear—they knew very well who had done the deed, and insisted on instant action; and by five o'clock, with Jeanne's assent, the civic guard had set out for Sweder's castle.

Too late to commence operations that night, the little band made camp at Vlesembeke, midway between Gaesbeke and Brussels, and consoled themselves by dreaming of the great things they would do on the morrow. But the morrow brought forth disappointment: Sweder, under cover of darkness, had made good his escape, and the assassins had fled with him. Anne was indeed at Gaesbeke, but she was wholly beyond their reach: her fortress, strongly garrisoned and well-stocked with supplies, was said to be impregnable, and, worst of all, one of their own brethren was her Commander-in-Chief, citizen Jan Van Hellebeke. How could a handful of burghers drag this she-wolf from her lair? The thing was not to be expected. What could they do but fire the hovels of Sweder's tenants and whimper to Duchess Jeanne. Nor was she deaf to their prayers. Soon they descried in the distance the shimmer of burnished mail drawing nearer and nearer to camp. It was the Lord High Seneschal of Brabant with his knights and men-at-arms, and in the midst of them was the ducal banner, borne aloft by the monks of Afflighem.[16] Nor was this all. The next few days brought help from every town in Brabant, feudal lords unsheathed their steel and shouted vengeance, the enthusiasm was universal—the enemy of Everard T'Serclaes was the common foe of the nation, and soon Sweder's stronghold was beleaguered by a mighty host.

Presently news came that his victim was dead. Better so. From the first there was no hope of saving him, and his poor broken body had been racked for ten days. They laid him to rest in the old church at Ternath, a stone's throw from the beautiful home which he had purchased two years before from the Lord of Westmaele, and where to this day each year as the anniversary of his death comes round there is still chanted for the repose of his soul a Mass of Requiem.

Shortly before Everard's death his nephew, Jan T'Serclaes had been chosen to take his place in the College of Aldermen. 'Juravit ante castrum de Gazebeke,' runs the brief note appended to his name in a contemporary list of city magistrates. This man, then, was in camp at the time of his election, and there, at the foot of the murderer's castle—that castle whose very existence was a menace to civic freedom, he had taken the oath which every magistrate was bound to take on assuming office, solemnly pledging himself to administer justice with an even hand, and to preserve inviolate the rights of the city. The scene was doubtless an impressive one, but many who witnessed it must have had grave doubts as to whether Jan would be able to make good his words, for things were not going well with the assailants, as yet they

THE OLD CASTLE OF EVERARD T'SERCLAES AT TERNATH.

had made no progress. Days turned into weeks and still the towers of Gaesbeke frowned defiance. The situation was growing critical. Sweder was collecting troops at Diest. The truce with Henry of Gelderland had all but expired. What if these two should join hands? The plan of campaign must be changed or the outcome would be disaster. Presently the plan of campaign was changed, and this is what happened.

The men of Louvain did what they always did in times of stress: they turned devout—wearied heaven with prayer, bare-headed and unshod followed the Crom Cruys[17] through the streets of their city chanting litanies, and then they sent word to their friends in the field to stand fast; the Duchess tried diplomacy, she would fain have convinced Anne of Linange that it was worth her while to capitulate; and the allies brought miners from Liége to solve the problem with gunpowder. Whereat, but not until operations had actually commenced, the Lady of Gaesbeke changed her tactics. She proposed a compromise. If only her life and the lives of her people were spared they might do what they would with her castle. The terms were accepted. On the morning of the 30th of April the murderess came forth, and along with the brave men who had protected her, set out for Hainault, and by sundown all that remained of Gaesbeke Castle were smouldering embers and tottering walls.

A year later Sweder and his wife were reinstated in their possessions, after having made solemn declaration not only in their own names, but in the names of their descendants, their relatives, their friends, their adherents, that they were wholly reconciled with the Duchess, the Barons and the good towns of Brabant, and had bound themselves by oath not to claim any damages for the losses which they had sustained, nor to in any way molest those of their vassals who had taken up arms against them.

As for the traitor Hellebeke, his life was spared in accordance with the terms of surrender, but he had sinned too deeply to hope for forgiveness, albeit for some reason or other his punishment was reserved until two years afterward. On the 2nd of June 1391 he was formally declared an enemy of the State and to have forfeited all his civic rights. 'And such henceforth shall be the lot of any man,' runs the sentence of his degradation still preserved amongst the archives of Brussels, 'who shall take sides with the foes of the city.'

CHAPTER XIII
Liberty at Last

It was not until some five-and-thirty years after the tragic death of 'the Saviour of Brussels' that the common folk of that city at last definitely obtained a direct voice in its government.

It was the old story. As it had been at Louvain so was it in the sister city: the patricians were divided amongst themselves, that was the cause of their overthrow. But if it was the old story, it was the old story differently told. At Louvain the cruelty and oppression of the ruling class and, above all, their incapacity and corruption, had sickened the people of aristocratic rule and they were ripe for revolt. A little band of patricians, partly from philanthropic motives, partly from private spleen, espoused the popular cause and placed themselves at its head; the Duke, for his own ends, connived at their proceedings, and after a long and bloody struggle the result was, as we have seen, victory.

At Brussels it was otherwise. When the craftsmen of Brussels at last obtained their hearts' desire, they had lived under an honest and capable government for at least fifty years, and if they had no voice in the legislature, they held the purse-strings and were thus indirectly able to make their influence felt, nor were they altogether excluded from offices of trust and emolument; and though, no doubt, they had not abandoned the hope of one day obtaining direct representation in the municipal senate, they seem to have so far acquiesced in the existing state of things that they had no thought of taking violent measures to change it. They were content to possess their souls in patience, and they were not defrauded of their expectation. By-and-by the fascinating dream of ages was a reality, and this was how it came about.

All that was best and all that was noblest in the three estates of Brabant had joined hands against the Sovereign—a wanton boy led astray by evil counsellors, who were squandering his wealth and the wealth of his towns, and suffering the honour of Brabant to be dragged in the dust; and when all seemed lost, when Brussels, betrayed by false brethren, was filled with German mercenaries breathing out threatening and slaughter, the energy and daring of the despised craftsmen had turned defeat into victory. And when the battle was won and the land once more had rest, these men received, by way of guerdon, the boon they had so long craved for.

The skein of the story is a long and intricate one, but it is worth the trouble of disentangling. It was during the reign of Duke John IV. that these things happened. John was a scion of the house of Bourgogne, which at this time was supreme in the Low Country, and as the events which we are about to relate were in large measure the outcome of the ambitious designs and selfish schemes of the Burgundians, it will be well for a moment to consider their origin and the means by which they mounted to power.[18]

The founder of the house was Philip of Valois, surnamed the Bold, a younger son of King John of France, and, like many other great houses, Court favour and a fortunate marriage were the foundation stones on which it was built.

Marguerite of Maele, the childless widow of her kinsman Philip of Rouvre, the last Duke of Burgundy of the old stock, was at this time the most to be desired of the marriageable princesses of Europe: she was young, beautiful, rich, heiress-apparent to the Counties of Flanders, Burgundy, Rethel, Artois and Nevers, and the only representative of the third generation of Duke John III. of Brabant. Among the princes who aspired to her hand was Philip of Valois, on whom, shortly after the death of her husband (1361), last of his race in the direct line, the French King had conferred his duchy (1363). After long and tedious negotiations and much haggling, for the Count of Flanders, her father, and the King of France, who conducted them, regarded one another with mutual distrust, the marriage treaty was signed (April 25, 1369), and in due course the widow of the last Duke of Burgundy of the old stock became the wife of the first Duke of the new dynasty (June 19, 1369).

A momentous marriage this, and one of which the consequences were far reaching. By it were presently united—when Louis of Maele died (January 30, 1384)—the two most formidable fiefs of the French crown; and the man who held them, a man of marvellous parts and vast ambition, unscrupulous, cunning, bold, had all the prestige of a prince of the blood, and, as the King's most trusted counsellor, all the resources of France at his back.

IV.—Genealogical Table of the Dukes of Brabant from John III. to Philip II.

John III., *d.* Dec. 5, 1355
```
                 |
  +----------+-----------+--------+----------------+
  |          |           |                 |
Henry,    Godfrey,    Jeanne, = Winceslaus   Marguerite = Louis of Maele,
```

```
d. 1349   d. 1351      d. Dec.  of                    | Count of Flanders,
               1406       Luxembourg,                 | d. Jan. 30, 1384
                     d. Dec. 8, 1383         | (he inherited at
                                             | the death of his mother,
                                             | Marguerite, daughter of
                                             | Philip V. of France, 1382,
                                             | the Counties of
                                             | Burgundy and Artois)
            +------------------------------+
            |
Philip of Rouvre, = Marguerite, = Philip of Valois, 4th son of John II.
Duke of Burgundy    d. March   | of France, who conferred on him
and Count of        16, 1405   | the Duchy of Burgundy in 1363,
Burgundy                       | d. April 27, 1404
(Franche-Comté)                |
and Artois, d. 1361            |
                    |
        +-------------+--+-----------------------------+
        |            |                 |
Marguerite, = John the   Marguerite = William, Jeanne de  = Anthony, =
Elizabeth = John the
only        | Fearless, d. March  | eldest   Saint-Pol | d. Oct. of Goerlitz
Pitiless,
daughter of | Count of   8, 1441  | son of    daughter  | 25, 1415
second son
Albert,     | Flanders,          | Albert,  of        |              of Albert
Count of    | Burgundy, etc.,    | Count of Waleran   |              of
Holland
Hainault    | on the death of    | Hainault of        |              d.
1425
and         | his mother (1405), | and     Luxembourg |
```

```
Holland,    | Duke of Burgundy    | Holland          |
d. Jan 14, | on the death of     | d. May 31,       |
1423       | his father (1404),  | 1417             |
           | resigned his        |                  |
   +-------+ interest in the     |                  |
   |         Duchy of Brabant    |                  |
   |         in favour of his    |                  |
   |         brother Anthony,    |                  |
   |         d. Sept. 10, 1419   |                  |
   |                    |    +----------+--------+
   |                    |    |                   |
Philip II.          Jacqueline, = John IV.,      Philip I.
(Philippe l'Asseuré),   Countess of  d. April 17, 1427  (Philippe de
Duke of Burgundy,       Hainault and                Saint-Pol),
Count of Burgundy,      Holland,                 d. Aug. 4, 1430
and Count of Flanders    abdicated 1433,
from 1423, Duke of      d. April 9, 1436
Brabant from 1430,
and Count of Hainault
and Holland from 1433
```

It was thanks, indeed, to this last mighty asset that Philip was able to prepare the way for the union of the Netherlands to the profit of his own house. His intimate connection with France obtained for him the friendship of Duchess Jeanne, always French in her sympathies, and through her good offices he was able to marry his eldest son, John the Fearless, and his eldest daughter, Marguerite, to the only daughter and the eldest son of Albert of Bavaria, heir-apparent to Hainault, Holland and Zeeland, and thus to secure these counties for one of his descendants. The double marriage took place on the 12th of April 1385, and it will be interesting to note that the prelate who gave the nuptial blessing was no other than John T'Serclaes, Count Bishop of Cambrai, a brother of 'the liberator of Brussels.' Again, when shortly after the death of Duke Winceslaus (1385) war broke out between

Brabant and Gelderland, and Jeanne, hard pressed, appealed to Philip for aid, it was with French troops and French gold that he was able to effectually help her, and thus to inspire—his main object in complying with her request—those sentiments of gratitude which later on, in 1390, induced her to acknowledge the right of her sister's child, Marguerite of Maele, to the reversion of her ancestral domains, and that, in spite of a previous engagement: in 1357, when smarting under the insult of the Flemish invasion, the work, as Jeanne firmly believed, of that same sister, she had pledged her word to the Emperor Charles IV., her husband's elder brother, that if she died childless her estate should not go to Marguerite of Brabant or to her issue, but to Charles himself, or, in his default, to his next-of-kin of the house of Luxembourg.

Thus much had French influence and French gold accomplished for the Duke of Burgundy, but he was not yet sure of obtaining the prize which he so much coveted. The burghers had something to say in the matter, and sentiments of gratitude and the glamour of France had little influence with them: they feared that the house of Burgundy would be too powerful for the security of their privileges; and also they were being pressed by Wenzel, King of the Romans, who claimed the reversion of Jeanne's heritage in virtue of the compact of 1357, to make a declaration in his favour. To neither claimant would they give a definite reply: it were time enough, they said, to consider the matter after Jeanne's decease. They were no doubt waiting to see which man would make the highest bid. At last Philip cut the knot by compelling his eldest son John to renounce his right to the succession in favour of his second son Anthony (1393), whom Jeanne, in 1401, with the assent of her people, formally acknowledged as her heir.

Nor was this all. At a meeting which took place at Paris, whither Jeanne had gone (1396) to see once more before she died 'the Princes of the Fleurs-de-lis,' she had arranged with Philip that young Anthony, now twelve years old, should reside with her at Brussels in order that he might thus learn to know the people over whom he would one day rule. No small advantage: if anything should happen to Jeanne, who was now seventy-four years of age, Anthony would be on the spot; but as weeks turned into months and months into years, and still the old Duchess clung to life, Philip began to tire of waiting and to wonder whether after all the cup would be dashed from his hands as he was carrying it to his lips.—If only Jeanne could be induced to abdicate, Anthony, who was now nineteen, could at once grasp the reins of government. Determined, if possible, to induce her to do so, he journeyed to Brussels early in April 1404, and once more his efforts were crowned with success.

It was his last triumph. In the midst of a sumptuous banquet (April 16, 1404) in honour of his son's inauguration as Regent of Brabant, he was struck down by a fever which was at that time raging in the city. On the ninth day after his seizure, when he was almost a dead man, at his own request they carried him on a litter to Hal and lodged him at the Sign of the Stag, hard by

Notre Dame de Hal from Chapel behind North Transept

the church, then famous, as it is now, for its miraculous image of Our Lady. He knew that he was past human aid, yet haply, he thought, the prayers of the Mother of God might even now save him; but the Angel of Death was inexorable, and towards nightfall on the morrow the great founder of the house of Bourgogne passed quietly away (April 27, 1404). His body was embalmed and carried to Dijon, and they buried it in the Carthusian monastery which he himself had founded there, but his heart was enclosed in a precious casket and laid up before the altar of Our Lady at Hal.

Death was at this time busy with the great ones of the Netherlands. Within eight months of Philip's demise (December 12, 1404), Albert of Hainault and Holland was gathered to his fathers and his son William reigned in his stead; shortly before the new Count's accession, Marguerite de Bourgogne had given him a daughter (July 25, 1401), Jacqueline, famed for her beauty and her misfortunes, whose tragic story we shall presently tell. Three months later Marguerite of Maele joined her husband, and their eldest son, Jean sans Peur, who the year before had inherited from his father the county of Charolais and the duchy of Burgundy, now added to his possessions the county of Burgundy and the counties of Flanders and Artois. A personage to be reckoned with, this little, huge-headed, flat-faced man, without grace and without address, and who spoke so ill that his speech was almost unintelligible: he knew what he wanted and he knew how to compass his ends; he had subtlety and determination, and was untroubled with scruples. He strengthened his bulwarks if he did not enlarge his borders, and he struck his roots deep into the soil of the Netherlands; but the greatest thing he did for the accomplishment of their union was to beget a son, to whom he transmitted his great capabilities, if not his evil looks, and who gathered in the harvest which his father and his grandfather had sown—Philip, second of his name, whom men called the Good, a sort of fifteenth century imperialist, whose acquaintance we shall make later on.

On the 1st of December 1406, full of years and good works, died Duchess Jeanne. She was the last of her generation, and the liberal traditions of the house of Louvain died with her. She had outlived the man who had so long plotted for her heritage well-nigh three years, and, as she had wished, she was succeeded by her great-nephew Anthony. Though a brave and chivalrous prince, his ideals were not the ideals of his subjects, and in consequence he was always at loggerheads with them, but when he was gathered to his fathers, struck down at Agincourt (October 25, 1415),[19] the evil days of his son John made Anthony regretted. Not that John was a vicious man, but he was physically and morally weak—de petite et foible complexion, as his secretary and intimate friend De Dynter has it; and Chastelain: 'Peu estoit enclin au harnois, et avec ce de féminin gouvernement, car en lui avoit peu de fait et peu de malice. Et pour ce, aucuns estant entour luy, qui le réoient simple, le gouvernèrent à leur prouffit et peu au sien, ne à ses pays.'[20] Herein we have the source of the difficulties which continually beset his path, difficulties of all kinds and with all sorts and conditions of persons—with his clergy, his nobles, his burghers, his common folk, and, within his own domestic circle, with his brother, his mother-in-law and his wife. She was the greatest difficulty of all, and it would have been marvellous indeed if his marriage had proved a happy one. What could there have been in common with the indolent, feeble, dull-witted John of Brabant and his brilliant and beautiful cousin Jacqueline, who had inherited, with the shrewdness and the masterful will, all the energy and all the daring of her mother's ambitious race? No more ill-assorted match could well have been devised than that which William of Holland urged with his last breath on his only daughter, the apple of his eye, who at that time was a child-widow of sixteen. With his body gangrened from the bite of a dog, and his mind confused with horror and grief at the foul deed which six weeks before had deprived Jacqueline of a husband, the dying man saw a pillar of strength in his poor little rickety nephew. He knew that when he was gone she would need a protector; he dreaded the cruel ambition of his brother, the Bishop of Liége, who, he fondly believed, would hurl himself in vain against the bedrock of the house of Bourgogne. Jacqueline herself had no such illusion, her cousin of Brabant was known to her, her eyes were not blinded by the glamour of his race, and she was convinced he would prove a sorry champion. Moreover, she had loved the Dauphin, her first husband, with whom she had been brought up, and the tragic circumstances of his death—poisoned, as all men believed, by his uncle of Orléans—had embittered her grief at his loss, and made her the less inclined to hurry again into wedlock. But for all that the marriage took place: the family council, held shortly after William's death at Biervliet, in Zeeland (July 31, 1417), was unanimously in favour of it, and in spite of her reluctance, and in spite of the opposition from interested motives of the Bishop of Liége, the hapless Jacqueline was presently constrained to give her hand to the poor stripling whom she loathed.

On Sunday, the 1st of August 1417, John and Jacqueline publicly plighted their troth, and it was arranged that they should be united in wedlock as soon as the necessary dispensation could be obtained from the Holy See. A matter this not easy of accomplishment, owing to the opposition of the Bishop of Liége, who naturally objected to a marriage intended to prevent his making good his claim to his niece's heritage, to which he maintained he had the better right—Holland and Hainault, as imperial fiefs, being not transmissible in the female line.

This man at the family council, dissembling his real intentions, had not only acknowledged Jacqueline's right to the whole of her father's dominions and approved of the proposed match, but had actually volunteered himself to procure the requisite dispensation, and afterwards he had prevailed on the men of Dordrecht to receive him as their Sovereign; and from thence, on the 3rd of September, he had secretly sent letters to Constance representing to the Fathers assembled there for the purpose of electing a new Pontiff and other matters, that if this incestuous union were sanctioned the country would be plunged in civil war.

Appointed to the See of Liége in 1390, a dissolute boy of seventeen in sub-deacon's orders, in spite of the reiterated protests of his canons and to the no small scandal of his people, John the Pitiless had persistently refused episcopal consecration. For a sub-deacon to be freed from his vow of celibacy he knew was not impossible, perhaps, as his enemies said, it was in his mind to found a house and convert the ecclesiastical state over which he presided—a republic then in all but the name, with a mitred figurehead for president—into a lay principality to be handed down to his descendants. In any case, he would preserve a free hand in view of political eventualities. For twelve years the people waited, groaning under John's oppression, for one after another he suppressed all their liberties, and shamed by his evil life, and then, at the end of their patience, they hunted him out of the town, and chose in his place a worthier man, Thierry, son of the Lord of Perwys, who in due course received from Benedict XIII. episcopal consecration.

But John the Pitiless was not the man to accept defeat, he appealed to his brother of Holland and to his brother-in-law of Burgundy, and after a long and bitter struggle he was presently reinstated. The last stand was made at Othée, in the plain of Russon, on the 23rd of September 1408, when the men of Liége were utterly routed. Amongst the eight thousand slain were Bishop Thierry and his father, the Lord of Perwys. When all was over they found their dead bodies on the battlefield, side by side and hand in hand. Better so, for John's fierce triumph was a veritable orgie of blood. Such of his victims as were laymen he beheaded or hanged, and he showed his pity for their daughters and wives and his respect for the ecclesiastical state by casting the women into the Meuse, and with them the canons whom Thierry had appointed, and the priests whom he had ordained. Then it was that the Liége men first called him Jean sans Pitié.

Such was the man who now professed himself so solicitous for the purity of family life and so fearsome lest the loosening of ecclesiastical discipline should have for its outcome war. But the Fathers of Constance were in no way deceived by his specious pleading, and as soon as they had chosen a Pope (Martin V.) the dispensation was accorded. John, however, was not yet at the end of his resources; as a prudent man he had taken care to have two strings to his bow: he had not only written to the Fathers of Constance, but also to his friend the Emperor Sigismond, who, as soon as he learnt that the brief had been dispatched, compelled the Pope by threats of imprisonment to revoke it. Embarrassing this, no doubt, to the agents of the Duke of Brabant, but they seem to have been equal to the emergency; for the clerks whose duty it was to affix the pontifical seal to the new rescript, dated Constance, January 5, 1413, conveniently forgot to do so for several days, and thus it came about that when at last it reached the interested parties the marriage had already taken place.

Edmund De Dynter, Duke John's secretary, tells us how it all happened:— Late on the evening of Thursday, March 10, 1413, the dispensation arrived at the Hague, where the Courts of Holland and Brabant and Burgundy had been anxiously awaiting it for over three weeks. The same night John and Jacqueline privately plighted their troth, and immediately after the ceremony, says Edmund De Dynter, who seems to have been present, they were conducted to the bridal chamber. Doubtless they had some inkling at the Hague of what had taken place at Constance, but in reality there was no need for haste, the newly-married couple had time to visit Mons and other towns of Hainault, where their sovereign rights were acknowledged, and Jacqueline had been welcomed as Duchess of Brabant at Brussels and Louvain and Bois-le-Duc before the second rescript was placed in the hands of Duke John. Shortly afterwards 'two venerable masters in theology' arrived at the Coudenberg, where the Court was now installed, bringing with them a sealed letter from Martin V. informing John that he might give full credence to what the bearers said. They told him that as the revocation had been extorted by force, it was to be regarded as null and void, and that as soon as the Pope had crossed the Alps and was out of the Emperor's power, he would dispatch a third rescript confirmatory of the first. And the Pope was as good as his word: in due course the promised letter arrived, dated Florence, August 27, 1418.

Though baffled in the matter of his niece's marriage, John the Pitiless had otherwise strengthened his position. The better to prosecute his claim to her heritage he had resigned his See, obtained a dispensation from his vow of celibacy, and married a rich widow—Elizabeth, Duchess of Luxembourg, step-mother to John of Brabant. Shortly afterwards the Emperor had publicly invested him with the disputed fiefs, and in Holland at least, especially among the burghers of the great towns, he had a very considerable following. Meanwhile he was still at Dordrecht, and presently he felt himself strong enough to openly declare war against Jacqueline and her husband.

The Estates of Brabant, well aware that in face of so redoubtable an adversary half measures would be useless, urged the Duke to attack Dordrecht by land and sea. John's counsellors, however, were of a different opinion. The expedition, they said, must be conducted with due regard to economy, and to expend money on ships were an altogether unnecessary outlay; and thus it came about that the siege of Dordrecht very soon had to be raised. John, who had at first taken the field, now retired to Brussels; city after city and fortress after fortress fell into the hands of his opponent; Philip of Burgundy, to whom his father, John the Fearless, absent in Paris, had left the care of his affairs in the Low Countries, offered his mediation, and a compromise was effected. On the 13th of February 1419 the Duke of Brabant ceded in fief to John the Pitiless a portion of his wife's domains, permitted him to take the title of Regent, and paid him a handsome indemnity into the bargain—100,000 English nobles.

The burghers of Brabant were enraged and disgusted, and Jacqueline was beside herself with indignation, the more so as they and she had each a personal and most intimate grievance against the men whose parsimony had caused this shame. The burghers never forgot that for years past these harpies had fattened at their expense, considering neither the interests of the State, which they starved, nor of the Sovereign, whom they cajoled and fleeced, for John never failed to apply to his towns whenever he found himself short of cash; and Jacqueline believed what was whispered at Court as to how the vilest of them, William of Assche, erst treasurer of the ducal household, now amman of Brussels, and his son-in-law, Everard T'Serclaes—the eldest son of the Deliverer—had obtained the baneful influence which they exercised over her feeble lord: Assche at the cost of his daughter's fair name, and T'Serclaes at the sacrifice of his own honour and the honour of his wife. Poor little John was bewitched seemingly by the charms of Lauretta of Assche, or at all events Jacqueline thought so, and she was proportionately jealous. But it was not these men, but that grasping old fox, Treasurer Vandenberghe, who was the first to experience the people's wrath. 'Ever swift to sweep in coin, and tardy, yea, of a truth most tardy, in the matter of payments,'[21] he it was who had been the chief promoter of the cheese-paring policy which had brought forth such disastrous results, and hence he was condemned by the Estates to exile, and declared to be for ever incapable of again holding office in Brabant. Nor was this all: Brussels and Louvain informed the Duke that they would grant him no further aid until the sentence had been carried out. It was the first passage of arms in the great struggle between John and his bonnes villes. The friends of the Duchess had been the first to strike, but her opponents were not slow to hit back. At Brussels her arch foe, William Assche, refused, quite illegally, to publish his colleague's condemnation, but the aldermen made him pay for it: they would no longer acknowledge him as amman, and flung him into gaol. Of the whole college one member only withheld his assent—Everard T'Serclaes, and in consequence he was declared to have forfeited his rights of lignage and to be for ever incapable of holding municipal office.

Meanwhile John and the Treasurer had betaken themselves to Mons, where the latter presently endured a worse punishment than exile: on the 23rd of March 1419, during the absence of the Duke and the Duchess hawking, Vandenberghe, sick and slumbering in his chamber, 'was suddenly aroused by the bastards of Holland' (Jacqueline's natural brothers), 'who very soon sent him to sleep again, and so soundly that no man shall ever wake him more; for without any respite they struck him stone dead, and forthwith went their way.' 'Spite,' says Secretary De Dynter, 'because he had stopped their pensions'; and Monstrelet adds, 'The Duchess, according to common report, was a sufficiently consenting party to what her brethren had done.'

Be this as it may, the removal of Vandenberghe was certainly, for the moment, of advantage to Jacqueline and her friends. For three days John was inconsolable, but at the expiration of that time his Duchess managed to appease him, and Rotslaere, a man devoted to the popular cause, was appointed Treasurer of Brabant (April 12, 1419). Maybe that John, in acting thus, was dissembling to gain time; maybe that, brooding over his wrongs alone (for shortly after the murder the ducal couple had separated), he was presently impelled to go back on his decision; certain it is that within a month after their appointment the new ministers were dismissed.

Before the end of April the Court had returned to Brabant: Jacqueline to Vilvorde, and John, cast down and restless, flitting from place to place— sometimes at Tervueren, sometimes at Antwerp, never at Brussels, where Assche was still in prison, at last he found himself at Bois-le-Duc, and by that time he had made up his mind.

The 15th of May 1419 was a noteworthy day in the life of Duke John of Brabant. Between sunrise and sunset he accomplished several things, and experienced some sensations of a sufficiently varied and exciting nature for a nervous youth of delicate constitution:—A morning ride from Bois-le-Duc to Crayenhem, unknown to Rotslaere—grandement embesogné, good man, *et moult esbahis*, when presently he heard of it; a secret meeting there with former counsellors, at which a plan was devised for taming Jacqueline; a journey next to Vilvorde, and there, beneath her windows, insulting proclamation, outcome of the morning conclave; then, swift flight to Tervueren to escape the consequences; and then—grand finale, when he flattered himself he had reached cover, the hurricane of his wife's indignation burst over his head; for Jacqueline, when she saw her lord departing, had at once taken horse, accompanied by one lady and three servants, and reaching Tervueren almost before he had recovered his breath, she forced her way into his chamber in spite of the remonstrance of the guard, and there, in the presence of his favourites, rated him soundly for two good hours. And Jacqueline had reason to be discontented, for Rotslaere and her friends had fallen, and the corrupt sycophants, who had been the cause of all her miseries, were once more in power, and, worse still, her own personal attendants—the Dutch ladies, whom she loved and who had served her all her life—had been summarily ordered to pack up their baggage and get themselves back to Holland. And who were the women who were to take their place? 'The noblest and best in the land,' said John. And no doubt he thought so: they were the wives and daughters of his boon companions, and amongst them was Lauretta of Assche.

Though John displayed admirable firmness so long as his wife confined herself to tears and supplication, he quailed before the bitter invective which his heartlessness presently called forth; and if it had not been for his fear of a like scene with Lauretta, maybe the Duchess would have carried the day. As it was, she was fain to content herself with her lord's reluctant consent to her retaining four of her women, and there, for the moment, the affair ended.

Meanwhile matters were not mending at Brussels. Assche was still in prison, and neither John's threats nor entreaties could induce the burghers to release him; and presently, when election time came round and the patricians as usual sent in their triple list of candidates, the Duke, by way of retaliation, refused to make any appointments, and for three weeks the city was without magistrates. At last, thanks to the good offices of Antwerp and Louvain, a compromise was effected, which was in reality a triumph for Brussels. John, indeed, obtained the release of his friend, but he was not reinstated in office, and John Taye, who now became amman, was a persona grata to the burghers. Nor was this all: the city obtained a new charter, by which it was ordained that henceforth a deputy amman should always be appointed, who, in the event of the amman's refusal to act, or if he performed his duties ill, would be competent to act for him; that if the deputy, in his turn, failed to give satisfaction, the aldermen could replace him by a more suitable person; and that if in future any Sovereign should refuse to appoint magistrates, the outgoing magistrates might themselves name their successors.

Notwithstanding that peace had thus been patched up between John and the men of Brussels, his heart was so filled with resentment that he could not prevail upon himself to return to the Coudenberg till six months later, and shortly afterwards came the final rupture with Jacqueline.

It happened thus. Hardly a year had passed since the signing of the Treaty of Gorcum (February 13, 1419), when John the Pitiless, again growing restive, began to demand fresh concessions and to threaten that if they were not granted Brabant would be drenched in blood. So eager was the Duke to avert war that he did not hesitate to invest him with the regency of Holland and Zeeland for a period of twelve years, and to cede to him also the lordships of Antwerp and Herenthals—dependencies these last of the duchy of Brabant.

Whilst Duke John was thus weakly disposing of his own and of his wife's property, his faithful henchman, Everard T'Serclaes, now steward of the ducal household, was racking his brains as to how he might rid the Court of Jacqueline's Dutch ladies. By so doing he would confer a boon on his master, and, matter of greater moment, gratify his own spleen, for his hatred of the Duchess was commensurate with the injury which he had done her, and with the contempt which she openly showed for him. After much thought, he came to the conclusion that the best plan would be to starve them out, and under pretext of thrift, for the household expenses, he said, were extremely heavy, he refused henceforth to make any provision for their maintenance.

Jacqueline had just heard of the new treaty and was in no mood to brook further outrage. The meanness and pettiness of this last insult cut her to the quick, and she resented it with the pride and energy natural to her character. Marguerite of Burgundy, who had sought out John and remonstrated with him in vain, had withdrawn in tears to an inn called Le Miroir in the *rue de la Montagne*, and Jacqueline, after a violent scene with her husband, fled from the Court to her mother's lodgings. No effort was made to recall her, and next morning the two ladies left Brussels for the Castle of Quesnoy in Hainault, where Jacqueline was still Sovereign. This was early in May 1420.

When it became known that the Duchess had gone, throughout the length and breadth of the land there was a widespread feeling of indignation, which, however, seems to have been at first stronger in some places than in others, and, generally speaking, the rural districts, influenced as they were by the feudal lords—almost all of them, from sentiments of chivalry, ardent partisans of Jacqueline, were more hostile than the towns. At Bois-le-Duc, indeed, John's adherents were sufficiently numerous and influential to insure the loyalty of the city throughout the contest which was now impending; Antwerp, for a time, also refrained from active hostility, and so, too, Brussels. The common folk had 'wondered and wept' when they saw Jacqueline leaving the palace in tears and on foot, and attended by only one serving-man, and the heartless boy, who had driven her from home, had long ago forfeited their confidence and respect, but at Brussels the common folk did not yet count, and the patricians, though many of them shared their sentiments, were for the most part loth to quarrel again with their best customer; for the cloth trade was waning in face of English competition, and the Court was now the mainstay of their prosperity.

At Louvain it was otherwise. The Dukes of Brabant had long since forsaken the cradle of their race, the tradesmen of the capital had little to gain and little to lose from the smiles or the evil looks of the occupant of the throne, and their judgment was not warped by self-interest. Moreover, at Louvain, the people—always eager to resent injustice and to champion the cause of the weak, were directly and largely represented in the municipal senate, and a healthier, manlier, more independent spirit pervaded the whole town. Nowhere in the duchy of Brabant was John's unworthy conduct held in greater contempt, nowhere were men more firmly determined to deliver him from the evil counsellors who, for their own ends, had prompted it, and the burghers of Louvain, to their honour, took the first step in this direction.

Shortly after Jacqueline's flight John, again short of cash, had summoned the Estates of Brabant to meet at Brussels, and the aldermen of Louvain, knowing very well that liberty could hardly be assured in the Court city, utterly ignored John's invitation and invited the Estates on the same day to assemble in their own town. It was a bold step, but the issue proved the wisdom of it: when the appointed day arrived a few stragglers from Antwerp and Bois-le-Duc betook themselves to Brussels, and representatives of the first and second order from all parts of the duchy flocked into the capital. They found it in a greater state of commotion than any of them had anticipated, for news had just come to hand of a fresh act of tyranny—the Duke had presumed to violate one of the oldest and most cherished privileges of the time-honoured Church of Saint Peter.

Thus: Sieger, chief of the house of Heetvelde, was one of the mightiest nobles of Brabant in the far-off days of Duchess Jeanne, with whom he claimed kinship, for he traced his descent to a natural son of the great house of Gaesbeke, a legitimate though younger branch of the reigning family. The Van Heetveldes, in the course of ages, had acquired estates and manorial rights in all parts of the duchy; they were patricians, too, of Louvain, for a Heetvelde of bygone days had married a daughter of that city, and the status of patrician, unlike that of the feudal lord, was transmissible in the female line. Invested with all the rights and privileges of the various orders to which he belonged, at Brussels, where he habitually resided, old Sieger was too mighty a man to be loved; five lignages banded together against him, and one morning he was found in the Grand' Place with his throat cut. Who was the actual murderer was never known, but Sieger's sons suspected a patrician called Nicholas de Swaef, and publicly charged him with the crime, and hence there arose a feud between the family of the murdered man and the family of the man who, as he had sworn, had been falsely accused of the murder. For years the streets of Brussels were the scene of their bloody conflicts. In vain the burghers of Louvain joined their efforts to the burghers of Brussels as mediators. At their instance Duchess Jeanne ordained that the quarrel should be forgotten, menacing with death any man who should venture to reopen it; but her threats were wholly disregarded, and after twenty years the Heetveldes and the Vanderstraetens[22] were still flying at one another's throats. At last, about Easter 1417, the belligerents agreed to accept the arbitration of Duke John IV., provided he gave his decision within a twelvemonth. For some reason or other he neglected to do so, and it was not till the 20th of June 1420 that he summoned the brothers Heetvelde to his presence and informed them that he was about to pronounce judgment. To this they demurred, on the ground that the stipulated time had long since gone by. Whatever may have been the case three years before, the Vanderstraetens were now John's friends and the Heetveldes among his bitterest opponents, and naturally enough the latter feared he would not hold the scales of justice evenly. Whereat John sentenced them, there and then, to banishment as contumacious, and the Heetveldes, instead of submitting, fled to Louvain. They were Petermen, they said, and as such subject only to their own tribunal. What wonder, then, that the anger of the burghers blazed more fiercely than ever, or that the Estates, to which the Heetveldes had appealed, quashed the iniquitous sentence, and forthwith informed the Duke that no fresh aid would be granted until their grievances had been redressed. The miscreants who had deprived Jacqueline of her heritage, driven her from Brabant, wasted the resources of the realm, and who had not even feared to flout Saint Peter, must first be dismissed from office. Nor did John dare to refuse, but the men whom he named to take their places made his former counsellers regretted: amongst them was Everard T'Serclaes, the fons et origo of all the mischief. Whereat the Estates, convinced that it was hopeless to expect reform so long as John remained in power, did two things—they sent letters to 'Madame the Duchess of Brabant and to Madame the Widow, her mother,' proposing co-operation, and by 'the vigour of the replies which they presently received were greatly consoled and comforted'; and they despatched 'Friar Edmond' to Paris to bring home the Count of Saint-Pol. And in this too they were successful, for although the Duke, getting wind of it, had immediately written to his brother urging him not to come, Friar Edmond proved himself the better diplomatist, and on the 10th of September returned to Louvain, bringing the young prince with him. Shortly afterwards came ambassadors from the King of France and from the Duke of Burgundy with a mission 'to appease the strife which had arisen between Duke John of Brabant, on the one part, and Madame the Duchess and Madame the Widow, and the nobles and the good towns of Brabant, on the other'; and, better still, a few days later came 'Madame Jaque herself and Madame her mother,' and then, after much confabulation and much coming and going between Brussels and Louvain, a conference was arranged at Vilvorde for Sunday the 29th of September. Thither, on the appointed day, came the allies from Louvain, with 'Madame Jaque and My Lord of Saint-Pol' at their head. But Duke John did not come. Hardly safe at Brussels, where his friends had still the upper hand, he was far too wise to attend a meeting in a town where he knew his opponents were more numerous than his partisans. Excusing himself on the ground of indisposition, he kept close house, and at nightfall on the morrow stealthily crept out into the darkness and slipped away. To cover his flight Everard T'Serclaes gave out that the Duke was too ill to see anyone but a couple of trusty serving-men, who were in the secret, and who carried his supper into his bedchamber after his departure, as if he were still there, whereas in reality he had fled with the Lord of Ashe and four others, who led him by circuitous routes to Bois-le-Duc.

As soon as it was publicly known that John had left the city, the Assembly at Vilvorde, by the advice of the French ambassador, conferred the government on Philip of Saint-Pol, who on the following day (October 2), along with Jacqueline, her mother and the Estates, triumphantly entered Brussels.[23]

Five months before the Duchess of Brabant had left her home, accompanied only by a humble serving-lad. As she wended her way through the muddy streets to her mother's lodging in the *rue de la Montagne* the few stragglers who recognised her had stood silent as she passed, in sympathy and respect at her humiliation; and now she returned in triumph at the head of a brilliant cavalcade of churchmen, and knights and burghers; and the people welcomed her with shouts of acclamation, and with trumpets and clashing bells.

How different too was her position in the palace to what it had been in former days. The fears of her poor little husband had compelled him to leave it trembling, disguised, under cover of night, and by a back door, in more pitiable condition almost than she had been when she had fled from the Coudenberg. And the man without heart and without soul, who, having robbed her of her husband's affection, thought it almost an honourable thing to stoop to the pettiness of depriving her ladies of their dinner, he, too, had gone the way of his master and his dupe, and of the corrupt crew whose pride and debauchery had in days of yore rendered her life intolerable, not one was left within the walls of the Coudenberg.

She was now in the midst of friends and attended by her own people. Her will was law. She was Sovereign, and, such was the chivalrous devotion of the men who had rescued and restored her, that in the ardour of their first enthusiasm they placed her interests before their own. At the solemn assembly which took place next day in the Town Hall the Estates unanimously decided to forthwith equip an expedition to wrest from John the Pitiless 'the possessions of the Duchess which her husband had abandoned to him without her consent.' Soon a great host was assembled at Breda, hard by the cities it had been decided, in the first place, to take. Knights from every lordship in Brabant were there, and armed burghers from every town save Bois-le-Duc, and Jacqueline herself was in the midst of them.

On the 16th of October she was at the gates of Heusden. The city surrendered without a blow, and the next day she was solemnly enthroned there as Duchess of Brabant. Four days later she sat down before Gertruidenberg. On Saint Martin's Day the city went up in flames, and on the 24th of November, flushed with victory, she returned at the head of her troops to Brussels.

It was her last triumph. For a brief space her star had been in the ascendant, and now it was already beginning to wane. Henceforth sorrow was to dog her heel, and ill-fortune to confront her at every turn. The Estates were again sitting, sometimes in the Coudenberg, sometimes in the Town Hall, but the prelates and knights and burghers assembled had other food for discussion than Jacqueline's Dutch affairs—the country was threatened with invasion, perhaps with civil war: John at Bois-le-Duc was hatching mischief. What particular form his mischief would take no man could tell, not even the Duke himself, for he inclined sometimes to one scheme, sometimes to another. All that was certainly known was that he was endeavouring to recruit an army in the land between the Meuse and the Rhine, that men of adventure were flocking to his standard from the hope of obtaining loot, and that he had turned a deaf ear to the deputation which the Regent had sent to Bois-le-Duc to entreat him to desist from his evil designs. At Brussels amongst the patricians he was known to have a considerable following, though many of them dissembled their true sentiments. Several of the aldermen were suspected of disaffection: at best they were but half-hearted patriots, and Amman Cluting was known to be the Duke's man, and was divested of his office in consequence.

Winter was coming on, and the city was filled with distress, for at any moment the land might be plunged in the horrors of civil war, and business was at a standstill. All that could be done had been done: Philip had issued a proclamation in which he declared that at the request of the Estates he had undertaken the government during the absence of his brother, and the Estates, in their turn, had addressed a letter to the nobles and the cities of Brabant informing them of the motives which had inspired their action. There was nothing for it but to await the issue of events. But inaction to one of Jacqueline's keen and impetuous nature was altogether impossible, and shortly after the failure of the Regent's negotiations with John, she set out with Madame the Widow for Valenciennes. The men of Brabant were unable to help her; she must seek assistance elsewhere. Philip of Burgundy was impossible: he was playing his own game. The King of France was his puppet; there was nothing to be done with him. Someone suggested England, and presently, unknown to her mother, she flitted across the Channel, determined to enlist the sympathy of her distant kinsman, King Henry V. Better had she remained in Brabant: if only she could have possessed her soul in patience she might have accomplished something.

Meanwhile at Brussels and throughout Brabant the air was thick with rumours. What would the morrow bring forth? All trade was at a standstill, it was the last month of the year and the empty stomachs of men without work were already beginning to shrink from the grip of winter. Every honest burgher as he turned into his bed at night was firmly convinced that the tocsin would clang before dawn, and in the morning he was no less sure that something untoward would happen before sundown. For six weary weeks the good town of Brussels was on tenterhooks, and then, on the 20th of January 1421, she was basely betrayed into the hands of the enemy by her own magistrates.

It was common knowledge that some of the patricians were disaffected, but no one imagined how far the evil had really spread until John appeared before the Louvain gate with an army of Germans. Then the renegades hoisted their true colours and then it was known for the first time that no less than four of the patrician clans had cast in their lot with his; and though the remaining three were composed for the most part of good patriots, their representatives in the city council, flustered and dismayed at the situation which had thus been suddenly sprung on them, after some feeble show at resistance, yielded to their more energetic colleagues.

These men had for weeks past been in correspondence with John, and had arranged all the details of the plot at a secret meeting held in the Vroente a few nights before, and when the Duke and his party arrived at Tervueren early on the morning of the 21st of January, ex-Amman Cluting and three of the confederate aldermen were there to receive him. When John, as had been previously arranged, had re-invested Cluting with his wand of office, the conspirators informed him that he would find no difficulty in entering the city by the Porte de Louvain, for Alderman Kegel was in command there and he would at once admit him; and having delivered their message they returned to Brussels to make ready for his reception. What, then, was the surprise of the ducal party when presently they reached the appointed gate and found it shut! Some of the more faint-hearted were for turning back, others for forcing an entrance, but that was found to be impossible. Others again, not knowing what to do, eased their minds by cursing the lying burghers who had betrayed them. 'Gentle Knight,' crooned a hag, a hag, who had vainly asked for alms of the Lord of Heinsberg, loudest in fierce declamation, 'gentle Knight, do not worry yourself about entering the city, but when once you are within consider well how best you may come out again.' He took little heed at the time, says De Dynter, but later on he called to mind what the old woman had said.

In reality Amman Cluting and his friends had not broken faith with John, but when they reached Brussels they found that the news of his arrival at Tervueren had preceded them and that the city was in a state of uproar. Kegel had been removed from the Porte de Louvain, the Regent had just ordered all the gates to be shut, and a meeting of the Grand Council was actually taking place in the Town Hall. Thither, then, the conspirators turned their horses' heads, and their arrival in the Council Chamber was the signal for a stormy scene. At first the magistrates of the Regent's faction hardened their hearts and stiffened their backs—no power on earth should persuade them to consent to the Duke's return, but their opponents were many and blustering, and they were weak-kneed and few. Presently they began to hesitate, and at last, when they accepted a compromise which was in reality a surrender, they flattered themselves that their firmness had saved the situation.

The meeting had lasted the best part of the day, and darkness was falling on the good town of Brussels when her aldermen, arrayed in robes of state, solemnly went forth to the great act of betrayal.

Wending their way by the Rue de la Montagne, Saint Gudule's, and the road which skirted the northern side of the park—then a great wood well stocked with game and extending right up to the ramparts—they presently reached the gate outside which John had been kicking his heels, as De Dynter says, for more

THE TOWN HALL, BRUSSELS.

than two hours, and in due course made known to him the result of their deliberations The Duke, they said, was free to enter the city provided he would limit his escort to a hundred and twenty men, amongst whom there must be no foreigner or no public enemy of the State. John passed his word, the gates were thrown open, a hundred and twenty knights rode in, and then the command rang out for the rest to follow. Some of the bystanders were for resistance, but the renegades succeeded in restraining them. Quick as thought the whole army dashed up to the Coudenberg, and presently the Count of Saint-Pol rode quietly off to Louvain.

OLD HOUSES NEAR SAINT GUDULE'S.

Next morning the Duke went down to the Town Hall, where a great crowd of aldermen, councillors, deans of trade companies and other civic officials were expecting him. His policy, he told them, was one of general appeasement, and he would fain have their co-operation; but though no sign of dissent was made he was filled with misgiving. What if his brother Philip should return with reinforcements? And presently he summoned the aldermen to the palace and demanded of them the course which in that event they would pursue. Their answer was a politic one—if the Duke distrusted them they were quite ready to hand him the keys of the city gates, but John would not hear of it. He was well assured, he said, of their loyalty.

In reality the greatest source of danger was not from without but from within—in the growing discontent of the people at the greed and arrogance of 'these foreign gens de guerre,' who galloped through the streets with their swords drawn as if Brussels were a conquered town, and who openly bragged in hostel and tavern that they would not go back to Germany till they were all rich men, aye, and that they meant to have not only the goods, but the wives and the daughters of a host of wealthy citizens whom it was the Duke's intention, so they averred, to presently hang. What wonder then, when this state of things had been going on for the best part of a week, that a serving-maid, who perceived a lighted candle in the window of a certain foreign knight at an hour when all honest men should be a-bed, clean lost her wits, and ran up screaming to call her master; or that he, good man, when he had plucked up his courage to peer in at the casement, and with his own eyes had seen the knight arming, ran off at the top of his speed to tell the magistrates that a plot was on foot to murder all the burghers; or that they, no less scared than he, put a double guard at the city gates; or that a great host of craftsmen soon appeared in the Grand' Place armed and angry: and perhaps too they had reason. De Dynter is by no means sure that the alleged plot was altogether imaginary. 'As to the aforesaid conspiracy,' he says, 'it was found from information received, that the Germans that night went to bed in their armour, and hence the Communaulté held that the fact was sufficiently proven; but they, the Germans, on the other hand, denied all knowledge of it, alleging that they had only armed, when they heard the roar of the mob, not knowing what might be going to happen; and I, for my part, have not been able to discover the truth of the matter, and hence I can only note down what each party said.' Several of John's partisans, who afterwards fell into the hands of the Regent, not only acknowledged, albeit under torture, that a massacre had been in contemplation, but divulged its object, adding names and details: some fifteen hundred German knights, with Heinsberg and Amman Cluting at their head, were to rise at a given signal—the sounding of the bell of Saint Jacques sur Coudenberg, seize the Town Hall, and, having thus made themselves masters of the city, arrest all the popular leaders and put them to death. The object being to break up Philip's party at Brussels before he had time to return with the reinforcements which he had gone to seek at Louvain.

Be this as it may, so firmly convinced were the craftsmen that some great catastrophe was impending that they all turned out in the middle of Monday night, as we have seen, determined, if need be, to sell their lives dearly. So fierce and so threatening was their attitude, and so alarming were the rumours which presently reached the palace, that about eleven o'clock Duke John, who was not without courage in moments of emergency, determined to go forth himself and do what he could to calm the storm, but his efforts were met with shouts of derision; as he rode round the market from guild to guild, begging the rioters to go home to bed, and assuring them they had no cause for fear, 'Go home to bed yourself,' they cried, 'and sleep well; your own fears are groundless, not one of us would harm a hair of your head,' and they probably spoke the truth, for though his subjects despised him and detested his methods of government, John himself was not personally unpopular. Indeed, the people regarded him rather with pity than hatred, for, after all, he was but a poor little puppet, the men who pulled the strings were alone to blame. They were soon to have their reward, but not to-night: it was not until Wednesday morning that a great mob of armed craftsmen came surging up to the palace. John faced them. 'Why this tumult? What did it mean?' 'Heinsberg, and they meant to have him.' And soon Heinsberg was led forth, for there was no denying them, and, oh! the irony of it, by his fellow-conspirator, Cluting. It was the amman's last official act: two days later he was himself arrested, and afterwards endured, as we shall see, a worse fate than the man whom he now handed over to the aldermen, who, like their chief, had changed sides, to be dragged in chains to prison. Before noon every German in Brussels was taken: the knights fettered and cast into gaol, their followers stripped and with only a few rags to cover them turned loose into the winter fields, and towards dusk the cheering of the mob and the bells from a hundred steeples announced Philip's arrival with a great army of nobles from the countryside, and of burghers from Louvain and Antwerp.

That night the craftsmen of Brussels were in a wild frenzy of gladness—not only on account of their triumph, but because they knew that the wine for which they had so long thirsted, the glorious wine of liberty, would soon be gurgling down their throats; the fragrance of its bouquet already filled their nostrils and they were drunk in anticipation. Philip had hailed them as the saviours of Brabant, and he would never refuse to strong men flushed with victory the wages they had justly earned. Let patricians do what they would, self-government was now assured to them.

As a matter of fact, it was not in the power of the patricians, split up as they were into hostile factions, to offer opposition to anyone. The clans which had triumphed and which, had they been left to their own resources, would have been utterly wiped out, were bound hand and foot to the plebeian allies who had rescued them and given them the victory. Their vanquished opponents, utterly cowed, were considering only how best they might escape the consequences of their indiscretion. From these men, then, there was nothing to fear.

On the night of Philip's coming some of the most deeply implicated, amongst them Alderman Kegel and old William of Assche, desperate in the belief that if they remained in Brussels their doom was fixed, taking their lives in their hands sallied forth boldly into the streets, and passing through the crowd, unnoticed in the darkness and confusion, succeeded in gaining the open country and a place of refuge till the storm had passed. The rest, trembling behind barred doors and windows, expected each moment to be dragged forth and torn in pieces by an infuriated mob—phantom peril, offspring of their conscious guilt. The city, given over to rejoicing, was content to leave vengeance in Philip's hands, and Philip, good man, wearied out with the day's travail, had retired to bed. It was not until the morrow, after dinner, that he proceeded with a small escort to the Coudenberg and put all, or nearly all, of the members of the ducal household under arrest. The greater number, however, were set at liberty the same day, though none of them were reinstated in office. Indeed, in dealing not only with these men, but with the burghers who had opposed him, Philip certainly acted with singular moderation. His policy seems to have been to strike at the leaders only, and that, with no undue harshness, and to suffer the small fry to go scot-free.

Though the number of persons concerned in one or other of the recent conspiracies must have been considerable, probably not less than a thousand, some twenty only were deemed worthy of punishment, notable burghers all of them or nobles from the countryside. Fourteen who had been duly tried, and under torture had acknowledged their guilt, were sentenced to imprisonment for life in fortresses outside the city. A direct violation this of one of the most cherished privileges of citizenship, but doubtless inspired out of consideration for the personal safety of the prisoners, who would have run no small risk of being lynched if they had been detained in Brussels. Some three or four who had fled from justice were condemned in default to lifelong exile and to the forfeiture of their estates. Only two were brought to the block, ex-Amman Cluting and one of his sergeants. They were taken on the Thursday night, and their end came with tragic speed. 'On Saturday morning,' says De Dynter, who was perhaps an eye-witness of the scene he describes, 'the whole community being assembled in the market-place under arms, Jan Cluetinck and Arnulph Vander Hove were led bound into the midst, and when Gerard Vander Zype, who ruled the Regent, coming forth from the Town Hall, with a loud voice had cried out, "Now we are going to begin," Amman Diedeghem gave the signal, and straightway and without any interval their heads were struck off.'

Cluting had not only taken an active part in the betrayal of the city on the 21st of January, but he was said to have been a prime mover in the alleged German conspiracy to murder the leaders of the popular party; and seeing that Philip and his barons were firmly convinced of the reality of the plot and that his guilt was proven, they could hardly have done otherwise than condemn him to death. In all probability Vander Hove died for aiding and abetting his chief. De Dynter, however, does not tell us for what crime he suffered: he contents himself with simply recording the fact of his execution.

One cannot help being astonished at the moderation which the working population of Brussels at this time showed. The craftsmen were now masters of the city, they were seconded by a large number of the patricians themselves, and in all probability no demand which they had chosen to make would have been refused them. Yet, unlike their fellows of Bruges and Ghent, who had long since excluded their patricians as such from all share in municipal government, so that they could only take part in civic affairs by enrolling themselves in one or other of the trade companies, the craftsmen of Brussels were content with a half share in the government of the city. All the old institutions were preserved, but they were enlarged so as to admit the plebeian element, or new institutions were created alongside of them.

So complicated did the municipal machinery now become, that any detailed account of it is impossible within the limits of this volume; suffice it to say, that at the head of the administration were two burgomasters, the first a patrician and the second a plebeian, the patrician burgomaster being chosen by the craftsmen from a list of three names presented to them annually by the incoming aldermen, who as heretofore were all patricians, and the plebeian burgomaster being chosen by the aldermen from a list of three names presented to them by the trade companies. These officers were held to be the representatives par excellence of the city, its guardians and supreme chiefs, and they were invested with judicial powers to settle all trade disputes, in which the matter at issue did not exceed a demi livre vieux gros.

The magistracy proper, as of yore, consisted of a College of Aldermen of seven members and two patrician treasurers. No change was made in the manner of their appointment, but it was ordained that henceforth these offices should only be conferred on patricians resident in Brussels, and such as were not in the employ of the Duke or of any great noble, because, as the charter quaintly explains, such have been found by experience to be peu profitables. Added to the magistracy were eight plebeian members, viz., six councillors and two treasurers. These were selected by the aldermen from a triple list presented to them by the trade companies. Thus the magistracy consisted of seventeen members, of whom nine were patricians and eight plebeians. Also provision was made for a referendum to the people. When in the opinion of the burgomasters and the plebeian councillors such a course was desirable, they were competent to convoke the juries of the trade companies, but before doing so they were bound to advise the aldermen. Then when they had communicated to the craftsmen the opinion of the magistracy on the matter in hand they demanded their decision, and that decision seems to have been final. Thus, though the patricians had a majority of one in the town council, the last word practically lay with the people in all grave matters.

The articles of the new charter were agreed upon in a great assembly of barons and of deputies of the towns of Brussels, Antwerp and Louvain, on Thursday the 6th of February 1421. The charter itself was signed and sealed by the Regent on the following Tuesday (February 11), and its provisions were immediately put into execution.

Until now the proletariat of Brussels had willingly acquiesced in the wise and moderate policy of the Regent and his advisers. No constraint had been placed on the personal liberty of Duke John; the three aldermen of the popular party, in spite of their lamentable weakness in the matter of the great betrayal, had not been deprived of office. Of the many who were undoubtedly guilty, only a comparatively small number had been put on trial, and the light punishments meted out to them might well have called forth the resentment of those who had suffered from their crimes; and yet the working population had acquiesced in all these things, and when they had at length received their charter of enfranchisement the craftsmen were content to lay down their arms; but the mildness and confidence of these men was soon to give place to cruel suspicion and an insatiable hunger for vengeance.

Shortly after Jacqueline's flight in the summer of 1420 some of Duke John's most intimate friends had banded together in a secret and lifelong league to support the throne, and generally to defend the Duke against the machinations of his enemies. This at least was the ostensible object of the league, but there is little doubt that the action of its members, all of whom were partisans of the Straetens, was inspired less by love of John than by hatred of the brothers Heetvelde. The matter was kept so quiet that none of the Duke's opponents had any inkling of it until the close of March 1421, when Gerard Vander Straeten, Provost of Saint Jacques sur Coudenberg, and one of the greatest churchmen in Brabant, was arrested, on suspicion seemingly, of being concerned in the German plot, of which Hendric Van Heetvelde, rumour had it, was to have been the first victim.

Whatever the cause of his arrest may have been, the consequences of it were tremendous. His house was searched, and there in his chamber were found mysterious papers relating to the secret league, with the names of the members in their own handwriting, and with their signets affixed, and also a letter of approval signed and sealed by Duke John himself.

The men of Brussels were bewildered and dismayed. What did it all mean? But when the *i*'s were dotted and the *t*'s were crossed by the burghers imprisoned without the walls, constrained thereto by torture—for these miscreants were all implicated—dismay became frenzy, and bewilderment a mighty voice compelling retribution. Again the craftsmen flew to arms, again they surged into the market-place, and again, but not until three days had passed, Myn Here Vander Zype appeared in the tribune of proclamation. 'Children,' he cried, 'be of good heart, your prayer is granted,' and presently the sergeants led in 'Gedolphus of Coudenberg, Willem Pipenpoy and Lord Everard T'Serclaes, Knight,'—conspirators, all of them, on their own showing; for had they not set their hands and seals to the fatal roll in Vander Straeten's chamber? The name of T'Serclaes was second on the list, and he was probably the originator of the movement—evilest of John's evil counsellors, unworthy offspring of a noble stock, and yet, for his father's sake, they might have spared him; but no voice was raised on his behalf, and his head was struck off with the rest. Of Vander Straeten's ultimate fate, De Dynter, who tells the story, says nothing, but his name in itself was enough to damn him.

If Philip and his council had been left to their own devices, these men's lives would doubtless have been spared. It was only under compulsion that they at last yielded to the clamour of the mob, and if they had held out longer, not even the influence of Vander Zype, who, as De Dynter reiterates again and again, 'ruled the Regent and swayed the people,' would have availed to save the rest of the leaguers. As it was, he was able to induce the craftsmen to lay down their arms and to acquiesce, for the moment, in no further proceedings being taken against them. Shortly afterwards Duke John formally approved of all that the Estates and the Regent had done, confirmed the new charter, and solemnly promised that no man should ever be molested for anything that had taken place in the course of the revolution. 'Whereat,' says De Dynter, 'the common folk were so well pleased that those in authority, having pity on the burghers imprisoned without the walls, were emboldened to mitigate the rigour of their confinement.'

At Louvain they were even permitted to receive their friends and to eat and drink with them. Naturally they took heart. Some of them began to dream of pardon, and even, over their wine-cups, to utter threats of vengeance, which of course reached the ears of the craftsmen of Brussels, and of course bred uproar. 'These blusterers must be led to the block; that was the only way to deal with them. Public safety demanded it.' In vain Vander Zype urged that it were the grossest injustice to increase the punishment of men who had been already tried and sentenced; the insurgents answered that the sum of their infamy was not then known, and that, if this boon were not granted, they would have out the Germans and cut their throats.

That was enough. Sigismund was already pressing for his subjects' release, and the Regent knew that if any evil should befall them he would have to make ready for battle. On Saturday, then, the 7th of June 1421, the prisoners were led in chains to Brussels, and before sundown they were dead men. On the morrow, when Gerard Vander Zype rode through the Grand' Place along with the bride to whom he had just plighted his troth in the old Church of Saint Nicholas, the pavement was still red with their blood, and they were all of them his own kinsmen—gruesome prelude this to the banquet of which the newly married couple were about to partake in the ducal palace.

Had Jeanne Vander Zype no foreboding of the horrible doom in store for her husband? And if so, did her heaving bosom gleam with those priceless jewels, the wedding gift with which Heinsberg hoped, not vainly, to purchase his redemption?

Of these things De Dynter says nothing, but we know that, thanks to Gerard's good offices, the German knights were released shortly after his marriage, and that the craftsmen, mollified by the blood which he had shed, offered no resistance; and we know, too, that the man who had sacrificed his kinsfolk to avert war was made to suffer for it in his own person, but not yet.

One chronicler asserts that Duke John himself was present at the executions of the 7th of June; but if this had been the case, De Dynter would have almost certainly mentioned it; and, moreover, as Wauters justly observes, the story is a most improbable one: John was so grieved at the death of his friends that he left Brussels immediately after the executions, perhaps even before they had taken place, and refused to return to the Coudenberg for two years.

Things being now set in order, the councillors who had led John astray being all in exile or dead, and John himself having solemnly engaged to rule henceforth according to law, the Estates were for recalling him and reinvesting him with the government of his domains; but Philip, supported by the men of Brussels, was loth to lay down authority, and for a time it seemed as if there would be trouble. At last, however, when all the confiscated estates of John's favourites had been conferred on him by way of solatium, and a large cash payment to cover expenses out of pocket, he yielded, and on November 25, 1423, Duke John came back to Brussels.

Some turbulent spirits there were who, angered at the Duke's refusal to retain the services of the Lord of Bigard, whom the magistrates had appointed captain of the city, on the ground that as he, John, had now returned he would be able in future to perform the duties incumbent on that office himself, broke out into riot, but the vast majority of the craftsmen were little inclined to risk their new-born liberty in the fortunes of a fresh revolution. Philip's influence was now on the side of the authorities, the disturbance was soon quelled, and the Lord of Bigard having submitted to the Duke, by order of the city magistrates was relieved of his office.

When Philip of Saint-Pol resigned the regency, Duke John, compelled thereto, no doubt, by his brother, had named Gerard Vander Zype Controller-General of Finance and Chief Steward of his household—the most honourable and lucrative appointment in his gift. At first the Duke professed himself well pleased with Vander Zype's management, but presently he began to complain of his unconscionable parsimony: even his own board, he alleged, was insufficiently furnished, and he knew there was no lack of funds. Perhaps there was another cause for John's rancour, perhaps in his heart he resented the violence which his steward had done to so many of his friends. Still there was no open rupture, but the Duke's sentiments were well known, it was whispered abroad that Vander Zype's removal, by whatever means, would be welcome to him, and this is what happened.

On the morning of the 23rd of April 1424 Gerard Vander Zype rode out to Tervueren, where the Duke was at this time sojourning. Having transacted the business which called him there—what it was De Dynter does not say—he set out on the homeward journey early in the afternoon. The road from Tervueren to Brussels led, as it still does, through the forest of Soignes, in those days a much more wild and desolate tract of country than it is now. When he had accomplished half of his journey and was nearing Stockel, on the outskirts of the wood, he descried in the distance a horseman riding furiously towards him. It was 'Messire Jehan Blondeel, who hated him with a perfect hatred.' 'Death, death!' cried the knight as he hurled himself against his foe, and, dragging him from his saddle, plunged his sword into his heart.

Vander Zype was not unattended, but his servants, probably in Blondeel's pay, took to their heels at the first sign of danger, and the body of the great patriot was left alone by the wayside all night.

In the morning it was found by some country folk and carried to Brussels, and presently, by order of Philip, cut to the quick at the death of his friend, laid to rest in the Church of Saint Jacques sur Coudenberg with solemn dirge and requiem.

CHAPTER XIV
The Trials of Jacqueline

The enemies of Duke John of Brabant were disappearing one by one. The bitterest opponent of all, the injured and insulted wife, whose heritage he had yielded to her ruthless competitor, and whose honour he had trampled in the dust, about this time, too, endured the first of that long series of rebuffs which in the end crushed her.

Shortly after her flight to England Jacqueline had lodged an appeal to the Holy See for the dissolution of her marriage, on the ground that at the time she pledged her troth she was not a free agent. Whilst the case was still pending she had bestowed her hand on Humphrey Duke of Gloucester, and towards the close of the year 1423 she appeared in Hainault with the man whom she now called her husband and six thousand English archers.

The nobles almost to a man flocked to her standard, every town in the county save Hal acknowledged Gloucester as their lawful prince, even the Governor of Hainault cast off his allegiance to John and swore fealty to his rival. But Jacqueline's former friends in Brabant regarded her new marriage from another point of view. The men of Brabant had dreamed that their triumph would be hers; they flattered themselves that they would have been able to reconcile the ill-matched pair. They had looked forward to the birth of a son destined to unite under one sceptre his father's and his mother's domains, and they now turned their swords, not against the outraged woman whose wrongs they had sworn to avenge, and whose dignity, as the Consort of their Sovereign, they were bound in honour as loyal subjects to uphold, but against the wanton, whose delirious passion had shattered their hopes. And there were others, too, who were angered at the course which Jacqueline had seen fit to pursue:—John the Pitiless, who, opportunely dying by poison, it was said, shortly after her arrival, was unable to vent his spleen, and Philippe l'Asseuré, to whom John had bequeathed his claims, and who, in order to safeguard his interests as heir-presumptive to Jacqueline's dominions, effectually showed his displeasure by joining hands with her former husband. The men of Hainault and their English allies were unable to withstand the united strength of Brabant and Burgundy. City after city and fortress after fortress surrendered or went up in flames. When, early in March 1424, Braine-le-Comte was taken, Gloucester withdrew to England to collect fresh forces, and before he had had time to return his last stronghold was in the hands of his opponents, and his wife a prisoner in Ghent.

De Dynter relates a strange delusion on the part of the English, which led to the surrender of Braine-le-Comte during the opening days of the campaign, and that, in spite of the fact that the city was strongly fortified and well stored with supplies. They had descried, they said, from the ramparts, amongst the knights of Brabant, their patron, Saint George; his arms were displayed on his ensign, and he was seated on his traditional white charger. At sight of the apparition their hearts had shrivelled, and no strength was left in their bodies; it was a sure sign from Heaven that they were favouring an unrighteous cause. 'Now, amongst our knights,' explains De Dynter, 'was Myn Here Daniel van Bouchout, the horse he bestrode was a white one, and his family arms exactly resemble the arms of Monseigneur Saint Georges.'

Burghers from every commune in Brabant, save Bois-le-Duc, took part in the siege of Braine, and when all was over and the loot divided the great town bell was allotted to the men of Lierre. They carried it in triumph to their native city, where it still hangs in the tower adjoining the Town Hall.[24]

Of the events which led to the surrender of Mons and to her own imprisonment, Jacqueline herself gives a curious account in a letter which she dispatched to Gloucester early in July 1425, and shortly before the final catastrophe. Mons had been besieged since the middle of May by Duke John of Brabant in person, and the city had been reduced to such straits that the burghers themselves had opened negotiations with the enemy unknown to Jacqueline, who was daily expecting reinforcements from England and had obstinately refused to treat. Early in June conditions of surrender were agreed upon, which, though sufficiently favourable to the burghers, provided that Jacqueline should undertake to break off all relations with Gloucester and acknowledge her former husband as legitimate Sovereign of her domains until such time as the Pope should pronounce judgment on her appeal.

To these terms she refused to consent, and the city was in consequence on the verge of rebellion. In vain she had gone down to the Town Hall (June 16) and made a personal appeal to the honour and chivalry of the burghers.

'Not only did they refuse to help me,' runs the letter from which the above facts are culled, 'but they said that my knights were doing their utmost to compass their destruction, and then, in spite of me, took Sergeant Macquaert and cut off his head, and put no less than two hundred and fifty of your most devoted followers under arrest, and at last told me plainly that if I any longer refused to make peace they would themselves deliver me into the hands of my cousin of Brabant. I have only eight days' delay and then they will send me to Flanders, grievous affliction, and I shall never see you again unless you make speed to save me, my only hope, my sole and sovereign joy. All that I suffer is for love of you; for God's sake, then, have pity on your sorrowing creature if you would not bring about her ruin. I have some hope that you will help me, for never have I done aught to offend you, nor will I as long as I live, but on the contrary I am ready to die for love of you and of your person, so greatly doth your noble domination delight me, by my faith, most redoubted lord and prince. For the love of God and of my Lord Saint George, consider then my wretched plight, this you have not yet done and methinks you have clean forgotten me. Inform me of your good pleasure and I will do it with all my heart, as the Blessed Son of God doth know right well. May He grant you a good and a long life and give me the joy of seeing you. Written in the false and traitorous town of Mons on the 6th day of July 1425. Your grieving and devoted handmaid, suffering great pain by your commandment.—Your handmaid,

'JACQUELINE.'

This letter was intercepted en route and handed to Philip of Burgundy, but had it reached Gloucester it would probably not have touched him. If he indeed loved Jacqueline, she was not the sole mistress of his heart; her rival, Eleanor Cobham, had accompanied him to Hainault and returned with him to England, and doubtless the society of this lady was some consolation for the grief which, as Vinchant informs us, he had publicly displayed at parting with the woman he called his wife.

As for the hapless Jacqueline, she accepted the terms of surrender arranged on the 1st of June, and was presently conducted to Philip's palace at Ghent, where she was virtually a prisoner. She recognised John of Brabant as rightful Sovereign of her domains until such time as the Pope should pronounce judgment on her appeal: John, in his turn, undertook to provide for her maintenance, and in accordance with the terms of the treaty appointed Philip of Burgundy Regent of Hainault and Holland.

Jacqueline, however, was not yet at the end of her adventures. In Holland the Hoeks[25] were still devoted to her, a plan was contrived for her deliverance, and presently it was successfully carried out. Vinchant tells us how it all happened.

'One evening early in October two of her most trusty and loyal friends, Dirk Merwede and Arnulph Spyerink, arrived in the city of Ghent, and having left their horses saddled and bridled in a certain place, went to visit their lady, bringing with them, done up in a bundle, a suit of male attire, which she, whilst her people were at supper, hastily put on, and thus disguised departed with the aforesaid knights without being recognised by any of her guards, and riding hard all night never halted till she reached Wondelghem, and from thence she went to the castle of the Lord of Vianen, who received her gladly, and having arrayed her in some of his wife's garments led her to Schoonhaven, where all the town was marvellously glad at her coming. Next day she journeyed to Gouda, from thence to Oudenwater ... and wherever she went she was welcomed, caressed and entreated as Lady and Countess of Holland—always accompanied by the Lord of Vianen, whom she named her commander-in-chief.'

For three years this indomitable princess was able to defy her opponents, but the issue of the contest was from the first a foregone conclusion. Philip was able to pour into Holland the élite of his soldiery, 'tous exercités,' as Monstrellet says, 'et excités en armes et faits de guerre.' He had, too, the support, of the Duke of Gelderland and of course of John of Brabant, and in Holland itself the Church, the burghers, the great mass of the industrial population, were all in his favour.

What chance had Jacqueline of victory in face of such odds? At first, indeed, she had some help from Gloucester, who, in spite of his brother of Bedford, Philip's friend, made shift to send her three thousand archers, but on the 27th of January 1426, the Pope affirmed the validity of Jacqueline's former marriage, and Gloucester, constrained to sever his connection with the woman who had suffered so much for his sake, made her cup yet more bitter by espousing her rival, Eleanor Cobham, and by withdrawing his troops from Holland. Henceforth she stood alone at the head of her loyal Hoeks. Inspired by her heroic courage, her indomitable will and the glamour of her misfortunes and her beauty, these stalwart Dutch knights were able to prolong the unequal contest for nearly three years, and then at last she was constrained to own herself vanquished.

On the 3rd of July 1428, by the Treaty of Delft, she acknowledged Philip as Regent of her domains, delivered into his hands all her strongholds and solemnly engaged not to marry again without his consent, for Jacqueline was now a widow—on the 17th of April, 1427, Duke John of Brabant had gone the way of all flesh.

This last condition she did not scruple to break, and Vinchant tells us why. 'After four years had passed,' he says, 'in good peace and concord between Madame Jacqueline, Countess of Holland, and Duke Philip of Burgundy, it so happened that Madame Marguerite, the Countess Dowager, sent her by certain gentlemen a present of some beautiful jewels and several good horses; whereat Countess Jacqueline, finding herself without cash, having expended all her funds on the late war, and having nothing to bestow by way of gratuity on her mother's people, sent secretly to the Vicomte de Montform, who had formerly been her lieutenant in Holland, begging him to lend her the wherewithal to preserve her reputation in the eyes of the aforesaid gentlemen by bestowing on each of them, according to his rank, some token of her gratitude; but the Vicomte excused himself, saying that he had expended all his means in her service, and the aforesaid lady, much perplexed, sent to another of her friends and was treated by him in like manner. Whereat she was so grieved that she withdrew to her chamber weeping, and one of her servants, Guillaume de Bye, seeing his lady thus distressed, took pity on her and said, "Madame, an it please you, I will go to Messire Franche de Borselle, lieutenant of Zeeland, and explain to him your present straits, and I am not without hope that some good will come of it?" "What!" says she, "toute esplourée, he is our foe and has never received any kindness from us." "Yet," says Guillaume, "an it please Madame, *je l'esprouveray par quelque moyen que ce soit.*" "I fear," quoth the Countess, "we shall gain nothing by it, albeit go, and say I will soon repay the debt." And Guillaume went, de bonne grace, and presently the Lord of Borselle, counting out the money, "Go tell my lady that not this time only, but always throughout my life, she may dispose of me and mine according to her good pleasure." Wherefore Madame Jacqueline held him in high esteem and conceived so great an affection for him that she desired to give him her hand, which she afterwards did clandestinely in her own chamber.' But for all that Philip got wind of it and obtained possession of the persons of the newly-married couple, and Jacqueline, constrained to choose between the death of her husband and the loss of her crown—for the Treaty of Delft conserved to her the nominal sovereignty of her domains—preferred the latter alternative. On the 12th of April 1433 Philip the Good exchanged his title of Regent for that of Count, and some three years later (April 9, 1436), his victim died of despair and consumption at the old Castle of Teylingen, hard by Leyden.

Jacqueline left no issue and her cousin of Burgundy thus became the legitimate lord of her domains. Six years before he had received the heritage of Duke Philip of Brabant, who had died most opportunely on the eve of his intended marriage (August 4, 1430). Rumour had said poison; the physicians, a sudden chill; and the man who inherited his patrimony, that Fortune was invariably kind to him.

CHAPTER XV
Buildings and Builders—Romanesque Architecture

It was not till the days of Charlemagne that art was born in the Low Country, and Charlemagne may be not inaptly said to have been its progenitor. When that monarch planted the outposts of Christian Europe on the banks of the Elbe he made the Low Country—a land then of marsh and wood, whose inhabitants had hitherto lived apart, forgotten by the rest of the world, on the edge, so to speak, of civilisation—the central province of his dominions, and, as such, it in due course became the centre of contemporary culture: the common intellectual mart of the Teutonic regions of the East and the North, the Latin provinces of the West and the South, of Ireland, of England, and of the land of the Scot. The bishops, satraps, scholars, merchants, courtiers, courtesans who flocked to Aix-la-Chapelle from all parts of Europe, all of them passed through the Low Country and were constrained to sojourn for rest and refreshment in the only hostelries which the land possessed—the convents and monasteries sparsely scattered amid its forests and fens. The traffic on the old Roman road across the Charbonnière was now greater than it had ever been before; the Meuse and the Scheldt for the first time became highways along which were towed huge barges heavily laden with foodstuffs for the provisionment of the Court, and thus, as Pirenne has it, 'on this soil, formed by the alluvial deposit of French and German streams, there gradually sprang up a civilisation of like nature with the soil itself, a civilisation made up of divers elements—Latin, German, French, in a word, a civilisation not so much national in character as European.'

Nor was it only thus indirectly that Charlemagne promoted the civilisation of the people of the Netherlands. The rapid progress which was at this time made in humanising these rugged folk was in large measure due to the Emperor's personal initiative: he brought artists from England, Italy, Constantinople, to decorate his palaces at Aix and Nimègue, he established a school of art attached to the Court, he ordained that the churches should be adorned with mural paintings, and named inspectors to watch over the work and see that his orders were strictly carried out, and, most important of all, he charged himself with the task of providing foreign teachers for the novices of the few religious houses which at this time were established in the land, and where the culture of art and letters seems to have fallen wholly into disrepute. The scholars to whom the Emperor confided this task were among the most famous of their day. Men like his secretary and biographer, Eginhard—the architect of the dome of Aix-la-Chapelle—

whom he set over the twin abbeys of Saint Peter and Saint Bavon at Ghent; and Arnon, one of the most brilliant disciples of Alcuin, who became abbot of Elnone by Tournai; and the Italian mechanician Georgius, who taught at Saint-Sauve, by Valenciennes; and the great Irish scholar Sedulius, who later on (840-855) lectured in the frescoed hall of Bishop Hartgar's new palace at Liége.

Nor was this policy unprofitable. A spark was enkindled which soon became a burning and a shining light. Clerks began to polish their rusty Latin, monks to busy themselves with history, in writing the lives of local saints, and by erecting in their honour temples not unworthy of the patrons to whom they were dedicated. Cloistered women, too, devoted their leisure hours to art: they adorned their refectories and chapels with frescoes, and their choir-books with exquisite miniatures and capitals cunningly devised, and, for the service of the altar, made marvellous vestures of gold, wrought about with divers colours. A specimen of their illumination has come down to us: in the sacristy of the old church at Maeseyck there is a copy of the Gospels, painted by two sisters, Saint Harlinda and Saint Renilda, who, about this time, ruled over the great Abbey of Aldeneyck, on the outskirts of the town. This is the most ancient piece of miniature work in Belgium. In a word, the ignorance and grossness which had so long disfigured the Church in the Netherlands completely disappeared, the soil teemed with religious houses, each of which was an active centre of literary and artistic life, and there was soon no more flourishing province in Christendom than the land between the Rhine and the sea. But the glory of it all was short-lived: after the Danish Terror there was nothing left of it but a memory. Unless the subterranean Church of Saint Guy at Anderlecht, as some maintain, be of this period, in Brabant, at least, no vestige remains of Carlovingian architecture. For more than sixty years thick darkness enveloped the land. Isolated efforts, indeed, there were: the monks of Lobbe maintained an obscure school; Bishop Stephen at Liége, and, at Utrecht, Bishops Radbod and Balderic, did what they could, in the midst of the barbarism and anarchy of the times, to keep alive the lamp of learning; but it was not until 953, when the Emperor Otho placed the ducal crown of Lotharingia on the head of his brother Bruno, that there was anything like an approach to a general Renaissance movement. Under Saint Bruno's firm and gentle rule discipline was re-established. Art and literature followed in its wake. Everachar the Saxon, whom he named to the See of Liége in 959, was the founder, or at least the restorer, of the Cathedral School there—a school which was renowned almost from its origin, and which, under his successor Notger, became one of the chief centres of learning in the West. The masters of Liége lectured in all parts of the empire—at Mainz, at Ratisbonne, at Brescia, and even penetrated into France; and students from all parts of Europe flocked to drink in knowledge in the famous school of Saint Lambert.

The literary and artistic movement inaugurated by Saint Bruno and the imperial bishops was no doubt accentuated by the monastic revival promoted about the same date by Gerard of Brogne. Great cathedrals and abbey churches now sprang up in rapid succession, cloisters were everywhere enlarged or rebuilt, bishops' palaces were adorned with sculpture and painting, and the little edifices of wood, which on the countryside had hitherto done duty for parish churches, were replaced by more substantial buildings of stone or brick. German in origin for the most part, it was naturally to German architects that the bishops of Lotharingia entrusted their building operations. Thus the style in vogue in the valley of the Rhine spread rapidly towards the west. With the architects came artisans of all sorts—sculptors, hewers of stone, painters, woodcarvers, founders of copper and of bronze. These foreigners founded schools in the country, a host of apprentices joined them, who made such progress in their craft that soon they were able to compete with their masters. Thus was there gradually formed a native school of architects and artists, of whose talent and technical skill the remnants of their work which have come down to us bear witness; and we know that in their own day their fame was so great that Abbot Suger had recourse to their aid for the work which at this time he was engaged upon in the Abbey of Saint-Denis.

They did not, however, at first form a new style. For something like two hundred years they were content to walk in the paths which their German masters had traced for them. Not only in architecture, but in painting, in sculpture, in wood-carving, in metal work, in embroidery, the school of the Meuse, as M. Pirenne aptly puts it, was the legitimate daughter of the school of the Rhine.

Indeed, as long as the Church in the Low Country remained imperial, German traditions prevailed. Even the main body of the cathedral at Tournai, with its dome and its turreted apsidal transepts, which was only commenced in 1030, is distinctively German in character, and so, too, was the cathedral at Cambrai,[26] designed on similar lines, and this is all the more remarkable from the fact that it was not completed till nearly a hundred and fifty years later—some seventy years, that is, after the episcopate of Walcher, the last of the imperial bishops of this diocese.

THE CHURCH OF SAINT NICHOLAS

Of the buildings in Brussels and its immediate neighbourhood, which date from this period (950-1200), but few remain. Indeed, in the city itself there are only fragments. Foremost among the monuments which contain them note the Parish Church of Saint Nicholas in the Rue au Beurre, one of the oldest and perhaps the most interesting of the time-honoured sanctuaries of Brussels. The date of its foundation is not known, but it cannot be later, and may be considerably earlier, than the close of the ten hundreds. It is one of those old buildings which, by reason of their great age and thrilling memories, have attained individuality and almost become living things—a stalwart veteran who in the course of a long and honourable career has manfully endured an unwonted share of the trials and vicissitudes of life. It has gained many scars in wrestling with time and the elements, more in its conflict with man. It has been cast down and renewed, enlarged and curtailed, defaced and embellished, polluted and blessed over and over again; and though for the last fifty years it has been constantly threatened by municipal blockheads with total destruction, it still towers amid the nest of habitations which cluster round its walls and cling on to its buttresses, a picturesque and venerable pile in spite of its mutilations—not the least pleasing of the rare landmarks of old-world Brussels.

THE OLD CHURCH OF SAINT NICHOLAS, RUE AU BEURRE.

It is not, however, its intrinsic beauty which renders this church so fascinating. It possesses in common with many ancient things, not only buildings, but often trees, pictures, furniture, and notably jewellery, another attribute: there is about it a certain subtle influence which at once lays hold of the spectator and convinces him that it has a story. It has, and a thrilling one which, if it were written, would fill volumes and keep the reader spellbound from the opening words of the first sentence to the end of the last page.

This church, dedicated to Saint Nicholas, patron saint of burghers and merchants, and situated on the fringe of the Great Market, hard by their Town Hall and Guild-houses, has been, from time immemorial, the distinctive church of the bourgeoisie, in the same way that Saint Jacques sur Coudenberg has always been the distinctive church of the Court. Its life is bound up with the life of the city. It is the cradle of its liberties. Its hopes, its struggles, its victories, its defeats are intimately associated with it. In this church the city fathers were wont to assemble in the early days when they had no town hall. Its steeple was the town belfry—we say advisedly *was*, for it exists no more—home of the 'work-clock,' which every morning called the craftsman to his toil and in the evening sounded his release; and of the shrill tocsin, which in days of terror summoned him to arms, and when he had triumphed shouted victory. Here, too, in a lower storey, was the archive chamber where were laid up the records and the title-deeds—the charters which the town had bought at such great cost of blood and gold. Thrice burnt down and thrice rebuilt, until the close of the seventeen hundreds, this ancient tower was the pride and the glory of the men of Brussels, who regarded it as the outward and visible sign of their privileges as citizens and their rights as men. Nor is this all, the Church of Saint Nicholas is possessed of a mysterious power of attraction. Why men should single out this particular church in preference to all others is a question hard to answer. There is no ostensible reason for it: it is not the shrine of some great and popular saint, no famous relics are treasured here, nor miraculous image or picture. They are drawn to it in spite of themselves. Wherefore, who shall say? Enter when you will, it is never without worshippers, and what a motley throng they are! Of course that sex which the breviary so quaintly and aptly styles devout is the most in evidence. Women in shoals are there—women of every age and every complexion, all sorts and conditions of women: from the *grande dame* of ancient date, demure, aloof, dowdy, who, to her very rosary beads, is invested with an air of distinction, to the market-woman with her milk cans or her basket of fresh vegetables; from the fashion plate of the demi monde, perfumed and painted, to the snuffy crone in foul rags, who in the same breath asks an alms and tells her chaplet. And the men, if there be fewer of them, are no less heterogeneous—that sleek, smug-faced tradesman is trying a deal with Saint Anthony, he has made him an offering and promised more if only he will promote his undertakings; the youth in glorious apparel is commending, perhaps, to Saint Joseph an affair of the heart, or—who can tell?—perhaps he has a thorn in the flesh of which he would fain be rid; the shabby, middle-aged, sallow-faced wreck who stands before 'Onze Lieve Vrouw,' works, when he is not too drunk, as a journeyman tailor, in politics he is a social democrat, and if you were to ask him his religion, he would tell you that he was a libre penseur, but the woman who loves him is sick and believes, and he has slunk in here to put up a taper for her in honour of the 'Salus infirmorum,' the old man with trembling limbs and palsied head, who is painfully making the way of the Cross, was in his day a dashing spark who could make women's hearts throb and sometimes broke them. He has drunk to the dregs of the joys of life and experienced the after-taste, but all this is ancient history; he has long ago made his peace with God, and is quietly waiting now for the great metamorphosis. And there are children too, not many—for the neighbourhood is one of theatres, cafés, public buildings—ragged urchins some of them, with bare feet and pinched faces. The streets outside are cold and wet, or they are hot and dusty, and where else should these waifs seek shelter but in their Father's house?

Such are the devotees who frequent this mysterious shrine; and the visible objects of their devotion—the likenesses of the ghosts who haunt it, are no less varied than are they. Some of them are Neo-Gothic conceptions of the school of Saint Luke—tall, emaciated figures with gilded locks and pale, meek faces; others are of the time of the Renaissance, and are full-blooded, fleshy, human; others again are as old perhaps as the church itself, and these are the most interesting.

For how many centuries, for example, has the 'Man of Sorrows' sat by the western doorway silently asking of those who enter, 'Is it nothing to you, all ye that pass by?' A strangely pathetic figure this. The sculptor who modelled it must have had this text in his mind, 'There is no beauty in Him,' and this, 'The Lord has placed upon His shoulders the iniquity of us all.' The statue is of carved wood painted after life, but time and maybe the flare of tapers have rendered it almost black. It is quite nude save for a loin cloth, but someone, perhaps scandalised at this, has thrown a mantle of purple velvet now faded and moth eaten, over the shoulders. A relic is let into the instep of the left foot, which is defaced and partly worn away by the lips of innumerable troubled souls who have found consolation in their own sorrows by pitying the sorrows of Christ. For the rest, the church is not without charm from an æsthetic point of view—the axis of the choir is probably more decidedly inclined to the north-east than that of any other church that the visitor will call to mind: this and the divers styles of architecture in which it is built renders it at least picturesque. Moreover, though the stained glass which once glowed in its windows has long since disappeared, and though whitewash and plaster have effaced the frescoes and carving with which its walls were formerly adorned, the interior is still bathed in glowing tints: it is rich in old oak furniture, in objects of marble and copper and brass, in easel paintings and in devotional statues resplendent with colour and gold, and there are flowers too and red lamps, and withal and always a host of flaring tapers. But let not the reader be disappointed. There is much in this church which is tawdry, trivial, vulgar, which transgresses in a flagrant degree the canons of good taste; its splendour, it cannot be denied, is not always the splendour of truth. We have here the lustre of colour which, like charity, covers a multitude of sins, the fascination of old-world memories and the glamour of the picturesque. Added to this there are a few genuine works of art, notably some good pictures, which even the most fastidious need not be ashamed to admire; but since they are all of more recent date than the Middle Age, they do not come within the scope of these pages. And what, perhaps, it will be asked, has this farrago of modern idolatry for which space has been found to do with the Middle Age? This much—call it idolatry if you will, we have here mediævalism undiluted. The credulous folk who flock to the Church of Saint Nicholas are silly enough to believe, like their fathers in the thirteen hundreds, that the Sabbath was made for man, not man for the Sabbath.

It is difficult, perhaps impossible, to say anything definite as to dates in the case of a building like the Church of Saint Nicholas, which has endured so many vicissitudes and suffered so much at the hands of restorers, but there can be little doubt that the great oblong columns which support the vaulting of the nave, and perhaps too the walls of the aisles, or at all events some portions of them, formed part of the original structure. But whether these things be old or new is a matter of little moment. The burghers' church is doomed. The decree has gone forth, and as soon as the leases of the old houses which cluster round it fall in, it is to be sacrificed to the demon progress. A street has to be enlarged or straightened, or the site is needed for a cab-stand or a public-house, or for some purpose equally objectionable. Death indeed sits close to our old friend, hence this disquisition. Albeit, he has so often escaped by the skin of his teeth that it is hard not to believe that means will even yet be found for still further prolonging his days. One thing is quite certain. If this piece of vandalism be carried out, it will be for the indelible shame of the whole city. A disgrace alike to the authors of the crime, and to those who by their indifference or their lack of energy, have connived at it. In Belgium there is a permanent Government commission for the preservation of ancient monuments, and a private society likewise exists, of which the raison d'être is similar, yet it seems that neither of these bodies have as much as thought it worth their while to lodge a formal protest.

More important from an architectural point of view than the Church of Saint Nicholas is the Church of Notre-Dame de la Chapelle. The foundation stone was laid by Duke Godfrey Longbeard in 1134, and though the greater portion of the existing structure is of more recent date, some interesting fragments still remain of the original building, notably the little Chapel of the Holy Cross and the beautiful façade of the south transept, which is pure Romanesque and richly adorned with sculpture. The plans were modified as the work progressed, and the rest of the south transept, the north transept and the chancel are in the style of the Transition. A nave and aisles were also added at this period, but they were destroyed by fire early in the fourteen hundreds, and rebuilt in the course of the century in the style then in vogue.

The collegiate Church of Saint Michael and Saint Gudule was commenced by Duke Henry I. in 1170, and the eastern wall of the ambulatory, with its Romanesque windows, date from this period. It took the men of Brussels five hundred years to complete this beautiful building, and hence it contains specimens of every style of architecture, and is on that account none the less interesting. We shall have something more to say of each of these churches in another chapter.

The civil architecture of this period is represented only by some fragments of the fortifications with which Lambert Balderick surrounded the city in 1040. They are scattered about here and there in various parts of the old town. There is a picturesque bit of wall for example in the garden of Saint Gudule's Presbytery, another piece has been incorporated into a house in the Rue des douze Apôtres, there is more in the Steenporte, and, most important of all, a tower some sixty feet high between the Halles Centrales and the Church of Saint Catherine.

This picturesque relic, which is called 'la Tour Noire,' was discovered when some old houses were demolished in 1887. At first the Corporation was for pulling it down, but fortunately Brussels at this time had a burgomaster who was not only an artist and an archæologist of repute, but also an enthusiastic amateur of mediæval architecture. After a long fight, M. Buls, who is still living though he has now withdrawn from public life, succeeded in saving the old tower, and thanks to his indefatigable efforts, it was later on restored by the town.

THE CRYPT OF SAINT GUY AT ANDERLECHT

LA TOUR NOIRE.

It is not, however, in the city itself, but in the suburb of Anderlecht, a mile and a half beyond the line of the outer ramparts, that the most interesting specimen of Romanesque architecture is to be found. Here we have no mere fragment, more or less defaced, but something complete in itself, something which has never been tampered with, something older, too, than any of the buildings of which we have just spoken, older, indeed, for the matter of that, than any other building in Brabant. In a word we have here an antique jewel of rare beauty, which has never been re-set nor re-cut: the subterranean Church of Saint Guy at Anderlecht remains to-day what it was when the builders planned it.

The earliest archives of the collegiate chapter of Anderlecht have disappeared, destroyed, no doubt, when the Flemings invaded Brabant under Louis of Maele, and hence the date of its foundation is not certainly known. Some chroniclers mention the year 800, others 914. Tradition says that it goes back to an epoch when there were only two other chapters in Brabant, the Chapter of Saint Berlinda, a niece of Saint-Amand, erected at Meerbeck towards the close of the six hundreds, and the famous Chapter of Nivelles, founded by Saint Gertrude, a daughter of Pepin of Landen, in 645; and we know from the Anderlecht *Life of Saint Guy*, the earliest life that has come down to us, that a dean and canons were certainly established there early in the ten hundreds. In any case there can be no doubt that this foundation was a very old one, and in all probability the present subterranean church is the church in which the first canons of Anderlecht were wont to perform their devotional offices.

True, it is said in the anonymous *Life of Saint Guy*, written most likely by a canon of Anderlecht in the opening years of the eleven hundreds, that about the time when his relics were first translated (1076) the canons of Anderlecht decided to build a new church, and from this, M. Schaeys, in his *Histoire de l'architecture en Belgique*, concludes that the present structure dates from this epoch, but the style of the architecture denotes a much earlier period, and the MS. account of what took place, in spite of the passage in question, which, read with the context, has clearly another meaning than that which M. Schaeys attributes to it, rather confirms than contradicts the evidence of the architecture.

The writer informs us that at this time the church at Anderlecht, by reason of its great age, was almost a ruin; some of the walls had actually fallen down, and others were in imminent danger of doing so. The clergy and the people therefore decided with one accord to sell the rich gifts which for years past pilgrims had been offering at the shrine of Saint Guy, and with the fund thus realised to build a new and more spacious church. If, then, the present crypt, which only measures forty feet by forty-eight, was the outcome of this decision, the former structure must indeed have been one of exceedingly narrow dimensions.

Although 'the poor man of Anderlecht' had during his lifetime been regarded as a saint, he was not publicly honoured as such until some forty years after his demise. About this time (1054) what our author calls a basilica, no doubt a small mortuary chapel, had been erected over his grave, and as it adjoined the church it now became necessary to pull it down in view of the proposed building operations. Hence the question arose, What should be done with the saint's body? The matter was referred to the bishop of the diocese, Gerard II. of Cambrai, 'who had succeeded the Lord Lietbert of blessed memory'—this fixes the date, Gerard received consecration in 1076—and he ordained that the body should be disinterred and provisionally laid to rest in the centre of the church until the new building should be ready for its reception.

The bishop's instructions, our author avers, were duly carried out, and in the last paragraph of his narrative, he informs us that 'the elevation of Saint Guy' was made by Bishop Odard on the 24th of July, 1112. It would seem, then, that from the earliest times there have been two churches at Anderlecht, an upper church and a lower church; that the former, having fallen into a ruinous state, was pulled down in the year 1076 and rebuilt on a larger scale, and that the new structure was completed in the summer of 1112, certainly not later than that date. Further, that the lower church, which no doubt had been more solidly built than the upper building, seeing that it was intended to support a superstructure, was still in 1076 in good repair, and that hence it was left standing.

That this was 'the church' where the relics of Saint Guy reposed during the interval which elapsed between the disinterment of 1076 and the 'elevation' of 1112 there can be no doubt whatever. Not only do the terms employed by the writer render this point certain, but we have the additional evidence of the empty tomb which still stands in the centre of the crypt. As to the date at which this interesting building was constructed the style of the architecture points to the eight hundreds. In form it is distinctly reminiscent of the early Christian basilica: it consists of an apsidal nave of three bays and double aisles, those which are adjacent to the nave are separated from it by cylindrical columns with capitals, which recall the Tuscan order, and from the outer aisles by two great square shafts without capitals, around each of which are clustered four columns similar to the columns of the nave. There is also a series of half columns of like design at intervals round the walls. These, and the piers, and the pillars of the nave support the vault, which is a simple cross vault without ribs. Each of the outer aisles is pierced in its west wall by a small round-headed doorway which opens on a staircase leading to the upper church, and the building is dimly lighted by six narrow slits of windows, which are likewise round-headed. The original high altar has disappeared, but there are two side altars which are of great antiquity, probably as old as the church itself—huge oblong blocks of stone without ornament or inscription. Hard by to each of them is a small chamber built in the thickness of the wall. It has been suggested that one was a baptistery, the other a vesting-room. In the centre of the inner southern aisle is the tomb of Saint Guy, an oblong mass built up of stone covered by a granite slab rudely carved with a double cross, floriated with vine leaves. The monument is pierced by an aperture neither broad nor high, just large enough for a lean man to crawl through if he felt so inclined, as many did at one time—the edges of the opening are worn away by the countless pilgrims who, in days of yore, thus gratified their devotion. Strange as they seem to us now, practices of this kind were common enough in the Middle Age: when in the eleven hundreds the bodies of the saints were 'elevated' from the crypts in which they had hitherto lain to the temples which about this time were raised above them, and there laid up in gilded shrines, the empty tombs in which they had so long reposed still continued to be the objects of popular devotion. Sometimes the coffin was left open, in order that the saint's clients might stretch their own limbs in the place where his body had lain, sometimes an opening was made in the side of the tomb large enough for a man to peer through, or through which he might even thrust his head. Sometimes it was larger still, and women with sickly children would then place them for a moment within, and pray that God, through His servant's merits, would make the weakling strong. They as firmly believed in the virtue of these sticks and stones as the men of Judæa believed in the virtue of the cloths and handkerchiefs which the Apostles had touched, or of 'the shadow of Peter passing by.'

Of course the present upper church is not the church which the canons of Anderlecht built with Guy's treasure. That was pulled down in 1460, as the Anderlecht archives bear witness. The present structure was commenced then, and not completed until well into the fifteen hundreds. We shall have something to say about it presently.

NIVELLES

A little further afield, in the ancient town of Nivelles, there is another and very noteworthy specimen of Romanesque architecture. Nivelles was in former days a far more important place than it is now. It gradually grew up beneath the shelter of the great abbey which, as we have seen, Saint Ita and Saint Gertrude had founded in 625; and if so far as concerns its material welfare it was inferior to the great cities of Brabant, it excelled them all in the dignity of its social standing, for the little town was an ecclesiastical fief held directly from the Emperor[27] by an abbess who bore the illustrious title of Lady Princess. To this exalted office no mere plebeian could aspire, nor patrician either for the matter of that, unless she had the right to a scutcheon with at least sixteen quarterings. The abbess lived in almost royal state in a palace adjoining her minster, and the white-robed canons and the Augustinian nuns, who formed the chapter of Nivelles, and dwelt, the former in a cloister hard by the church, the latter, apart in the town, were submitted alike in spiritual and in temporal things to her jurisdiction. Even the lay aristocracy shone with an additional lustre reflected from her magnificence. What rights and privileges they enjoyed above their fellow-citizens were theirs not in virtue of noble birth, but as members of the household of Saint Gertrude. Their fathers were serfs on the abbey domain who had risen to positions of trust, they were men who had bartered their liberty for a servitude freer than freedom itself, had entered a great monastic family and become participators in its immunities, and these their descendants continued to enjoy for years after the days of bondage had ceased. The Hommes de Sainte Gertrude like the Hommes de Saint Pierre owed their title to distinction to the servile condition of their ancestors.

Though the rulers of Brabant had for years past encroached on her privileges whenever they had an opportunity of doing so, the abbess was still a grande dame, with ample means to support her high position when the end came in 1793, but the power which she then wielded, though still considerable, was only the shadow of what it had been in the palmy days when she was not only in name but in fact 'the Lady Princess of Nivelles.'

Nivelles never seems to have attained to anything like commercial pre-eminence. In the days when the fabrication of woollen goods was the staple industry of the Netherlands, her manufacturers perhaps did as well as their fellows in other small towns of like standing, but certainly no better. Later on, when the cloth monopoly was lost and men turned their attention to linen, she did indeed make some reputation for the excellence of her cambric, but she lost it after the riots of 1647, when her weavers migrated in a body to Cambrai and Valenciennes. Henceforth, until its suppression, the custom of the household of Saint Gertrude was the mainstay of her prosperity, and when that source was cut off by the French revolutionists in 1793, she very soon became what she is now, a little market town with a population of some ten or eleven thousand souls.

Nivelles is situated partly on the side of a hill and partly on the fringe of an emerald valley made fertile by the river Senne. Here there are snug homesteads nestling amid orchards and surrounded by well-tilled fields, and rich pasture-lands enclosed with hedges thick and high. There are woods too on the rising ground beyond, and here and there a windmill or the steeple of some village church. The landscape is one most pleasant to behold, and if only the fields were less carefully tilled and the cottages and farm buildings were not so numerous nor so well cared for, it might easily be mistaken for an English scene in one of the home counties.

The little town itself is tranquil, dreamy, clean. In its narrow, winding streets there are some curious old houses with high-pitched roofs and crow-stepped gables, and here and there are some curious old buildings with mullioned windows and Gothic doorways, which one is quite sure, if they are not now the homes of nuns, were at one time, and of course there is a sprinkling of those clean, comfortable-looking, substantial dwellings which are always to be met with in quiet nooks and corners in the country towns of Belgium. Sometimes they have courtyards in front, separated from the street by cunningly wrought iron railings and paved with cobble-stones, on which stand palms in tubs, or bay trees fashioned like umbrellas. Sometimes stretching out behind there is a trimly-kept walled garden of which the passer-by occasionally obtains a refreshing glimpse through some half-open door. They were built for the most part about a hundred and fifty years ago, and are the homes of local professional men or the winter abodes of the neighbouring country gentry, who, reckoning their incomes by hundreds, rather than thousands, are rich enough not only to vegetate comfortably and in a manner befitting their station, but to give alms with no stinted hand, and withal and always to keep very respectable balances at their bankers.

The most interesting feature of the town of Nivelles is, of course, the old Minster, with the exception, perhaps, of Tournai Cathedral, the finest Romanesque church in Belgium. It is a noble pile three hundred and twenty feet long, with three towers at the west end, single nave-aisles, strongly-marked transepts, and an unusually long rectangular choir built over a crypt. Within, however, it is disappointing, for the interior was so completely transformed in the course of the seventeen hundreds that no vestige of the original work was left visible. Efforts are now being made to repair the mischief. The beautiful crypt, which had been completely filled up with earth and rubble, has been excavated and restored, the walls of the choir and transepts have been stripped of the bastard Renaissance ornament with which they were disfigured, the bays which had been bricked up have been opened, a timber roof has been substituted for the plaster ceiling, and it is proposed, as soon as funds are forthcoming, to completely restore the whole church.

The restoration, it is pleasing to note, is being carefully and conscientiously carried out, but though every available fragment is being utilised, so much of the old work has disappeared that, alas, there is no hope of adequately repairing the havoc wrought by the ill-judged generosity of the canons of Nivelles in 1754.

En revanche, save for 'the golden stain of time' and the great tower, a child of the fourteen hundreds, without, the Church of Nivelles remains to-day what it was when Pope Leo consecrated it in 1047 in the presence of his imperial nephew. Not the only association this of Saint Gertrude's Abbey with Leo IX. Its bells, so runs the tale, were solemnly tolled by invisible hands when on the night of the 19th of April 1054 the soul of the great reformer passed out of the world. Whatever may be thought of this beautiful legend, it at least bears witness to Leo's popularity.

So glorious is the exterior of this grand old building, that did the journey from Brussels to Nivelles take as many hours as it does minutes, the sight of it would be ample compensation, and, too, there are cloisters as old as the church itself, in style pure Romanesque, so vast that forest trees flourish in the garth, without making it appear crowded. The south, the east and the west sides have suffered considerably from over-restoration, but the north colonnade is still intact, and built over it is all that remains of the ancient monastery. We have here one of those silent, old-world nooks which are still redolent of the incense of the Middle Age.

The Church of Nivelles is not only interesting on account of its architecture: Pepin of Landen is buried here in the centre of the nave, and beside him his wife, Saint Idenberge, and their daughter Begga, whom the Beguines regard as their patron saint. Here, too, are the mortal remains of another of Pepin's daughters, Saint Gertrude, foundress of the abbey. They are treasured in a shrine of copper gilt, adorned with sculpture and bas-relief, and encrusted with precious stones, a veritable triumph of the goldsmith's craft, designed by Jaquemon, monk of Anchin, and wrought by another Jaquemon, a townsman of Nivelles, with the assistance of one Nicolon, who seems to have been a citizen of Douai. The names of these men are meet to be had in perpetual remembrance.

For the moment this marvellous piece of metal-work is laid up in the sacristy. Presently, when the restoration of the chancel is completed, it will be restored to its former position above the high altar.

Of the remaining fragments of Romanesque architecture in the immediate neighbourhood of Brussels, most remarkable, perhaps, is the great square tower of the Church of Saint Jacques at Louvain, which probably dates from the beginning of the eleven hundreds. Within are some curious cylindrical columns, adorned with floriated capitals of good design and workmanship. The Abbey Church of Parc, hard by the same city, was commenced in 1225, perhaps earlier, but not completed till 1297. This building exists to-day, but it has been so frequently altered by successive abbots that no trace of the original Romanesque work is visible, save a little round-headed doorway alongside the main entrance and some narrow slits of windows in the chancel.

For the rest, in the villages and hamlets, which are so thickly sown in the country round Brussels, there are not a few churches or portions of churches which date from the period we have just been considering. It is impossible, however, within the limits of this handbook to give even a list of them. Those who are interested in this matter will do well to consult Mr. Weale's *Belgium*. Here will be found descriptions, with numerous historical notes, of the village churches in the neighbourhood of the chief towns of the kingdom and along the main lines. It was published nearly fifty years ago, and of course since then many archæological discoveries have been made, and, alas, much ancient work has disappeared, but no other handbook with which we are acquainted contains in so small a compass such a vast mass of generally reliable information concerning the architecture and the art of the Low Countries.

Gothic architecture seems to have been first introduced into the Netherlands from France by way of Tournai. The stately choir, second to none in Europe, which that great church-builder, Bishop Walter de Marvis, added to his cathedral there during the second quarter of the twelve hundreds, was probably the first purely Gothic structure erected in Belgium. It is altogether French in plan and in method of construction, and it may well have been designed by a mason of the Ile de France. Men's minds were at once captivated by its beauty, and the new style spread rapidly throughout the land.

It could hardly have been otherwise: Tournai was not only the religious capital of Flanders, it was also the artistic capital of a very considerable portion of the Low Country; here was established a school of architects and sculptors, which at this time was among the most famous of the North; when the architects of Tournai adopted the new style it was bound to make headway. Flanders, Holland, Zeeland, without quarries of their own, and without native masons, were constrained to bring from Tournai, the nearest point where stone was to be had, alike their building material and their builders. These men had drawn their inspiration from beyond the Rhine, and perhaps, too, from Normandy, and had already attained in their craft a very high order of excellence. When fascinated, then, by the beauty of Bishop Walter's choir, they determined to follow the new French fashion; they showed themselves no servile imitators, but modified their old plans and their old schemes of ornament in such a manner as to suit the needs of the new methods of construction: thus they gradually evolved a distinct style of their own, and the flat apse, the octagonal towers, the round turrets, adorned with pilasters with capitals delicately carved on either side of the western gable, the high, narrow lancet windows, without mullions or tracery—all distinctive features of Tournai work, are to be met with over and over again, not only in Hainault and in Flanders, but even in Picardy and in Holland.

Less marked was the influence of the Tournai school on the architecture of Brabant. Brabant had quarries of her own, and builders, inferior, indeed, to the builders of Tournai, but for all that well skilled in their craft; and thus what Tournai was doing for the rest of Belgium Brabant was able to do for herself. Though at first her architects seem to have taken as their models the buildings which their rivals of Tournai were constructing in Hainault, in Holland, and in Flanders, even their earliest Gothic work is in no way lacking in originality. Witness, for example, the choir of the Collegiate Church of Saint Gudule at Brussels, one of their first efforts. As time progressed the distinctive features became more and more pronounced, and presently a style was developed more original and also more beautiful than anything produced at the same time by the Tournai school. Indeed, the Gothic architecture of Brabant of the fourteen, fifteen and sixteen hundreds, if it be equalled, is certainly not surpassed by the Gothic architecture of those centuries in any other land. So far as concerns civic buildings, Brabant certainly holds the palm. Neither France nor Germany nor England can show anything which can be compared, for example, to the Town Hall of Brussels or the Town Hall of Louvain, or even with the Gothic portion of the Town Hall of Ghent, which was designed by Brabant architects.

So great was the fame of the architects of Brabant from the commencement of the fourteen hundreds that their services were in request all over the Netherlands, and later on, in the days of the Emperor Charles V., in Germany, in France, and even in far-off Spain; and, strangely enough, some of their latest efforts are as nobly conceived and as carefully executed as in the days when their art was at its zenith.

Nothing could well be finer than the Parish Church of Saint Jacques at Antwerp, which was commenced in 1491 and not completed till 1694, the work having been discontinued from lack of funds in 1530, and not renewed, owing to the religious troubles, until 1602. This grand old building, which was designed for a simple parish church, has all the characteristic features of a great cathedral—triforium, clerestory, double aisles, ambulatory chevet, transepts, and a host of side chapels. The plans were drawn up by Herman De Waghemakere, a burgher of Antwerp, and an architect famous throughout the Low Countries, who not only designed many noble buildings, but begot two sons, Herman and Dominic, to whom he transmitted his talent, and whom he trained to his own calling. When he died, early in the fifteen hundreds, they were able to worthily continue the work at Saint Jacques' which the old man had so successfully commenced, until 1530.

At this time no portion of the church was completed, and the choir was not even begun. When, some seventy years afterwards, building operations were again resumed, the original plans were strictly adhered to, and it is worthy of note that the more recent work is as carefully and skilfully executed as that which was carried out under the eyes of old Herman himself.

This church is rich in stained glass of the fourteen, fifteen and sixteen hundreds, which, considering the period, is of a very high order. If the designs of some of the windows be faulty, the scheme of colour is in each case perfect. It has retained more of its old furniture—tapestry, metal-work, wood-carving and the like, than most churches in Belgium. It contains some good pictures—notably, in the Lady Chapel, an altar-piece by Rubens, which was placed here by his widow, and, in a vault beneath it, all that remains of 'this prince of painters and of gentlemen.'

In the sublime tower of Saint Rombold's at Mechlin we have another late creation, though not so late as the Church of Saint Jacques at Antwerp. The foundation stone was laid on the 1st of May 1452, and they seem to have worked at it intermittently until 1583, when the stones destined to complete it were carried off to Holland by the Prince of Orange, and employed by him to build the town of Willemstad. Even in its unfinished state it is a colossal building. At its base it is fifty-three feet wide without counting the buttresses, which advance on each side to a distance of nearly fifteen feet. Its actual height is over 320 feet, but if the spire had been added, of which the original plans are still in existence, it would have risen to the prodigious height of 544 feet, and would thus have been the loftiest steeple in Europe. This mighty tower was designed by Jan Kelderman, master-mason, of Louvain, not many months, perhaps not many weeks, before his death in 1445; at which time he was in all probability between seventy and eighty years of age. The foundation stone was laid under the direction of his son Andrew, and for over a hundred years one or other of his descendants busied themselves with carrying out the old man's designs.

A remarkable family, the Keldermans: architects, sculptors, painters, almost all of them, during many generations. The first of whom we have any record was Jan van Marsdale, sculptor, of Brussels, who, for some reason of which we are ignorant, adopted the family name by which his descendants are generally known. He was probably born some time during the second quarter of the thirteen hundreds, and died at Brussels not earlier than 1415. In his day he was an artist of renown, but nothing which can be certainly attributed to him has come down to us. We know that he was the author of the richly-sculptured tomb of François van Halen, which was placed in the first apsidal chapel on the south side of Saint Rombold's at Mechlin in 1415, and demolished in 1810.—Of this marvellous work of art there exists in *Le Théâtre Sacré du Brabant* an engraving—and we know, too, that he was the father of the Jan Kelderman who designed Saint Rombold's tower. This man was a burgher of Louvain, and city architect there from the 7th of October 1439 till his death in 1445. He directed the building of the Council Chamber in the Hôtel de Ville, which had been designed by his predecessor, Plyssis van Vorst, and which still exists. Of his three sons, Rombold, the eldest, was a painter of glass, and one at least of his works has come down to us: a beautiful window in the old church at Lierre, the first on the north side—representing Godefroid Vilain XIV. and his wife, Elizabeth d'Immersule, donors, along with their patrons, Saint Peter and the poor man of Assisi. This window was painted in 1474, and the sum which the artist received for it was forty-two golden florins. Rombold was born in the year 1420. He married before 1447 Catherine van Voshem, whose sister Elizabeth was the wife of the famous painter, Dierick Boudts, and inhabited his own house in the Rue de Diest at Louvain, where he died on the 17th of March 1489. Matthew, Jan's second son, followed his father's trade, and he also busied himself with painting and sculpture: the indentures of an apprentice whom he undertook to instruct, in three years, in the art of painting are still in existence, and we know, too, that some of the carved beams in the Town Hall at Louvain are his work. For the rest, he in due course took to himself a wife, who presently bore him a son, whom he named Hendrick

Saint Rombold's Cathedral

and trained to his own calling. No record of any work that he executed has as yet been found, but he seems to have done well in his profession, for in

1505 he purchased a house in the Cattle Market at Mechlin, hard by the Chapel of Saint Eloi, and here in 1521 he received Albert Dürer, who in his journal notes that at Mechlin he was the guest of 'Maister Heindrich.'

Andrew, the youngest son of old Jan Kelderman, was a man more famous than either of his brethren. He was city architect of Mechlin, and supervised the carrying out of his father's design of Saint Rombold's tower for thirty years; and when he died, in 1485 or thereabout, it had risen as high as the bell-chamber. He was the author of divers beautiful rood-screens, amongst them that in the church at Bergen-op-Zoom, which he wrought in 1471 with the aid of his son Anthony, who, it will be interesting to note, dwelt in a house at Mechlin which is still standing—No. 13 Aux Tuileries.

This man, succeeding his father, directed the building of Saint Rombold's tower until he in his turn died, on the 15th of October 1512. He was the author of two famous buildings—the Town Hall of Middelburg, in the island of Walcheren, and, in his native city, the Church of *Notre-Dame au-delà de la Dyle*, and the father of two sons who were not unworthy of the family name, and each of whom set their mark on the family tower. The younger was aptly enough called after the saint with whom the Keldermans had been so long associated; honours were presently his, and wealth and a wide reputation, if he were not the greatest of his race, at least he was the most successful, of Rombold Kelderman II. we shall have much to say later on; the elder was named, after his father, Anthony, and though he died young, he lived long enough, but only just long enough, to design a monument which still

NOTRE-DAME AU-DELÀ DE LA DYLE.

proclaims his genius—the old Broodhuis at Brussels, now called La Maison du Roi. Some three days before the foundation stone was laid young

Anthony was gathered to his fathers (December 5, 1515), and the guerdon which he would have received was paid into the hands of his widow.

LA MAISON DU ROI.

There were other members of this talented family of whom the record of some of their labours has come down to us. Notably Matthew, a younger son of Andrew Kelderman, who worked at Antwerp Cathedral under Herman De Waghemakere from 1487 to 1498; his son, also Matthew, who migrated to Louvain, was named city mason there and directed the building operations of the Church of Saint Peter from 1503 to 1527; and Laurence, who plied his trade, for the most part in Brussels, helped to build the Maison du Roi, and was perhaps a nephew, perhaps a son, of the great architect who planned it. The city records from which these bald facts have been culled in comparatively recent years by those who have or have had the care of them, divulge something of the nature of an anecdote concerning Laurence Kelderman. We learn from certain entries in the town accounts of Brussels that in the year 1513 he was mulcted 30 florins for wounding one of the amman's serjeants, and the same document informs us too how it came about.

Kelderman and two other famous masons—Hendrick van Pede, the author of the Town Hall of Oudenaarde, and Ludwig van Beughem, who later on built for Marguerite of Austria the famous Church of Brow in Bresse— were at this time at work, most fortunately for them as it afterwards turned out, on the beautiful palace which the Count of Nassau was erecting for himself in Brussels with that gold, as all men believed, which he had wrung from the vanquished burghers of Bruges in 1490, and every evening it was their wont, when their work was done, to drink together at the Sign of the Star, a tavern of note in the Great Market, which seems to have been at this time much frequented by men of their craft. To this house of entertainment, then, on the 13th of February, at their accustomed hour they repaired, and each man having bade the drawer bring the liquor he liked best, they proceeded to pledge one another in bumpers, but their potations that night were not destined to be of long duration. Perhaps there was strife in the cups of some of their boon companions, certain it is that one of them drew his knife, and, as luck would have it, at the same moment the amman's serjeant walked in, who, fearing mischief or feigning to do so, forthwith disarmed the fellow; whereat our masons, enraged at this insult to a free citizen, hurled themselves on the officer of justice, wrenched away his sword, and in so doing inflicted on him a flesh wound. The offence, according to the strict code of Brussels, was no light one, and serious consequences would have undoubtedly followed had it not been for the Count of Nassau, who, loth to lose the services of such capable workmen, exerted his influence in their behalf, and thus they were quit with a fine. Later on we find the names of two of the delinquents again associated, but in very different fashion. When it was decided in 1532 to add to the Church of Saint Gudila a new Sacrament chapel, the Maîtres de la Fabrique commissioned three architects to prepare plans for the proposed structure, and two of them were our friends of the tavern brawl, Hendrick van Pede and Ludwig van Beughem. Peter van Wyenhoven was the third competitor, his designs were adjudged the best, and he it was who constructed the actual building. Bernard van Orley, the famous painter, made the fair copy of his plans for him on two large sheets of parchment, and received for so doing, it will be interesting to note, £2, 10s. 9d., and the foundation stone was laid on the 8th of February 1535.

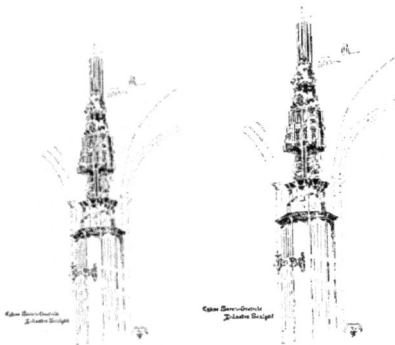

Eglise Sainte-Gudule Pilastre Sculpté

The plan of this chapel is exceedingly simple. It consists of a nave of four bays with a flat apse pierced by a vast window enriched with flamboyant tracery. The building is also lighted by five other windows of similar design and like dimensions, of which four are set in the north wall, and one in the last bay of the south wall. They are all of them filled with beautiful stained glass, which is as old as the chapel itself, and the picture which glows in one of them—the second on the north side—was designed and painted by Bernard van Orley. The shafts, or piers, or pilasters—it is difficult to know exactly what to call them—from which spring the numerous prismatic ribs of a rich and intricate vault, are strangely and elaborately fashioned. Below they are bold, octagonal columns, or rather half-columns. Higher up they break out into a mass of tabernacle work in the form of two canopies, which shelter saints, and when at last they emerge from behind the pinnacles and crockets, we find that they have ceased to be columns and are now slender reeded shafts, which presently spread out like palm leaves and become the ribs of the groining.

Though Van Pede's designs were not accepted, the Sainte Chapelle des Miracles is none the less a perpetual memorial of his genius: the cunningly wrought sculpture which it contains is almost all of it his handiwork. The honoured name of Kelderman too is linked with this building, but that association is now only a memory: the high altar which Peter Kelderman reared has long since been cast down.

But to return to Peter's more famous kinsman, old Anthony Kelderman's second son, Jonkhere Rombold van Marsdale, for thus the honest mason styled himself after Charles V. had ennobled him. Maybe he thought the ancient family name sounded more aristocratic than the name which his great-grandfather had adopted.

Though Rombold was undoubtedly an architect and artist of a very high order, and though he remained to the end of his career a man of energy and enterprise, and at last died in harness, full of years and honours, strangely enough his memory is not kept alive by any monument which he alone can be certainly said to have designed and carried to completion. In his early days he was largely engaged in completing the work of other men, or in adding to, or embellishing, or restoring buildings which already existed. Later on he entered into partnership with Dominic De Waghemakere, and henceforth most of his designs were not the outcome of his unaided genius. Together they planned many glorious structures. Some never got beyond paper, others were commenced and left unfinished, for they lived in troublous times; only a few were brought to completion, and of these but one remains, the Steen of Antwerp, spoilt by restoration.

Rombold Kelderman had honours, riches, renown. His career from this point of view was certainly a most successful one, but an untoward fortune seems to have dogged his steps in the matter of his craft, and this was so not only with his own creations but also with the buildings which he reared and the plans which he made conjointly with Dominic De Waghemakere.

THE STEEN OF ANTWERP.

Thus, for example, he was commissioned by Charles V. to transform the unfinished Cloth Hall of Mechlin into a place of assembly for the Grand Council of Brabant. He drew out plans; they were all that could be desired—the original drawings are preserved amongst the city rolls; somewhere about the year 1529 the foundation stone was laid, and at first the work was pushed on bravely, but before it was half finished came the troubles of Philip's reign and it had to be abandoned, but Rombold grieved not at it, he had long since paid Nature's debt.

Otherwise, and yet more deplorable, was the disaster which baulked the realisation of Kelderman and De Waghemakere's magnificent scheme for the reconstruction of the choir of Antwerp Cathedral.

During the two centuries which had elapsed since the commencement of this great church the ground around it had gradually risen by reason of numerous interments to a very considerable distance above the pavement; hence the church was always cold and damp, and in wet weather not unfrequently flooded. To remedy this, it was decided early in the fifteen hundreds, to erect a new choir with a crypt beneath it in such a manner that the pavement of the upper building should be on a considerably higher level than the ground outside. Kelderman and De Waghemakere prepared the plans, and in due course the Emperor himself laid the foundation stone. For nearly ten years they worked at the new structure, and then came the catastrophe which sooner or later almost always frustrated Kelderman's most strenuous endeavours: a fire broke out which wrought such havoc on the main body of the cathedral that the repairs absorbed alike the money and the material which had gradually been amassed for the building of the new choir. Thus was the ambitious scheme of these two great architects nipped, so to speak, in the bud, for ambitious scheme it undoubtedly was: if it had been carried out Antwerp would have possessed a cathedral vaster and, if contemporary witnesses are to be trusted, more beautiful than any other city in Christendom. Of this we have no means of judging, for though the plans were carefully treasured among the city rolls for some two hundred years, at last they mysteriously disappeared. There was reason to believe they had been stolen, and though every effort was made to trace them, from that day to this they have never been found; but of the vast proportions of the proposed edifice there can be no manner of doubt, the foundations still exist, and here and there they are visible. Moreover, a few years ago, there was discovered, hidden away in the archive chamber, a contemporary sketch of the ground plan, from which it appears that Kelderman's choir would have occupied a

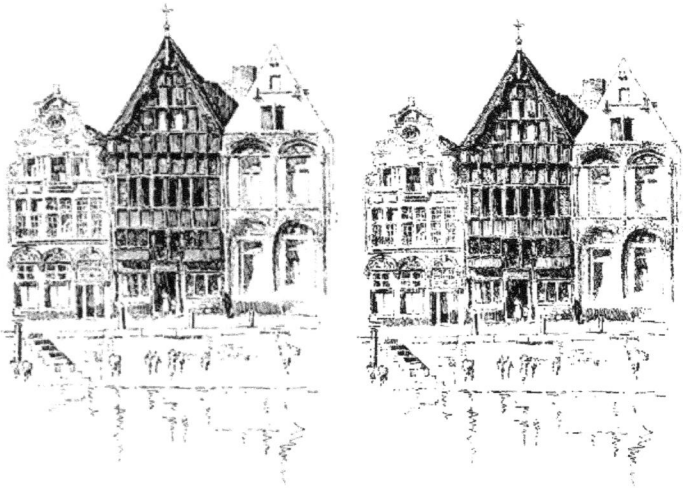

QUAI DE L'AVOINE, MALINES.

surface just twice as large as that covered by the actual choir including the ambulatory and the chevet. Now Antwerp Cathedral in its present state is not one of mean dimensions: it is somewhat longer than Westminster Abbey, without the lady chapel, and exceeds it in breadth at the transepts by over ten feet and at the nave by no less than a hundred.

Kelderman and his partner were happier, or perhaps it would be more apt to say not quite so unfortunate in their undertakings at Ghent. Here their endeavours were at least crowned with some measure of success. Early in the year 1518 the city fathers of Ghent commissioned our masons to erect for them a new Town Hall, as we learn from the contract passed between them on that occasion. The original deed is still in existence; it is very curious and interesting, and throws much light on the customs and methods of the builders of the day. In it Rombold and Dominic bind themselves to inspect the work three times a year—in April, in August, and somewhere about the Feast of Saint Bavo, at which last visit they promised to bring with them designs for sculpture, ironwork and so forth, to be executed by the workmen in winter time, when building operations were invariably suspended, and they also undertook to come to Ghent at any time throughout the year when their presence was deemed necessary, provided their travelling expenses were paid and they were given four, or at least three, weeks' notice. Moreover, the magistrates reserved to themselves the right to name other architects in place of De Waghemakere and Kelderman, in the event of their not giving satisfaction. They had no occasion to exercise it; the plans were perfect, Rombold and his partner performed their duties with the greatest assiduity, and the burghers began to flatter themselves that soon Ghent would be endowed with the grandest Town Hall in the Netherlands. Their expectations were not realised—the building progressed slowly, perhaps on account of the threatening state of the political atmosphere. On the 15th of December 1531 Rombold Kelderman died, and it was not yet half finished. Albeit, they did not lose heart; Dominic, in virtue of a clause in the agreement, named Laurence Kelderman to succeed his uncle; for four years longer the work dragged on and then at last it came to a standstill. Who could think of building operations amid the hubbub and whirl of rebellion? Or afterwards, when the riot was quelled, whilst Alva was begging for the destruction of the town, or whilst the city fathers with ropes round their necks were humbly sueing for pardon? It was not till the close of the century that the burghers were once more able to turn their attention to their unfinished Town Hall. Dominic had long since joined his partner on the other side of the stream, the art in which these men had so excelled was now almost dead, Ghent was beginning to be captivated by the spurious charms of the Renaissance, and in completing her Town Hall she followed the bent of her fancy. The new architects, however, left the work of their predecessors intact, and we have this much too to be thankful for: the original plans still exist. By a clause of the agreement of 1518 it was provided that in the event of the decease of both the architects before the completion of the Town Hall the plans should be restored by their heirs to the city magistrates; this clause was faithfully carried out, and the plans, along with the contracts, are still preserved among the city archives of Ghent.

However much we may regret the setting aside of the plans of Kelderman and De Waghemakere, it cannot be denied that they deserved the fate which overtook their labours, for they themselves had shown scant respect to the memory of their predecessor, John Stassins, an architect of no mean order, who, as early as 1481, had made plans for the new Town Hall, plans which were accepted by the city fathers, and which, until his death in 1517, he had done his utmost to realise. So much labour lost, Kelderman and De Waghemakere discarded them and cast down his unfinished building; but in Ghent John Stassins has his memorial: he it was who planned and reared Saint Bavo's stately tower, not the least beautiful of the many beautiful towers which still adorn the cities and the villages of the Low Country.

The mention of the tower of Saint Bavo's naturally suggests the church itself. Here we have perhaps the most beautiful of all the Belgian cathedrals, certainly the most interesting. Founded in the course of the nine hundreds, and not completed till the latter half of the seventeenth century, this time-honoured building contains specimens of almost every period of architecture. The crypt, or at all events a portion of it, is part of the original structure; it is divided into four naves and is the largest crypt in Belgium. Here lie the ashes of Hubert van Eyck and those of his sister Marguerite. The choir, of blue Tournai stone, severe, ample, stately, is of course Tournai work of the closing years of the twelve hundreds, all of it save the vault, which dates from four centuries later, and is so perfect an imitation of primary Gothic work that did we not know that the choir of Saint Bavo's, like so many early churches in Belgium, was originally covered with a wagon-head roof of timber, and were it not for the cathedral records which remove all doubt as to the period of its construction, it would certainly be assigned at latest to the opening years of the thirteen hundreds. For the rest, the fifteen ambulatory chapels are of the thirteen and of the fourteen hundreds; the tower, as we have seen, dates from the closing years of the latter period; and the nave and transepts, the aisles and adjoining side chapels were built in the middle of the fifteen hundreds.

That the western half of Ghent Cathedral was the work of a Brabant architect, is more than likely, for though there is no documentary evidence to show who was its author, it has all the characteristic features of the Brabant style. The position and character of the tower—lofty, massive, bold, proudly standing at the head of the church, with its lower stage as wide and as high as the nave and incorporated with it; the peculiar treatment of the triforium—not an arcade, but a simple gallery of sculptured stone; the triangular oculi in the gables of the transepts, and the vast windows, divided by great Y-shaped mullions, which light them, these and a host of other things too numerous to mention proclaim with no uncertain voice what manner of man made it.

In every age and in every land it has been the aim of Gothic masons to make their buildings, and especially their religious buildings, the incarnation of this mandate—Sursum corda. Almost always they succeeded, but often, and this is notably the case in England, their most successful efforts are cramped and narrow, or at all events from their great height seem so. The Gothic architects of Brabant set themselves a harder task, which, in spite of its difficulty, they not infrequently accomplished. Their churches should, indeed, sing Sursum corda as loudly as the rest, but they should add to it no less loudly this other refrain—*In loco spatioso*. The builder of the cathedral at Ghent in this respect triumphed magnificently: Saint Bavo soars like an archangel, and it would be hard to find a church which more emphatically preaches breadth. Not only is the building in reality broad and high, it looks so; nay, it has the appearance of being broader and higher than it actually is. In order to invest it with a large atmosphere the architect who designed it not only gave breadth to his ground plan but made all his openings broad, taking care that those most in evidence should be broader in proportion than the rest. Thus the surface covered by the nave and aisles is almost a perfect square. Indeed, the distance from north to south is slightly greater than that from east to west. Of this vast space the central avenue embraces, roughly speaking, two-fifths, the adjacent avenues each about one-fifth, and each of the outer avenues one-tenth. In other words, the nave is twice as broad as the inner aisles, and these bear much the same proportion to the outer aisles. Also, in order to give them greater breadth, he economised his openings, and in the case of windows reduced the intervening masonry to a minimum. Thus the nave, notwithstanding its great length, has only four bays—the object of this was no doubt to give breadth to the cross vistas— and consequently in its clerestory there are but eight windows, four on each side, and the same number in the walls of the outer aisles. In spite of the vast span of the arches, the several arcades have by no means a stunted appearance. They are too lofty for that, and also in the case of the central avenue the rich moulding which adorns them springs from the bases of piers without capitals, and thus we have a series of unbroken lines ascending from plinth to apex, which marvellously increases their height.

Arcades are often thus treated in tertiary Brabant work, and even too sometimes in buildings of the second period. Not that the architects who designed them despised capitals, or were ignorant of their æsthetic value, but they knew where they could be suppressed with advantage and where they could be added with effect. None of their buildings are wholly devoid of them, and at Saint Bavo's they are numerous and highly developed, a very noteworthy feature in the scheme of ornament: alike in transept, nave and aisles, the ribs of the vault spring from them. They are all of like fashion: bell-shaped, considerably larger above than below, and adorned, but not over adorned, by closely clinging conventional leaves. They crown cylindrical columns, sometimes single, sometimes in groups of three, five, or more, which, though they are in reality of no mean girth, by reason of their great height and of the vast bulk of the piers to which they are in each case attached, seem slender, but not so slender as to suggest weakness. One feels quite sure that each stately shaft can easily carry the burthen which rests on its beautiful head.

As we have already remarked, there is no direct evidence to show who made the plans of the western half of Saint Bavo's, or at all events, of the nave, but the following facts are significant. It is undoubtedly the noblest ecclesiastical structure which Brabant produced in the first half of the fifteen hundreds; of the Brabant architects of this period the greatest was Dominic De Waghemakere, and he was constantly at Ghent during the early days of its construction busy with the new Town Hall. We suspect, then, with Monsieur Louis Cloquet, that Dominic at least had his say in the matter.[28]

Glorious, however, as these late Gothic buildings are—and there are others in Brabant no less beautiful, and how many, perhaps, still lovelier which exist only on parchment, never realised, or by the hands of iconoclasts cast down?—they are but the aftermath, the last and the loveliest flowers of a tree which when it produced them, was already almost dead. By a supreme and mighty effort it had forced the little life that was in it into one favoured branch, which thus clothed with fairest blossoms and with the freshness of their beauty still upon it, withered away like the rest. If we would contemplate the tree in its vigour we must go back to the fourteen hundreds, and more especially to the days of Philippe l'Asseuré—to the long peace of thirty years which followed the Treaty of Arras (September 21, 1435). Then it was that Gothic art in Belgium reached the zenith of its magnificence, then it was that she first became unrivalled in the abundance and in the quality of her fruit, that each day saw some great work completed or the foundations of some grand building laid. Many of these monuments have perished, but such of them as remain, though they have suffered much at the hands of enemies and of friends, bear witness alike to the genius of the artists who created them and to the public spirit and the devotion of the burghers and craftsmen who provided the funds with which they were built, and who, hard-headed, close-fisted, cautious men, as many of them were, counted it no loss to have invested so much of their capital in these unremunerative securities. In those days Brabant was rich and free, and possessed of the faith which removes mountains.

The years which immediately preceded the advent of the house of Burgundy (1384) had been throughout the length and breadth of the Netherlands evil. War everywhere and of every description, not only with alien foes, but province against province, city against city, class against class; the staple industry gone or fast going, and half the population swept away by famine and pestilence. Flanders, with its fields untilled and its dykes unmended, had become what it was a thousand years before—morass and jungle, the home of wolves which preyed on the meagre flocks that remained, and of vast herds of stag and boar which ravaged the scanty patches of grain which here and there the dwindled peasantry had made shift to raise; and though other provinces had suffered less, there was dearth and wretchedness everywhere. Yet of these same stricken fields some fifty years later Philippe de Commines was able to say, '*Ils se pouvoient mieulx dire terre de promission que nulle aultres seigneuries qui fussent sur la terre.*' The geographical position of the land, the energy and enterprise of its people, the advantages resultant from the union of all the provinces under one prince, and, above all, the blessing of peace; therein lies the explanation.

In no quarter was the recovery more rapid, nowhere was the meed of prosperity so great as in the duchy of Brabant. Not only had Brabant suffered less than the other provinces, but its soil was naturally more fertile, and the burghers of the great towns, now that their long-standing strife had been settled, showed themselves more apt than their fellows in Flanders for example, in developing new industries and in adapting their methods of trade to the changing conditions of the commercial situation. Whilst the three *bonnes villes* of Flanders—Bruges, Ypres, and Ghent, were vainly striving to foster their dying industry to the no small detriment of their trade, by imposing exorbitant duties on foreign made goods, and at last by altogether prohibiting the importation of English cloth, the 'good towns' of Brabant found salvation in the development of new industries, notably the manufacture of linen and tapestry, or, as in the case of Antwerp and Bergen -op-Zoom, by enlarging the doors of their markets. Antwerp, indeed, found a gold mine in her free fairs open to all the world without toll or tribute, and, thanks to the liberal policy which she pursued in regard to aliens, presently succeeded in diverting to her shores the foreign merchandise which had formerly found its way to Bruges. Also, the towns of Brabant were directly or indirectly aided by the personal action of the princes of the new dynasty, who seem to have exerted their utmost endeavours to promote their welfare: Louvain was indebted to Duke John IV. for a boon not to be despised, for in planting his new university in the ancient capital, he practically gave to her a fresh lease of life; Mechlin was helped later on by that stern and gloomy Sovereign, Charles le Téméraire, who made the city of Saint Rombold the seat of the national parliament; the interests of Antwerp were invariably pushed by the entire dynasty, often at the expense of Bruges; and Brussels, which for years past had been in reality, though not in name, the capital of Brabant, now that that duchy was held by a prince who was also Sovereign of each of the adjoining states, became, to all intents and purposes, the common capital of the Netherlands, the home of a prince whose revenues were larger and whose expenses were heavier than those of any other prince of his day, whose wont it was to astonish the world by the splendour of his feasts and pageants—advertisements, costly if you will, but, from the credit they gave him, well worth the money he paid for them, of a prince whose very economies—for if Philip knew how to spend, he knew too how to count and how to save—were a source of wealth to his subjects: the vast sums which he annually sank in building operations, or invested in precious stones and precious stuffs, in goldsmiths' ware, in sculpture, in pictures—so many gilt-edged securities which, if need be, could be turned into cash, and, if he had luck, at a profit—represented the sum of his savings, and much of it found its way into the pockets of Brussels tradesmen.

Brussels, then, at this time had a market in her midst for the product of her newly-developed industries: linen, tapestry, plate, and liquor of various kinds—ale, nut brown, pale, and black, 'swart-bier,' seemingly a sort of archaic stout, and wine from her own vineyards, some of it, amongst others, from that famous vineyard of which a portion of the site is now occupied by the Jardin Botanique. Hers was the profitable task of providing for the costly needs and costlier follies of the richest Court in Europe, of a Court of which not a few of its members less distinguished for length of pedigree than length of purse, sought, after the manner of nouveaux riches, to blind men's eyes to the newness of their shields by the glamour of their new wealth; for Philip would have none but capable officers, and in naming them did not restrict his choice to one class. He knew how to choose, and chose where he saw ability: there were great nobles at his council board, and beside them sat men of humble origin; and these were, amongst the most highly placed, the wealthiest and the most trusted, men like Chancellor Rolin, the son of a plain citizen of Autun, or Peter Bladelin, who, from a dyer of buckram, became Controller-General of Finance. Times had changed since the days when at Bruges and elsewhere 'men with blue nails' were debarred even from the rights of citizenship.

With a prince who could afford to be lavish, and whom policy and inclination alike prompted to expenditure, and a Court made up of new men and men of ancient race, whose pride compelled them, coûte que coûte, to emulate these mushrooms, gold was poured out like water, and Brussels flourished amazingly. Every public event and every private happening was made the excuse for a revel, and what revels they were! 'Convis et banquets' to quote the words of Philippe de Commines, '*plus grands et plus prodigues qu'en nul aultre lieu ... baignoiries et aultres festoyements avec femmes grands et désordonnez, et à peu de honte*;' but Philippe adds a saving clause: 'Je parle,' he says, 'des femmes de basse condition.' And what strange, fantastic, grown-up children were those who took part in them! The decoration of the great pavilion of wood, conveyed by water from Brussels to Bruges for the wedding of Charles the Bold and Margaret of York, in 1468, had occupied during many months hundreds of artists and artisans from all parts of the Netherlands, amongst them masters of the first order. One of the features of this marvellous construction was a tower forty feet high adorned with apes and wolves and wild boars, which, by mechanical means, were made to dance and sing, and in the great hall there were a host of other quaint creations, amongst them a whale sixty feet long, which was able to move about, several elephants, a pelican, from whose beak streamed hippocrass, and a female figure wrought in gold, with its breasts spurting wine. These strange mechanical toys were much in vogue in the fourteen and fifteen hundreds, and some of them have come down to us—'the oldest citizen of Brussels, the famous "mannikin" of the Rue de l'Etuve is still doing what he did in the days of Philippe l'Asseuré.'

Never before in the course of its history had the city of Brussels been so prosperous. Within the circuit of its ramparts now dwelt some sixty thousand souls—more than double the population of Louvain, and nearly double that of Antwerp. If Brussels were not the richest city in the Netherlands, it was at all events the city where the evidences of wealth were the most visible, and amongst them dissipation. When men can afford to indulge the wayward humours of 'Brother Ass' they not unfrequently do so, and the men of Brussels at this time rode him with an exceedingly loose rein. They drank of the joys of life to the dregs, and some of them were nauseated: suicides were more frequent than of yore, and so were religious vocations.

But it was not only by reason of human frailty that Brussels at this time sinned: the days which had passed had unchained a devil which still continued to haunt the town, albeit those evil days were now but a memory. The wars in which so many of the inhabitants had taken an active part, and the deeds of violence which had so often accompanied the revolutions and counter-revolutions incident on the struggle for freedom in almost all the great cities, had accustomed the people to horrors, and bred in their hearts a veritable lust for blood. Hence when strife arose the sequel was often death in some shape or other, and the chief effect which these crimes produced on public opinion was to fill men's minds with a morbid and universal dread of poison and of the assassin's knife. No one knew whom he could trust, friend looked askance at friend, and sturdy burghers abroad at night turned cold as they passed dark corners. The highest in the land were commonly believed to have had recourse to these methods in order to rid themselves of foes, or of friends whose existence was a bar to the realisation of their desires, and though these rumours were often groundless, the fact that they should have been so widely credited, and that those whose fair names were sullied by them should have in consequence fallen so little in popular estimation is in itself significant, and so, too, is what Chastelain says concerning a repast of which Duke Philip once partook in the hut of a peasant. Riding alone and at night from Brussels towards Hal he had lost his way in the Forest of Soignes, and the man in whose house he took refuge believed him to be an ordinary wayfarer; the meal which was set before him was a very humble one—cheese, black bread and onions—but at least 'he ate,' old Chastelain notes, 'without fear of poison.'

Here we have one side of the picture as contemporary chroniclers have painted it. Perhaps they put in the shadows too black, and maybe the scheme of colour is too glaring. Vice makes more stir in the world than virtue because it is something abnormal—a monstrosity, which from its very nature compels attention; and because, too, it is more interesting than virtue, men talk more about it, and write more about it, and in doing so they are often apt for the sake of effect to exaggerate its dimensions. All this should be taken into account, and also, there is another side to the picture.

It was not all frivolity and bloodshed in the 'good towns' of Brabant in the days of Philippe l'Asseuré; the gold which was so lavishly poured out was assuredly not all squandered on the pride of the flesh, and the pride of life, and the pride of the eye. Men were by no means devoid of public spirit, nor were they unmindful of the poor; splendid as were some of their own habitations, their splendour was eclipsed by the greater glory of guild hall and market and church. Somehow or other, too, in spite of their revels, they found time for serious business: never were the towns of Brabant so ably administered or the affairs of the duchy in such capable hands. It was an age of much literary and artistic activity, and the burghers showed themselves alike collectively and, when they could afford it, individually, generous patrons of letters and of art; also the Christian religion was still a living reality for all sorts and conditions of men, and though many failed to live up to its principles there were not a few, and some of them amongst the most highly placed, who were keenly alive to the ills which afflicted society and indefatigable in their efforts to correct them, efforts which were presently crowned with no small measure of success. For strangely enough the ebullition of evil which characterised this epoch was synchronal with one of those marvellous outbursts of religious fervour which occurred periodically in the Netherlands all through the Middle Age. Perhaps it was not so strange after all, for each was the outcome in some degree of the turmoil and wretchedness which, as we have seen, formed the keynote of the preceding period. These things act differently on different natures: some under their influence become devout, others seek relief in dissipation.

No people throughout the whole course of their history have continuously shown themselves more deeply impressed by sentiments of faith and Christian piety than the inhabitants of those lands which are now embraced by the kingdoms of Belgium and Holland.

We have seen how eagerly in the early days the nobles of Brabant and Hainault and Flanders helped on the work of Gerard of Brogne, how staunch they were later on in their support of the Cluniac movement, and to what excesses they were sometimes led by their intemperate zeal in furthering it. So, too, when Peter the Hermit preached his first crusade, nowhere did he find so many recruits as in this quarter of Europe, and in no other land did the sons of Saint Francis obtain a heartier greeting: they were received with open arms by all classes of the population; even the patrician burgher, who often warned off monks, for he dreaded their wealth and influence, opened alike his doors and his purse for the followers of 'the poor man of Assisi.'

Again, no cities in Christendom were so richly endowed with charitable institutions as the great commercial centres of the Low Countries. They were all of them served by religious, but, mark this, all of them, or nearly all of them, under municipal control. For the burgher would be master in his own house, and, to tell the truth, in spite of his faith and his good works, was something of an 'anti-clerical'—very keen to resent the interference of the clergy in his affairs, no less eager, whenever he could, to trench on their domain. He always read between the lines in interpreting the charter of his own privileges, but scrupulously adhered to the letter of the law when theirs were called in question.

Albeit, though now and again there was a sharp tussle, like that for the management of the schools, in which he proved himself the better man, as a rule his relations with the priesthood were fairly cordial: the secular clergy, cut off from their chiefs, whose Sees for the most part were in foreign lands, were too feeble to resist aggression; the great monastic houses were nearly all of them without the towns, and thus it rarely happened that their interests clashed with his; as for the Franciscan friars, in spite of their democratic tendencies and their sympathy undisguised for the toilers whom he so often oppressed, he could not afford to quarrel with them: the services which they rendered to the sick and the poor were not to be dispensed with, and also he found them a useful check on the secular clergy whose labours and whose profits they shared, and with whom, from the force of circumstances, they were naturally often at loggerheads.

This independence of spirit, this impatience of ecclesiastical control, was not peculiar to the patrician class. Outcome of the national love of liberty, it manifested itself in various ways in all classes of the urban population: the trade companies provided themselves with private chapels, and seem to have claimed the right of naming their own chaplains; a host of religious confraternities were formed, more or less free from ecclesiastical control, and, for those who were inclined to be more devout, numerous lay communities of both sexes, as we shall presently see, and, in at least two cities of Brabant—Tirlemont and Léau—there were regularly constituted chapters of canons composed exclusively of married laymen.

The influence of these lay institutions—of these, so to speak, half-way houses between the world and the cloister, was far-reaching and profound. Their members were held in higher esteem than either the monks or the secular clergy; hand in hand with the mendicant orders they directed the current of religious thought.

Curiously enough, too, there seems to have been something in the temperament of these people which, in spite of their anti-clericalism, their phlegm, their commercial pursuits, rendered them strangely susceptible to the fascination of the interior life: in the spiritual complexion of the towns there was an undercurrent of mysticism which waxed and waned intermittently all through the Middle Age. Now it would flow so deep down and so sluggishly that it seemed almost to die away, and then it would suddenly swirl to the surface and become a rushing stream, which sometimes surged over the bounds of orthodoxy and produced the wildest extravagancies. Its normal rôle was to do for the foolish things of the Gospel—for poverty, for purity, for meekness, what chivalry did for the pride of life and the pride of the eye, and what minstrelsy did for the pride of the flesh: surround them with a halo of romance; but it acted differently on different temperaments, and in divers times manifested itself in divers ways, according to the circumstances which called forth its energy and the various kinds of material with which it came in contact.

Thus it peopled the forests with hermits, humble, harmless, prayerful folk, who, working out their own salvation as best they could alone with nature and with God, saw visions and dreamed dreams, always marvellous, often beautiful, sometimes grotesque—if they did nothing else for their fellow-men they at least put a little poetry into their lives—and it raised up too, false prophets, or, by assuring them a following, made false prophets possible—fiery zealots, some of them, who before they deceived others had first made dupes of themselves, and some of them mere impostors with one object—pelf.

To which class Tanchelm belonged who shall say? The only contemporary account of him which has come down to us was not written by his friends. Fool or knave, in this man we have a picturesque personality, and an interesting one, too, in several respects. He lived in those days of stress and whirl when the atoms which were presently to form the great communes of Brabant were striving to come together: we first hear of him at Antwerp somewhere about the year 1113. Who he was, whence he came, what his calling, no man could tell, but the women whispered it about that the mysterious stranger was a prophet, and at last Tanchelm broke silence and publicly proclaimed in the market-place that he was indeed a prophet, and more than a prophet—the incarnation of the Paraclete. Half the population believed him. Churches were consecrated in his honour. He lived in royal state, and when he came forth he was attended by a bodyguard of armed men.

Riot and bloodshed were the outcome, and in the midst of it he fled, disguised as a monk, to Rome, where, strangely enough, he was not molested. When the storm had had time to lull he set out on the homeward journey, but at Cologne he was arrested by the Archbishop, who, less complaisant than the Pope, or perhaps better informed, set him in gaol. Somehow or other he contrived to escape to Antwerp, where he did as he had done before, like results followed; Duke Godfrey meditating his arrest, the fanatic got wind of it, and again determined on flight; but as he was on his way to the wharf, whence he would have taken shipping for England, he was stabbed by a man 'full of zeal,' as an ancient writer has it. Thus did Tanchelm end his chequered career. His fate was not unmerited, for he himself had slain Alaric, Burgrave of Antwerp, but in the eyes of his disciples he was a martyr, and the sect which he had founded did not die with him.

It was not till the close of the eleven hundreds that religious peace was at last established throughout the length and breadth of the land, for the movement at Antwerp was not an isolated one. Heresy was everywhere in the air. The infection was carried from place to place by merchant and artisan, and fierce outbreaks were continually occurring, sometimes in one place and sometimes in another, all through the century. 'The social and moral disturbance provoked by the communal movement,' notes M. Pirenne, sufficiently explains this state of things,'[29] and doubtless he is right; but the fewness and the incapacity of the parochial clergy must also be taken into account.

For six years the canons of Antwerp had vainly striven to bring back their wandering sheep. Not matter, perhaps, for wonderment. When the Tanchelm trouble began there was only one parish priest in the city, a man of loose life. At last they gave up the task in despair, and invoked the aid of a stranger—Norbert, the famous mystic of Laon, who had lately founded a missionary order which the world was beginning to talk about.

This man, who was born at Xanten on the Lower Rhine, of a rich and powerful family, had taken orders because he thought that for one of his brilliant parts and with his wealth and influence the shortest road to distinction was by way of the Church. And the Church did something for him: she assured him a lasting reputation, she presently set his name down in her register of canonised saints. That was not the kind of fame which Norbert had in those days looked for, but if earthly glory escaped him he had only himself to thank for it.

Shortly after his ordination he was named Court chaplain to the Emperor Henry V., later on he obtained a canon's stall at Cologne, and then one sultry afternoon he took it into his head to ride over to a neighbouring village. A storm arose, a flash of lightning struck him from his saddle, and when he came to himself he was a changed man. He resigned his prebend, bestowed his goods on the poor, and for two years, ragged and barefoot, wandered about France and Germany preaching penance. He spoke well, had the gift of address, the charm of personal beauty; he was all things to all men, as his biographer says of him, and he reckoned his converts by thousands.

But Norbert was not satisfied. Of all the sheep he had brought to the fold how many would have never strayed if the shepherds had been faithful! The care lessness and incompetency of the parochial clergy, that was the crying evil of the day, and he would do what he could to remedy it.

To this end he withdrew to the forest of Coucy, near Laon, with a little band of disciples, and presently there rose up in the midst of a secluded valley which Norbert called Prémontré because, as he said, the place had been pointed out to him in a dream, a rude habitation with a church alongside of it and a few outbuildings. It was the first home of the great Premonstratensian Order, an order whose members, whilst leading the lives of monks, devoted themselves, at the same time, to pastoral work and to preaching.

Such was the man and such were the men who now undertook to convert Antwerp, and thanks to their indefatigable labours the Ghost of Tanchelm was at last laid. Whereat the canons, loth to lose their services, ceded to them their own collegiate church and themselves migrated to the Chapel of Saint Mary, a very humble structure in those days, without the city walls, and it will be interesting to note it gradually grew into Antwerp Cathedral.

Two of the monasteries with which Norbert's White Canons were about this time endowed are still standing, and are still in the possession of the order: the Abbey of Tongerloo, in the heart of the Campine, founded by Duke Godfrey Longbeard in 1130, and the great Abbey of Parc, hard by Louvain, founded by the same Sovereign a few years earlier. This is a most picturesque and charming spot and is well worth a visit. Very little of the original work remains, but the Gothic cloisters date from the close of the fifteen hundreds and they are exceedingly beautiful, so, too, the chapter-house and a most delightful old water-mill of the same period; also there is a large and valuable collection of ancient manuscripts, amongst them the original charter of endowment signed by Godfrey Longbeard, and in the church and in the guest-house there are a few good pictures.

BEGUINES AND BEGHARDS

The national tendency to mysticism was fostered rather than thwarted by the new evangelists: when the people returned to orthodoxy they were more than ever inclined to the interior life, and soon the Béguinage appeared—that manifestation par excellence, as a recent writer has it, of urban religiosity clothed and in its right mind.

In the early days of the eleven hundreds, perhaps even before Norbert began to preach, there were women in Belgium who lived alone, and without taking vows devoted themselves to prayer and good works. At first there were not many of them, but as the century grew older their numbers increased: it was the age of the Crusades, and the cities teemed with desolate women—the raw material for a host of neophytes. These solitaries lived, not in the forest, but on the fringe of the town, where their work lay, for they served Christ in His poor. Presently, somewhere about the beginning of the twelve hundreds, some of them, for the sake of mutual protection, grouped their cabins together, and the little community thus formed was the first Béguinage.

Whence the name is hard to say. Various explanations have been suggested. Maybe it is derived from the old Flemish word beghen, in the sense of to pray, not in the sense of to beg, for the Beguine never asked alms; maybe from Saint Begga of Nivelles, where, it is said, the first institution of this kind was established; maybe, again, from Lambert le Bègue, a zealot of Liége, who died in 1180, after having expended a fortune in founding on his own estate a church and cloister for women whom the Crusades had deprived of their natural protectors. The cloister has long since disappeared, but the church is still standing, it is dedicated to Saint Christopher, and is a very beautiful specimen of transition work.

The Beguine was only half a nun. The vows which she took were not irrevocable; she could return to the world when she would, nor did she renounce her property. If she was without private means she neither asked nor accepted alms, but supported herself by her spindle, or by taking in needlework, or sometimes by teaching the children of burghers. During the time of her novitiate she lived in the house of the 'Grand Mistress' of her cloister, but afterwards she had her own dwelling, and, if she could afford it, was attended by her own servants. The same aim in life, kindred pursuits and community of worship were the ties which bound her to her companions. There was no common rule, each Béguinage fixed its own order of life, and was submitted only to the jurisdiction of its own superior, though later on many of them adopted the rule of the third order of Saint Francis. Nor were these communities less varied as to the social status of their members: some of them, like the Béguinage of Bruges, only admitted ladies of noble birth; others, like the little Béguinage of Louvain, were exclusively reserved for persons in humble circumstances; others, again, opened their doors wide to women of every condition, and these were the most densely peopled—several of them, like the Great Béguinage of Ghent, numbering their inhabitants by thousands.

Such was this semi-monastic institution. Admirably adapted to the spiritual and social needs of the age which produced it, it spread rapidly throughout the land, and soon began to exercise a profound influence on the religious life of the people. By the close of the twelve hundreds there was hardly a commune in Belgium without its Béguinage, whilst several of the great cities had two, or three, or even more, and, mark this, each of these institutions was an ardent centre of mysticism. There was a Béguinage at Brussels before the year 1245. Witness a Bull of this date of Pope Innocent IV., authorising the Beguines of that city to recite the Divine Office, and by the close of the century it seems to have attained considerable prosperity. It occupied a large tract of land, says Wauters, between the Chaussée de Laeken and the Couvent des Dames Blanches, and contained several streets and spacious gardens. It possessed its own church, which, by concession of the Dean and Chapter of Molenbeke, was, in 1252, made extra-parochial, its own water-mill, granted by Duke John I, in 1290, and a hospital for sick poor, founded by the same Sovereign four years later. The community was suppressed at the time of the French Revolution, and no relic of it remains save the church—not the original building, but a reconstruction of 1657. It now serves as a parish church, and is dedicated to Saint John the Baptist.

The Grand Béguinage at Louvain was probably founded early in the twelve hundreds. Two inscriptions rudely carved in stone, and now placed on each side of the northern doorway of the church, respectively attest that the cloistral buildings were commenced in 1234, and the church itself a year later. This structure consists of a long rectangular nave, with a clerestory, but no triforium, and single lean-to aisles, which are of the same length as the nave. There is no steeple, but a small bell turret marks the entrance to the choir, which is lighted by a huge east window filled with beautiful tracery. The interior is singularly plain, and, save for the capitals, rudely carved with foliage and grotesque figures, there is no sculpture, or at all events there is none visible, though doubtless if the plaster were removed from the walls some relics of stone carving or moulded brick would be brought to light. We have here a typical Béguinage church of the latter half of the twelve hundreds. The Church of the Béguinage of Bruges, for example, which dates from the same period, is almost a facsimile, and this type prevailed, at least in its main outlines, until the end of the Gothic period, and even in some cases until later.

From the Béguinage Louvain

The Béguinage of Louvain is one of the most picturesque in Belgium. It is situated on either side of the Dyle, here a narrow stream, which winds through a labyrinth of crooked streets, and presently, after passing through a little bridge, disappears behind the hospital, which gives on the churchyard, where there are yew trees and a great stone crucifix. It is a very quiet, homely spot this Béguinage, full of old-world memories, and the widows and maidens who dwell there while away their lives in much the same way as their predecessors did in the thirteen hundreds.

There were Beguines at Mechlin as early as 1207. At this epoch their cloister was in the centre of the town, but its exact site is not known. In 1259 they migrated to a spot beyond the ramparts, on the western side of the city, between the Dyle and the Chaussée d'Anvers. This cloister was totally destroyed during the religious troubles of the fifteen hundreds. Towards the close of the century, when order was once more established, the Beguines, having obtained permission of the civic authorities, returned to the centre of the city and erected for themselves the cloister which they at present inhabit, and later on (1629-1647), the imposing temple in which they still worship. This Béguinage was again suppressed at the time of the French Revolution, and again re-established during the opening years of the eighteen hundreds, but only a portion of their property was restored to the community, and at present the greater number of the houses are occupied by private individuals.

Many other Béguinages still exist in Brabant, and, indeed, all over Belgium, but many more have been suppressed, and the buildings which once sheltered the religious are now used for secular purposes. The largest of the existing communities of this kind is that of Ghent, which numbers nearly a thousand members, and the smallest is probably that of Dixmude, which has only three.

The religious movement of which the Béguinage was the outcome brought forth also, about the same time, or perhaps a little later, several similar institutions for men. Of these the Beghards, or, as they were sometimes called, the Brethren of Penance, were the most widespread and the most important. Their members were all of them laymen, and, like the Beguines, took no vows, observed no fixed rule of life, and were subject only to their own superiors, but, unlike them, they had no private property: the brethren of each cloister had a common purse, dwelt together under one roof and ate at the same table. They were, for the most part, of humble origin — weavers, dyers, fullers and such like, and were often men to whom fortune had not been kind—men who had outlived their friends, or whose family ties had been broken by some untoward event, and who, by reason of failing health or advancing years, or perhaps on account of some accident, were unable to stand alone. Each establishment was self-supporting; the members plied their wonted trades, and lived as best they could on the meagre product of their united toil. If, as Monsieur Pirenne observes, 'the mediæval towns of Belgium found in the Béguinage a solution of their "feminine question,"' the establishment of these communities afforded them at least a partial solution of another problem, which pressed for an answer—the difficult problem of how to deal with the worn-out working-man.

It should be borne in mind, however, that the primary object of all these institutions was not a temporal but a spiritual one. Their members, who for the most part had received so small a share of this world's good things, had banded together, not, in the first place, that they might be able to keep the wolf from the door during the few years of life that remained to them, but in order to ensure for themselves in the next world, as they confidently believed, an eternity of bliss. Nor, whilst working out their own salvation, were they unmindful of the spiritual welfare of their neighbours, nor, for the matter of that, of their temporal welfare either. The Celites, a kindred community to the Beghards, were wholly occupied in tending the sick and burying the dead—and, thanks to their intimate connection with the trade companies, they were able to largely influence the religious life, and to a great extent to form the religious opinion of the mediæval towns of Belgium, or, at all events, in the case of their working population, during more than two centuries. They did not, how ever, escape the fate which, sooner or later, overtakes all human institutions: before the close of the Middle Age they were, most of them, in full decadence. Not, as so often happens, that their life was crushed out by the weight of gold: though, as time went on, they acquired endowments, they never attained to wealth or anything like it; they waned with the waning of the cloth trade, and, when that industry died, gradually dwindled away. Their crazy ships were sorely tried by the storm of the fifteen hundreds. Some of them went to the bottom, some weathered its fury, but were so battered that they afterwards sank in still water; a few, somehow or other, managed to keep afloat till another and a fiercer hurricane at last dashed them to pieces.

The Brethren of Penance rapidly spread all over the Low Countries, and even penetrated into France and into the provinces beyond the Rhine. There were Beghards in Brussels as early as 1274, perhaps even at a still earlier date, and they observed no fixed rule till 1359, when they became Franciscan Tertiaries. They earned their livelihood by weaving cloth; indeed, until 1474, when the cloth trade was practically dead, no man could join the order unless he were a member of the Weavers' Company, and, naturally enough, they lived in the weavers' quarter behind the Town Hall. Their convent was situated in the street which still bears their name, or rather in the *Rue des Alexiens*, a continuation of the Rue des Beghards, and which at one time seems to have formed part of it. It stood at the foot of a steep hill, and the brethren called their home Mariendael, or Mary's Valley. Beghards and Beguines were everywhere renowned for their tender devotion to the Madonna—a devotion which they sometimes liked to emphasise in the mystical names they gave to their dwellings. Thus the Béguinage of Vilvorde, for example, was 'Our dear Lady's Consolation,' 'Onze Lieve Vrouw-ten-Troost,' 'Solatium Sanctæ Mariæ.'

The Zacites or Brethren of the Sack were also established in Brussels at a very early date; they were never a numerous community, and in 1480, having dwindled down to seven aged brethren, their convent was suppressed by the civic authorities, and its revenues bestowed on the new Carthusian priory which the city was at this time founding at Scheut. As for the expelled Zacites, six of them were placed in charitable institutions, and the seventh, who was by profession a surgeon, received a small life pension. Their chapel still remains; it is situated in the Rue de la Madeleine, and is well worth visiting—not so much on account of its architectural beauty, for it can never have been anything else than a very plain and unpretentious building, and, moreover, it has been spoiled by clumsy restoration; but it is interesting from its great age—it dates from the close of the twelve hundreds—and because it is the last remaining relic in Brussels of a very curious group of religious communities composed entirely of laymen.

The ardent spirit of mysticism, which had raised up in the course of the twelve hundreds the Beguines and the Brethren of Penance, waxed rather than waned as time went on, fostered and nourished by these institutions; nor is it surprising that some of their members, untrammelled as they were by ecclesiastical control, should presently have developed opinions not in harmony with the Christian faith. Amongst them, in the opening years of the thirteen hundreds, Sister Hadewych, who, in the vulgar tongue, wrote glowing prose and frenzied verse, in which she illustrated the Divine charity by profane comparisons, couched in the language of earthly and carnal love; and—unless she were the same individual, which is not unlikely—the famous Brussels mystic, Bloemardine, who boldly proclaimed that man in this life could attain to such a state that sin would be impossible to him, and likewise progress in virtue, and that then he could give free rein to his passions without fear of incurring guilt. Crowds were captivated by her burning eloquence; even at Court she had numerous disciples; they gave her a silver throne, which, when she had sat in it, was said to be invested with miraculous powers; it was currently believed that she was attended by two seraphim when she approached the Holy Table; and it is significant of the trend of public opinion, that the opposition of Jan van Ruysbroek, himself a mystic, but of a very different order, and at this time the best beloved and most influential of the Brussels secular clergy—we shall have much to say of him later on—gained for him only the contempt and ridicule of the people, who made him the subject of ribald songs, which were howled after him in the streets.

Nor was Bloemardine the only devotee whom an extravagant mysticism had deprived of mental ballast: there were Beghards and Beguines all over the country who were the victims of like delusions; the wildest opinions were held and publicly proclaimed to be orthodox—opinions, some of them, which seem to have differed little from the religious and political opinions professed by anarchists to-day. Of course the people gave ear to them, in all the great towns of the Netherlands these fanatics had numerous disciples, and the violent outbreaks against the Jews, which occurred periodically all through the thirteen hundreds, were in great measure due to their teaching. The bulk of their adherents were among the most abject of the population—weavers, dyers, fullers and such like, who, underpaid and without resources, living from hand to mouth, were often compelled, when sickness came or when work was slack, to have recourse to Shylock, and sometimes they made him pay the penalty of his extortions. If to slay the Jew were no sin, why not thus obtain freedom? Why not wipe out the debt in the blood of the man whose fathers had shown as little pity to Christ as he himself had to them? A riot of this kind occurred in 1308, and it needed all the energy and decision of Duke John II., who, like most of the sovereigns of Brabant, favoured the Jews, to hinder a general massacre.

Their houses were pillaged and wrecked, but they themselves escaped to the Castle of Genappe, which John had placed at their disposal; and he at last succeeded in quelling the mob which was clamouring round its walls for their lives.

After the great pestilence of 1348, when the poverty and wretchedness of the lesser folk had increased tenfold and the people had been lashed to frenzy by the preaching of the Flagellants, a more serious outbreak occurred. A certain Jewish convert was at this time one of the most trusted servants of Duke John III. Aware of the peril which threatened his compatriots, he commended them to his master's protection. 'Be of good heart,' said John, 'not a hair of their heads shall perish.' But it was beyond his power to make his words good. Prince Henry, in order to curry favour with the people, placed himself at their head, a score of Hebrews were cut down, and amongst them, despite his conversion, John's servant; and twenty years later the advent of the Dancers, a kindred sect to the Flagellants, was the signal for a fresh massacre.

The trouble which overtook the Jewish colony at Brussels in 1370 must probably be placed in a different category: it seems to have been the direct outcome of the bigotry and fanaticism, not of the Christians, but of some of the Jews themselves. Albeit, this should be borne in mind: we have only the Christian version of what took place. If some Hebrew scribe had recounted the story he would doubtless have given it a different complexion. The only official document which has come down to us anent this affair was drawn up some thirty years after the event; but since the redactors had themselves presided at the trial of the incriminated Jews, they must have been at least acquainted with the main outlines of the case, though possibly their memory may have failed them as to details. Doubtless they shared the prejudices and superstitions of the age in which they lived, but there is no reason to suspect their good faith, they were educated men of high social standing in the city of Brussels, and they seem to have enjoyed the respect and confidence of their fellow-townsmen. The following is the gist of the story of the famous Miraculous Hosts as they relate it. Towards the close of the year 1370 a certain Hebrew fanatic, one Jonathan of Enghien, furious at the numerous conversions which had recently taken place amongst his co-religionists, determined to show his contempt for the Christian faith by outraging that which those who believed in it held to be most sacred. To this end he purchased the assistance of John of Louvain, a Jew who had lately discarded the Hebrew faith. This man contrived to purloin from the Parish Church of Saint Catherine at Brussels sixteen consecrated wafers which, as had been agreed, he brought to Jonathan at Enghien, who forthwith summoned his friends, and in their presence made the Sacred Species the subject of his scorn.

Three days afterwards he was found dead in his garden—slain by a dagger thrust. His widow, believing that this misfortune had come upon her on account of the stolen wafers, had them secretly conveyed to the synagogue at Brussels—perhaps that strange old house in the Rue Ter Arken which from time immemorial has been called La Maison des Juifs—where soon a great throng of Hebrews assembled to examine the Christians' sacred bread; and some of them with the points of their daggers pricked the Hosts, whereat, so runs the legend, there spurted out drops of blood.

Dismayed at the prodigy, they took counsel as to how they might best be rid of 'this bread of evil omen,' and at last persuaded a Jewess named Catherine who had recently become a Christian, to carry it to Cologne. Hardly had she set out on the journey, however, than she was seized with qualms of conscience and retraced her steps, sought out the priest of Saint Catherine's, told him all that had happened, and restored to him the consecrated wafers which John van Loven had stolen six months before from his church.

Presently the matter was brought before Duke Winceslaus. Such of the Jews whom Catherine had denounced, and who had not already fled, were at once put under arrest, and in due course tried, found guilty, and sentenced, some to lifelong exile, others to be burnt at the stake, and all of them to the forfeiture of their estates. Accounts vary as to the number who suffered the death penalty—three, five and seven being severally mentioned.

As for the informer Catherine, she was kept in close confinement by way of precaution until the whole matter had been cleared up. Her prison, it is said, was an upper chamber above the baptistery of the Church of Saint Gudule, in which it was at one time customary to detain suspicious characters. It will be interesting to note that this cell is still in existence, and that the east wall is pierced by a little window giving on the interior of the north aisle, by means of which prisoners were able to assist at Mass without leaving their place of confinement.

SAINT CATHERINE'S, BRUSSELS.

Bearing in mind the punishments in vogue at this time—to be buried alive, for example, was the penalty due to treason, and the vintner found guilty of falsifying his wine was burned in the vat containing the adulterated liquor— the Hebrew fanatics, whose excesses we have just recounted, do not seem to have been treated with any extraordinary harshness on account of their nationality. If any Christian burgher had committed a like offence, no less severe a penalty would assuredly have been meted out to him.

The city of Brussels still contains a memorial in stone of this weird tragedy: the beautiful Sacrament Chapel which was added to the Church of Saint Gudule in 1535 was built as a shrine for three of the 'Miraculous Hosts.'[30]

But to return to Ruysbroek. His campaign in favour of orthodoxy had not promoted his temporal weal. Bloemardine, as we have seen, had friends at Court, and it was perhaps owing to their opposition that he still filled, at the age of fifty, the humble post of vicar, or as we should say, curate, of Saint Gudule's, and that, in spite of his acknowledged worth, and the great name his spiritual writings had already made for him. But in truth his dress, his manner of life, his whole bearing was not such as to commend him to the friendship of the world of wealth and fashion, often then as now the shortest road to preferment. If he were not of the people, he lived amongst them, and fared as they did. Like them he was squalid, ill-housed, half-clad, very often hungry. What time he could spare from his pastoral duties he devoted to contemplation and to writing, not in Latin, but in his own rude native tongue, some of those marvellous mystic treatises which later on gained for him world-wide renown and the title of Father of Flemish prose. Union with God and to assuage the sufferings of Christ in His poor, this was his highest ambition: fat livings and comfortable stalls were things which he never thought of. Ruysbroek, however, was not destined to remain to the end of his days an obscure curate: in the year 1343 a circumstance occurred which caused him to change the scene of his labours, and presently he was called upon to fill a more responsible and dignified position. It happened thus.

Franz Coudenberg and Jan Hinckaert, friends of Ruysbroek's, were near kinsmen, and each of them occupied a canon's stall at Saint Gudule's. They sympathised with the aspirations of the people, had, perhaps, been mixed up in one of their abortive attempts to obtain liberty, and on this or some other ground, early in the year 1343, Coudenberg was accused of treason to Duke John III., who, with a view, perhaps, to ridding the town of a dangerous agitator, offered him a tract of land in the Forest of Soignes at a place called Groenendael, which for the last forty years had been the site of a hermitage now occupied by Coudenberg's friend Lambert, a solitary whose family name is not recorded, on condition that he should build a monastery there for five brethren, of whom at least two should be priests. Perhaps the offer was one which Coudenberg was not free to refuse, perhaps it was tantamount to a sentence of exile, which included within its scope Hinckaert and Ruysbroek as well. In any case, Coudenberg did not refuse it, and when early in the following year he withdrew to Groenendael, these men went with him. It was not, however, till five years later that the new community was regularly organised and that the brethren adopted a definite rule. On the 10th of March 1349 Pierre de Clermont, Bishop of Cambrai, clothed them with the habit of canons regular of the Order of Saint Augustine, and shortly afterwards they chose Jan van Ruysbroek for their prior. Not only did he know how to maintain discipline in his own monastery, but he was able to restore order in a host of others, and so great was his influence outside the cloister that within a few years of the founding of Groenendael a whole group of new religious houses sprang up—Rouge Cloître, Corsendonck, Sept Fontaines, Bethléem, Ter Cluysen—which owed their origin to one or other of his disciples, and though they were not at first submitted to Groenendael, observed the same rule and were intimately associated with it by ties of the closest friendship: for the brethren of every one of them Ruysbroek was 'the master.'

Meanwhile he did not discontinue his literary work, and as a man of letters no less than as a theologian and a reformer, Ruysbroek deserves to be studied. Writing in prose and in the vulgar tongue, he addressed himself in the first place to the people, for the art of reading was at this time sufficiently widespread, but in what he wrote there was no tinge of grossness or sensuality. His mystical treatises breathe the spirit of the *Imitation of Christ*, of which indeed they may be said to be the prototype, and by reason of the loftiness of his sentiments and the purity and the beauty of the language in which they are expressed he merits to be placed in the first rank of the spiritual writers of the Middle Age. He himself used so say that he wrote under the immediate inspiration of the Holy Ghost, and a story related by his biographer and disciple, Hendrick Bogaerden, goes to show that at least in his own cloister such was believed to be the case.

Rouge Cloître

It was Ruysbroek's custom to write as he walked in the forest, and one day having prolonged his ramble beyond his wont, the monks grew alarmed and dispatched one of their number to search for him, and presently this man discovered the Prior of Groenendael. He was seated beneath a linden tree with his tablets in his hand, and he was surrounded with rays of light. Perhaps the sun had suddenly pierced through a dark cloud, but the picture is none the less a pleasing one, and it shows in what estimation Jan Ruysbroek was held by his spiritual sons. Nor was it only in his own cloister or in his native land that Ruysbroek was regarded as a saint. In Germany, in Flanders, in Holland, wherever his books were read, his name was held in veneration, and Groenendael was constantly besieged by pilgrims, many of them from distant lands, who had come there for no other reason than to hold converse with its prior. Nor was his head turned by so much adulation. To the end of his days he remained the humble, gentle, unassuming priest he had been in the days when he was an unknown Brussels curate, and it was ever his delight to perform the most menial offices in his priory.

He died on the night of the 2nd of December 1381, in the eighty-ninth year of his age, and 'on that night,' note the chroniclers of Groenendael, 'the bells of the Church of Deventer, where dwelt his friend Geert Groote, were solemnly tolled for him by invisible hands, and another friend and disciple, the Dean of Saint Sulpice at Diest, dreamed that his soul had passed from this world, and after remaining in purgatory half an hour, was carried by angels to heaven'; and they also tell us that fifty years after his death, his body having been disinterred, was found to be still incorrupt, and that it was exposed in the cloister of Groenendael for three days and seen by thousands of people. Strange stories these, typical of the age in which they were first told.

The literary and religious revival which Jan Ruysbroek had inaugurated did not die with him. The brethren of Groenendael and of the neighbouring monasteries at Rouge Cloître and Sept Fontaines continued to busy themselves with spiritual writings, which were largely read by the people, and amongst which may be found the flower of Flemish literature of the end of the Middle Age; and Geert Groote, the most famous of Ruysbroek's immediate disciples, in founding shortly before Ruysbroek's death the congregation of the Brethren of the Common Life, had placed at the disposal of fourteenth-century mysticism an organisation no less active than the Béguinage had been two hundred years before. Groote, who belonged to a rich burgher family, was born in the year 1340 at Deventer in Holland. Having read at Cologne, at Paris, at Prague, he took orders and soon obtained preferment. But his relations with the Gottesfreunde of Cologne and, too, the books of Ruysbroek—it was not till later on that he became personally acquainted with their author—gradually inclined him to mysticism, and on his recovery from a dangerous illness in 1373 he resigned his rich livings, bestowed the greater portion of his patrimony on the Carthusians of Arnheim, and bade farewell to the world. For a time he lived in strict seclusion, devoting himself wholly to meditation and to books, and it seems to have been during this period that he made the acquaintance of Ruysbroek. But for a man of Geert's exuberant energy a hermit's life was impossible: he had found a pearl of great price and he yearned to make it known. Moreover, he was consumed with indignation at the worldliness of the Church, and presently he was wandering from village to village and town to town calling men to repentance, proclaiming the beauty of Divine love, and bewailing wherever he went the decadence of ecclesiastical discipline and the degradation of the clergy. The effect of his preaching was marvellous; thousands hung on his lips; the towns, says Moll, were filled with devotees; you might know them by their silence, their ecstasies during Mass, their mean clothes, their brilliant eyes full of sweetness. From amongst these a little band attached themselves to Groote, and became his fellow-workers—they were the first 'Brethren of the Common Life.' Of course the reformer was opposed by the clerks whose evil lives he denounced, but the cry of heresy was vainly raised against a man no less zealous for purity of faith than he was for purity of morals, and whose success in combating error had gained for him the surname of Malleus Hereticorum. The best of the secular clergy, to escape the contagion of the prevalent disorders, sought refuge within the ranks of his society, which in due course was approved by the Holy See. Geert Groote, however, did not live long enough to perfect the work he had begun. He died in 1384, and his mantle fell on the shoulders of his henchman, Florence Radewyes. This man founded two years later the famous Augustinian monastery of Windesheim, which henceforth became the centre of Geert Groote's association, and to which later on Ruysbroek's houses were also affiliated.

The confraternity of the Common Life resembled in several respects the Béguinage and the Brotherhoods of Penance, now decadent. The members took no vows, neither asked nor received alms, and earned their daily bread; but their houses were more closely knit together, and brothers and sisters alike busied themselves exclusively with educational work and literature, and in the case of priests by preaching.

When Groote began his campaign learning was at a low ebb. The fame of the schools of Liége had long since become but a memory; save for a few clerks here and there who had read at Paris or Cologne, there were no scholars in the Netherlands; even amongst the higher clergy there were some who knew nothing of Latin, and the burgher was quite content if, when his children left school, they were able to read and write. Groote and his friends determined to change all this; their efforts were crowned with success, and success came quickly; the schools which the Brethren of the Common Life founded all over the land became so many ardent centres of spiritual and intellectual life. Amongst the famous men whom they educated, or who served in their ranks, note Thomas à Kempis, Gabriel Biel, and the Dutch Pope, Adrian VI.; in a word, a widespread literary and religious revival was the outcome of their endeavour, and it had not yet begun to wane in the days of Philippe l'Asseuré.

Such was the moral complexion of the Low Country when her art reached the acme of its magnificence, and what a marvellous conglomeration of anomalies and contradictions that moral complexion must have been—an inconsequent medley of coarseness and refinement, of luxury and restraint, of avarice and generosity, of cruelty and compassion, of heroic virtue and crying vice, and with it all a rampant spirit of vulgar commercialism, which somehow or other was not incompatible with the culture of literature and music and art, nor, stranger still, with a firm conviction of the reality of spiritual things.

The God whom the men of Brabant worshipped was no vague personification of nature or natural forces, no hazy abstract conception of righteousness, order, law, but a personal God, a living, loving, life-giving God, who was the founder and father and friend of the human race, the creator and master of heaven and earth, and of all things therein contained—almighty, eternal, immense, incomprehensible, infinite in intelligence, in will, and in all perfections. The saints whom they adored were no vague, shadowy heroes who lived only in the memory of the great things they had accomplished when they were on earth. They had passed through the valley of the shadow of death, but death had no dominion over them: their hand was not thereby shortened, they were still mighty to save. Nay, the virtue in them was now greater than it had been in the days of their sojourning: if by their charity and their sweetness they had then been able to soothe the sick and console the afflicted, they could now bestow health and joy. If they had then reclaimed the desert and taught the husbandman how to tend his flock and to handle his plough, they could now ward off pest and murrain and assure him a bountiful harvest. So great was their love for the children of earth that no request was too trifling to claim their attention, and such was the efficacy of their intercession that no boon was beyond their power to confer. They held the first place in the heavenly court, they were the ministers and the intimate friends of the Most High, and He delighted to manifest His glory in them. Even their bones, and the clothes that they had worn, and the things that they had touched, were believed to be endowed with miraculous powers. They were always close at hand, and sometimes when the days were evil and the people needed heartening, they appeared to them in visible form all glorious in shimmering raiment and attended by cohorts of angels.

When the famous relics of Aachen were exposed in 1447, so great was the concourse of pilgrims that it was impossible for the Estates of Liége to assemble. The patricians of Bruges attributed the victory of Rosebeke to the direct intervention of the Mother of God, and it was Saint Michael, the patron of Brussels, who obtained for the craftsmen of that city the great charter of 1421.

Whatever may be thought of the religious convictions of these people, that their art was profoundly influenced by them is a fact which cannot be denied: the remnant of their work which has come down to us bears ample testimony to it, from the stateliest sanctuary to the meanest wayside shrine and from the grandest municipal palace to the carved lintel of some poor workman's cot. Stories from the Old and the New Testament are sculptured on the façade of the Town Hall of Louvain, the original statues which peopled the niches of the Town Hall of Brussels were all of them the statues of saints, and on the highest pinnacle of that network of stone which forms its spire stands Saint Michael slaying the dragon, symbol of the ultimate triumph of good over ill. Nor are these things unusual, we find them over and over again throughout the Low Country.

This is all the more remarkable because the art of the period was in no sense hieratic: the masons and sculptors and painters of Belgium at the time of which we are writing were ordinary working men, members of one or other of the craft guilds, and the patrons who employed them were not as a rule ecclesiastics but, for the most part, plain tradesmen; and yet their art was nothing less than the solemn profession of faith of the burghers and the craftsmen who created it—their creed made manifest in piled up brick and sculptured stone, in oak, in cedar, in iron cunningly wrought, in the saffron sheen of hammered brass, in the glister of gems, the glow of silk and in the burnished splendour of gold: a harmony magnifical of perfect forms and perfect tints in honour of Him who is above all and in all and through all—the Alpha and Omega of the universe. Herein we have the secret of their success—the faith that was in them, their vivid realisation of things unseen. This was how it was that in an age overflowing with luxury, a nation of merchants and manufacturers, who from the very nature of their pursuits must have been for the most part occupied with sordid things, were able to produce an art wholly untainted by sensualism, an art so glorious and so nearly perfect that it has hardly ever been equalled and never yet surpassed. Thus it has ever been and thus it will ever be. The average man is too commonplace and too practical to be moved by an abstract notion. It needs something which he believes to be a living reality, something which he is convinced is immeasurably above and beyond himself to enkindle in him the enthusiasm necessary to conceive and to carry out any really great idea. Art for art's sake is a formula which has sometimes hypnotised individuals of a sensitive and romantic temperament, but it has never yet converted the herd.

Some of us have been warring against the Philistines beneath an oriflamme emblazoned with this shibboleth for the best part of half a century, and what has been the outcome? A modicum of success in the matter of wall paper and a magnificent collection of pictorial bill posters. Nor can we begin to hope for any more solid results until we are at least as firmly convinced as were the sinners of Brabant in the fourteen hundreds of the truth of those words which Thomas à Kempis uttered, and which in one phrase sum up the philosophy of his great spiritual ancestor, old Jan van Ruysbroek—'Vanitas vanitatum et omnia vanitas præter amare Deum et illi soli servire.'[31]

CHAPTER XVI
Buildings and Builders (continued)

In an old collegiate church not far from Brussels there is a very curious mural tablet in memory of a certain canon who in his day was seemingly a man of some distinction. The inscription is undated and it runs thus:—

D. O. M.

AC

MEMORIÆ

R.adm. Dñi, D. FRANCISCI

VANDEN ABEELE

qui

ex Curato 3ᵃ Portionis hujus

insignis Ecclesiæ dein Primæ

Per 25 annos sedulus et laudabilis

Canonicus-Curator fuit;

Sed FUIT:

nunc cinis, ossa, vermis

Putredo NIHIL

Hæc sors mortalium

Nasci, laborare, mori.

Tu qui vivis, oculos

Deorsum conjice,

Et attende.

We, throughout many pages, have been hymning the glory of Brussels in the days of the Burgundian Dukes. That glory is among the things which have been. It was, but it has long since vanished. In the words of Canon Abeele's epitaph—'Fuit; sed FUIT: nunc ... NIHIL' in very large letters.

The public buildings in Brussels of this period—that is within the circuit of its ancient ramparts—can be counted on the fingers of one hand, and at least, so far as concerns decoration, they have entirely lost their pristine beauty. It is not to be wondered at. First came the fury of the Calvinists—that was towards the close of the fifteen hundreds; almost all the old buildings of the Netherlands endured many things at their hands; then the French bombardment of 1695, when the Grand' Place was shattered and fourteen churches and something like four thousand houses were burnt to the ground. 'An utterly wanton piece of destruction,' notes the contemporary author of *Les Délices des Pays-Bas*, 'but in two years,' he continues, 'the city had risen from its ashes more beautiful than ever,'

Hardly so, but still the men of Brussels had reason to be proud of their achievement: the Guild Halls in the Grand' Place date from this period. Too soon came the age of whitewash and plaster, when Gothic art was held in contempt. Much havoc was wrought then, throughout the whole country, more a few years later (1794), when the French revolutionists invaded the Netherlands. The cities suffered more from their antics than from those of any of their predecessors. Churches and convents were cast down, municipal buildings wrecked, and they carried off all the art treasures they could lay hands on. At last came the Gothic revival, and with it the restorer: he is hard at work still, and some say he has already wrought more havoc than all the iconoclasts put together, from the Gueux to the Sans-Culottes. Remarks of this kind are frequently made by little poets and by decadent painters who, because they have an eye for the picturesque, flatter themselves that they know all about architecture, and without any knowledge of the laws of construction or the principles of design, fancy that they are perfectly qualified to pass judgment on the work of professional experts who have devoted, perhaps, a lifetime to these subjects.

GUILD HOUSES IN THE GRAND' PLACE, BRUSSELS.

Of course there have been mistakes: in the early days of the movement this was inevitable, and, even since then, and when there was less excuse, the most lamentable blunders have from time to time been committed, blunders which never ought to have been made, and which in some cases entailed mischief which is altogether past reparation.

Thus when the élite were fascinated by the great name of Ruskin, and their fingers itched to lay everything bare, there was a veritable holocaust of frescoes.

Whatever may have been the case in other countries, the mediæval architects of the Netherlands never hesitated to conceal the natural appearance of their building materials whenever it suited their purpose to do so. Rough and unsightly walls they covered with plaster, which served as a ground work for coloured decoration, and if the hue of their stone was not to their liking, they had no scruple about painting it, for in their eyes no building was complete unless it glowed with rainbow tints. Though these things are now generally acknowledged, even at the present day there are restorers in Belgium—not very many, thank God, but still there are some,—who obstinately persist in ignoring them. It is not so very long ago since the mural paintings in Ghent Cathedral were ruthlessly sacrificed in order that 'the splendour of the true' might shine forth in all its glory, and the man who did this thing now has it in his mind to flay Sainte Walburge of Furnes, a church where distinct traces of mural decoration have been found; and who shall say how many frescoes lie hid beneath the whitewash?[32] But if a few men, here and there, have occasionally been found wanting in matters of this kind and in others no less serious, we nevertheless owe a very large debt of gratitude to the restorers, for if it had not been for their efforts many of the grand old monuments which now excite our admiration would by this time have fallen down, and, on the whole, the necessary task of restoration, always a delicate and difficult one, has been carefully and conscientiously carried out. And also this should be borne in mind, the works of art which the restorers have brought to light or preserved from destruction vastly outnumber those which have perished through their carelessness or ill-judged zeal; and in the case of frescoes we are practically no worse off than we were before, for they were all of them completely obliterated by whitewash. Of course this might have been removed. The operation is not an easy one, but it has been performed in very many cases with the happiest results, notably in the Church of Our Lady at Hal and in the Church of Saint Guy at Anderlecht, where some very remarkable and very beautiful mural paintings have been laid bare, and those at Anderlecht are almost in a perfect state of preservation. In Brussels itself there are no mural paintings save some faint vestiges in the Sablon and in Notre Dame de la Chapelle, and this is one reason why we said that the Burgundian buildings of the capital had lost their pristine beauty. Beautiful they are still, but for the most part they have been pitilessly scarified, and their beauty is like the faded beauty of death, cold, rigid, grey. Brussels, in a word, has lost her complexion, but he indeed would be a bold man who would set his hand to restore it.

NOTRE-DAME DU SABLON

Of the great ecclesiastical monuments of Brussels wholly constructed during this period only one remains—the church commonly known as

Notre-Dame du Sablon, but which is in reality dedicated to Our Lady of Victories. It was originally the private oratory of the great military guild of Crossbowmen—the one mediæval guild of Brussels which still exists— hence the invocation, and as most of the brethren were, by trade, either carpenters or builders, there is little doubt that this structure is the handiwork of some of them, and it is not unlikely that the master-mason who designed it was himself a Crossbowman. Nor is this all. Not only does the church on the Sablon Hill owe its foundation to the members of this guild, thanks to their prowess it passed unscathed through the religious troubles of King Philip's reign. The Calvinists had sworn its destruction, but when on the night appointed they reached the church and found it full of armed guildsmen prepared, at all costs, to defend their property, they contented themselves with howling outside, and made no further attempt to wreck it. The Crossbowmen retained possession of their beautiful oratory, and continued to administer its revenues through a committee of four members, whom they annually elected for this purpose, until the close of the seventeen hundreds, and when those stormy days had passed, and order was re-established, it became what it still is, a parish church.

NOTRE-DAME DU SABLON.

Though there was a church on this spot early in the thirteen hundreds, and one seemingly of no mean proportions, for we learn from a contemporary register that in 1391 it was served by five chaplains, for some reason or other it was pulled down, or perhaps wrecked by fire, before the close of the century, and the actual building only dates from the fourteen hundreds. The church records were destroyed during the bombardment of 1695, and hence we possess little information concerning the details of its construction. The most ancient portion is the south porch, which was built about 1410. The choir must have been finished before 1435, for frescoes bearing this date were discovered here when the choir was restored about fifty years ago, and in all probability the best part of a century had elapsed before the whole building was completed, or rather before the building operations ceased, for the church is not yet finished, and in all probability never will be.

From first to last the original plans seem to have been scrupulously adhered to, save only that for some reason or other, probably from lack of funds, the idea of a tower was abandoned. This made no difference in the interior arrangement of the church: the great columns and arches at the west end of the nave, which were intended to support the projected tower, still exist, and it would not have appeared otherwise if the tower had been actually built. What was done was this—the roof of the nave was continued over the unfinished tower, and the outer walls were built exactly like the walls of the nave, and the church was made to terminate with a very elaborate western façade, which has only been completed recently, and thus, though the foundations and the lower stages of the tower still exist, as seen from the exterior, there is no indication whatever that such a feature was originally contemplated. The building is one of considerable dimensions, the plan is a Latin cross with a polygonal apse to the choir, and it measures 213 feet by 121 feet at the transepts, and 85 feet at the nave, and is very nearly 60 feet high. It had originally double aisles, but the outer ones have been converted into fourteen side chapels, several of which in days gone by were the private chapels of some of the trade companies. Here we have a typical Brabant church of the fourteen hundreds. It is not, however, one of the best specimens of the period. The exterior is undeniably fine; the most captious critic could hardly quarrel with it; nothing could well be more beautiful than the choir and the south transept, with that cluster of outbuildings nestling in the corner between them, which give the required touch of the picturesque, and are not high enough to mar the buttresses or the tapering beauty of the graceful lancet windows. If we could see the interior without having first seen the outside, perhaps we should go into ecstasies, but after having feasted our eyes on so much loveliness without, the feeling which one experiences on entering the church is distinctly one of disappointment. The proportions are good and some of the essential features—the triforium, for example, the clerestory, the vaulting throughout—are excellent, but the details leave much to be desired, the moulding seems skimpy, there is an unusual dearth of sculpture and of ornament of every kind, the whole building is stiff, cold, naked. Surely that it should appear thus was not in the mind of the master-mason who planned it: he contemplated an elaborate scheme of coloured decoration, though perhaps it was never fully carried out. It was customary to secure for work of this kind the best artists of the day, men like John van Eyck and Roger Van der Weyden, each of whom there is documentary evidence to prove were 'illuminators of stone,' and naturally they demanded and received a high price for their services. But that something was done in this direction is quite certain: frescoes have actually been discovered in the chancel, and too, alas! wiped out, the illumination of the keystones of the vaulting still exists, and in other parts of the church there are some faint vestiges of mural painting, nor has the whitewash yet been everywhere removed. Doubtless, when this is done, more will be brought to light. For the rest, no lover of mediæval art will think of leaving Brussels without having first visited this most interesting building.

NOTRE-DAME DE LA CHAPELLE

The Church of Notre-Dame de la Chapelle has been for many centuries[33] what it still is, a simple parish church, the parish church of a district which has never been a rich one, and which, when the foundation stone was laid, and for more than three centuries afterwards, was the poorest quarter of the city. In those days this stately structure towered high above the squalid huts of turf or wood which the weavers called their homes; fires were frequent then, and in the great conflagration of 1405, which destroyed fourteen hundred houses, the old sanctuary, where so many generations of downtrodden toilers had brought their woes and grievances to the throne of the Most High, was all but burnt down. The choir and transepts were not so injured as to be past reparation, but the nave and the aisles and the tower were wholly destroyed, and it was decided to rebuild them in such a fashion that the poor man's church should be second to none in the city. For something like fifty years they laboured at it, and when at last the work was completed, not even the great collegiate Church of Saint Michael and Saint Gudule was more lovely than the chapel in the weavers' quarter. Saint Gudule's was

NOTRE-DAME DE LA CHAPELLE.

of course, a larger church than Notre-Dame, but in those days the difference in size of the two buildings was not so great as it is at present: Saint Gudule's has waxed both in size and beauty since then, as we shall presently see, and Notre-Dame has waned. Villeroi shattered the spire in 1695, and some forty years before, two very beautiful side chapels on the north of the chancel were made one, which is not beautiful, and perhaps, too, when the church was restored after the French bombardment, the arrangement of the roof was altered: the more recent portion of the building is very considerably higher than the earlier work, and the junction is not very happily effected, at all events as seen from the exterior. This can hardly have been the original arrangement, unless, indeed, it was only regarded as a temporary one, with a view later on to the reconstruction of the transepts and the chancel, in the same style and on the same magnificent scale as the rest of the building. If this were the original plan of the architect, and if it had been successfully carried out, Brussels would have been possessed of the chef-d'œuvre of Brabant architecture, but on the other hand she would have lost a very beautiful specimen of early transition work, perhaps the most beautiful in the Low Countries.

The plan of the nave of Notre-Dame de la Chapelle is very similar to that of the Sablon, but it is a longer and broader and higher building, the columns are bolder, the mouldings richer, and the capitals are more elaborately and more delicately carved. If the Sablon church could be re-invested with the gold and colour which, we believe, it originally possessed, its glory would be outshone by the greater glory of the bare walls and the white windows of *Notre-Dame de la Chapelle*. For this church, too, has been scraped, and no vestige of its ancient stained glass remains. The old story: the Calvinist, the whitewasher, and the restorer. There are still, however, some faint traces of fresco work: there is a ruddy glow on one of the massive columns which separate the south transept from the outer south aisle, which, if one steadily gazes at it, presently assumes the shape of an aureoled figure draped in crimson robes; and here and there on the walls there are large patches of a delicate hue, like the tint of faded rose leaves. At first one imagines that they are patches of that beautiful pink stone—a species of porphyry—with which so many of the churches in the Rhine Valley are built, between Mainz and Coblenz, but on closer inspection it will be found that they are remnants of mural painting.

The removal of the whitewash from this church took place at a sufficiently distant date for that cunning illuminator, Time, who works swiftly nowadays in our smoky northern cities, to accomplish something in the Church of Notre Dame of which he need not be ashamed. The glacis with which he has enamelled the bare stone in nave and aisle and transept, if it is not as brilliant as the blue, the vermilion, the burnished gold with which

John van Eyck or Roger Van der Weyden would have adorned it, is at least more beautiful and more lasting than the pigments which would have been employed if any modern master-painter had taken the matter in hand.

There are two rare and striking features in this building to which we would draw the reader's notice: the triforium, perhaps the most perfect existing expression of the Brabant architect's ideal of what a triforium should be; and the clustered cylindrical columns beneath the tower, which itself forms, as is the case in most Brabant churches, the first bay of the nave. The treatment of these columns constitutes almost a reversion to the method of treating grouped columns during the first period of Gothic architecture. Each group consists of a central column of the same form and dimensions as the columns which support the other bays of the nave, and four columns attached to it of like form, but more slender. This method of treating groups of columns, though not so rare in Brabant as in England in third period work, is nevertheless

NOTRE-DAME AU-DELÀ DE LA DYLE.

sufficiently uncommon, albeit groups of this kind are occasionally to be met with even in the latest Gothic work. Witness the group in the chancel of *Notre-Dame au-delà de la Dyle* at Mechlin.

Symmetry, simplicity, unity, these are the most striking characteristics of Notre-Dame de la Chapelle: the great cylindrical pillars on each side of the central avenue are all made after the same model, the clustered columns which separate the inner from the outer aisles are alike, nearly every capital throughout the building is carved in one fashion, triforium answers to triforium, spandrel to spandrel, arch to arch, each window, alike in aisle and clerestory, beholds in the window opposite the reflection almost of its own fair face. And yet in crystallising the child of his fancy, the designer of this church was able to impress his handiwork with the charm of the picturesque. How did he accomplish this feat? Artist as he was to his finger-tips—all architects were artists in those days, and this man was surely the first of his craft—he knew very well that if a building were perfectly and geometrically symmetrical it would be as cold and as stiff and as lifeless as a statue designed under similar conditions, and he subtly introduced into his ground plan a modicum of irregularity: he made the western bay of his central avenue slightly narrower than the three succeeding bays, these of like dimensions, and the fifth and the last, which are not equal to one another, each of them a trifle broader. The discrepancies are so minute that they are not at first sight perceptible, but their influence extends, it goes without saying, to every part of the building. Further, such was his sublime contempt for the sacrosanct law of precision, that he ventured on something bolder still: he determined not to make the central line of his nave the true central line of the building; in other words, that each of the northern aisles should be narrower than the corresponding aisle on the other side of the church. And here again the dissimilarity is imperceptible, and that, though the difference in width of the inner aisles is something like two feet, and in the case of the outer aisles no less than four feet seven inches.

Most impressive is the view of the nave as one stands beneath the chancel arch, no less pleasing is the view athwart the church as seen from the baptistery chapel with the face turned towards the south-east, but choose what coign of vantage you will, and you shall behold visions of loveliness.

SAINT MICHEL ET SAINTE GUDULE

The saint to whom the mother church of Brussels is dedicated, is, and has been from time immemorial, almost a phantom saint, a half-forgotten memory, little more than a name—Gudule, or as the earlier chroniclers have it, Gudila.

Of her life's story hardly anything is certainly known. If any scribe of her own day wrote of her, no trace of his writing remains. The manuscript, if it ever existed, was no doubt destroyed at the time of the Danish Invasion, and when the storm had passed, and a new generation of chroniclers began to gather up the fragments—to collect, that is, and to note down from the lips of the few monks who had survived its fury, whatever they had to relate of the sayings and doings of the saints whose acta had perished, they seem to have been able to learn very little of the life of Gudila, save that she was among the forbears of Charlemagne's race, that she dwelt in a castle hard by Alost, at a place called Mortzel, and after having lived an exemplary life, died there in the odour of sanctity somewhere about the year 712.

The earliest life that has come down to us, however, was not penned by any of these chroniclers: it dates from a much later period and cannot have been written before 1047, for it gives an account of the translation of Saint Gudila's relics which took place in that year

SAINT MICHEL ET SAINTE GUDULE.

It is dedicated by the author, one Hubert, perhaps a canon of *Sainte Gudule*, to his 'beloved brother Albert, who had given him an old manuscript containing a few scanty notes—rare jewels, but ill cut and ill set—concerning the virtues of gentle Gudila,' in order that he might turn them into good Latin. This seems to have been the main source of Hubert's information, and being seemingly an honest man who scorned to draw on his imagination he has very little to tell us of his heroine's intimate life. 'In my opinion,' he says, 'it is a holier thing to keep silence than to tell lies.'

That 'gentle Gudila' was in reality what is called a saint seems to be sufficiently probable. The fact that she has always been held to be such by the inhabitants of her native land is in itself prima facie evidence that she deserved to be so regarded: the verdict of the multitude in cases of this kind is not to be lightly set aside. Albeit a very great Roman ecclesiastic seems to have had his doubts on the matter—Pope Julius II.'s famous legate, Bernardino Carvajal, better known from his titular church as the Cardinal di Santa Croce. It is related by the monks of Afflighem that it was his wont when he visited the mother church of Brussels thus timidly to invoke the patron saint to whom that church is dedicated—*Si es sancta ora pro me.*

The name of Gudila has been associated with Brussels since the days of that unfortunate sovereign, Duke Charles of Lotharingia. The Abbey of Mortzel was at this time in the hands of a certain feudal chief, one Wulfger, whose father under pretext of protecting the nuns, had obtained possession, of their property, and established himself in their abode. When Charles ascended the throne (977), he did what he could to evict this man, but though Wulfger refused to budge, and the Duke was not strong enough to coerce him, he was able at last to obtain possession of his kinswoman's bones. In 979 he carried them to Brussels and laid them up in the Chapel of Saint Géry, an ancient sanctuary hard by his own dwelling, and which was said to have been founded by Gudila's grandfather—old Pepin of Landen. Here her relics remained for something like seventy years.

Meanwhile the village of Brussels was beginning to grow into a little town, the old fortress on the banks of the Senne had been abandoned, and the rulers of this part of the country, who now sometimes styled themselves Counts of Brussels and sometimes Counts of Louvain, had migrated to a new habitation on the hill called Coudenberg, somewhere about the spot where the royal palace now stands.

On a neighbouring height stood a humble oratory dedicated to Saint Michael: its exact site is unknown, but it cannot have been very far from the place at present occupied by the Church of Saint Gudila. No man could say when it was built or who was the founder; it had been there from time immemorial, nothing more was known of it. It was a very humble structure, little more than a wayside shrine, but no place of public worship was nearer his abode, and perhaps it was for this reason that Count Lambert II. determined to rebuild it on a larger scale and in worthier fashion, and to establish there a chapter of canons.

He did so, and early in 1046 the new church was consecrated to Saint Michael and Saint Gudila, whose relics were the same day translated thither from their former resting-place in Saint Gery's.

This old church, since the removal of the Court, had been suffered to fall into decay, and Lambert himself tells us that he found the tomb of his ancestress in a state of deplorable neglect, and that this was the reason why he transferred her relics to his new church on Saint Michael's Mount. Here they were reverently treasured for over five hundred years: in Lambert's church as long as it stood, and afterwards, in the church which succeeded it, until 1579. The Calvinists were busy then purging the land, as they said, of idols, destroying, that is, works of art, wrecking and plundering wherever they could the temples of the old faith. On the night of the 7th of June they visited the Church of Saint Gudila. Amongst the loot which they carried off was her costly shrine; it was of gold, studded with jewels, and God knows what they did with the ashes which it contained. Shrines and coffins, too, had been broken open in the hope of discovering treasure, and next morning the floor of the church was found to be strewn with human bones. These were afterwards carefully collected and buried in the Chapel of Saint Mary Magdalen, and it may well be that amongst them are the bones of 'gentle Gudila.'

The mother church of Brussels, the church, that is, to which all the other Brussels churches were formerly submitted, in origin the most ancient of them all, the largest, too, and the most interesting in many respects, perhaps not the most beautiful, but certainly the most picturesque, not only of Brussels churches, but of all the churches of Brabant, is not so much the monument of the people of Brussels as the family monument of the princes who governed them, and more especially of the princes of the great house of Louvain: from Godfrey III. onwards almost all of them had a hand in it. The work was continued by several of their successors, and was at last brought to completion during the reign of Duke Philip VI. (Philip IV. of Spain), in 1653.

During the latter half of the ten hundreds the original Church of Saint Gudila, which stood on the spot now occupied by the nave of the present building, had been greatly damaged by fire. No attempt seems to have been made to restore it, and when Godfrey III. ascended the throne in 1142 it was fast falling into decay. He therefore determined to raise up a new church, which should be second to none in the Low Country, and of such vast dimensions that it could be built over the old church, which would thus be available for public worship whilst the work was in progress.

This plan he presently proceeded to carry out; the old church was patched up, and in due course he solemnly laid the foundation stone of the present structure. This was somewhere about the year 1170. At first the work was pushed on with vigour, but for some reason or other, probably owing to lack of funds, when the eastern wall of the ambulatory was completed, things came to a standstill, and nothing further was done for nearly sixty years. Duke Godfrey died in 1190, and his son and successor, Henry the Warrior—a keen, unscrupulous, strenuous prince, with a passion for territorial aggrandisement, and never happy unless he were doing something to promote the prosperity of his beloved towns, was too occupied with intrigue and warfare until the closing years of his long and successful career to have any leisure for church building. It was not till 1226 that he at last began to seriously think of realising his father's project, and he did something more than think about it: in the beautiful Transition work in chancel, transept and ambulatory we have the result of his meditations.

Henry himself, in the deed by which he endowed the Chapter of Saint Gudila's with ten new stalls, informs us of the motive which had inspired him. The work had been resumed, he says, by his order 'in honour of the Blessed Virgin.' But was he impelled by no other motive than his devotion to the Mother of God? What we know of the antecedents of the man suggests an affirmative answer.

The famous road from Cologne to Bruges—that road on which, as we have already seen, the commercial prosperity of the cities of Brabant at this time wholly depended—before entering the duchy of Brabant passed through the Pays de Liége, and the bishop who ruled that little principality was thus enabled, whenever he would, to create a commercial crisis by closing up that portion of the great trade route which traversed his domains.

To this state of things the burghers of Brabant objected, and Duke Henry would fain have put an end to it by transferring the See of Saint Lambert to one of his own towns. Though after the disastrous battle of Montenaeken (October 14, 1213)—'Saint Lambert's triumph,' as the men of Liége called it—he had humbled himself before Hugh of Pierrepont and sued for pardon on bended knees, his reconciliation with the bishop was only a feigned one, nor had he in reality abandoned his scheme; and it is more than likely that when, in his old age, he at last set his hand to the task which his father had left undone, he flattered himself that the church he was rearing would one day be a cathedral.

During the long peace which Brussels enjoyed from the closing years of the Warrior's reign to the end of the reign of his great-grandson, Duke John the Victorious, the building operations at Saint Gudila's were carried on continuously, but the progress made was comparatively slow, for the Dukes were often short of cash, and were obliged to have recourse to all kinds of expedients to raise the necessary funds. In 1273, however, the chancel was completed and the greater part of the transept, and it is most likely that in the same year the old church was pulled down. All the work done during this period may be described as First Pointed. The tracery of the clerestory windows is, of course, flamboyant; it was substituted for the original tracery during the first quarter of the fifteen hundreds. In the course of the succeeding century the north aisle was added and the lowest stage of the nave, and at least the foundation of the towers, all this in the style then in vogue—Second Pointed. Here we have the work of three Sovereigns, John II., John III., and Duchess Jeanne, the last of the Sovereigns of Brabant of the old Louvain line. The building was completed by the Dukes of the Burgundian dynasty, and the distinctive features of Brabant architecture now become more emphasised. In the nave, for example, we have the beginning of that transformation of the triforium, which was so marked a feature in the Brabant style. Here it is still a separate story, still a passage in the thickness of the wall, but the arcading has completely disappeared, and in its place is a series of vertical bars which are simply a continuation of the mullions of the windows above. These are in the same plane as the triforium, and are only separated from it by bands of masonry so attenuated that they appear to be nothing more than transom bars. The effect is not happy: each section of the blind story with the corresponding section of the clerestory above, seems to be one huge window with the lower part bricked up. The exact date of this portion of the building is uncertain, but the nave must have been completed before 1446, for we know that in this year the Baroness de Heeze was condemned by Philippe l'Asseuré to fill the great west window with stained glass by way of a fine for having infringed the rights of the city. The present glass, however, is of much later date. It was presented by Everard de La Marck, Prince-Bishop of Liége, in 1528.

The north aisle with its lateral chapels is of later date than the fifteenth-century work in the nave, and the architecture is of a more pleasing character. The general design is much the same as that of the south aisle, but the details differ considerably: instead of clustered columns we have here richly-moulded prismatic piers. Save those of the first two bays, which are of earlier date than the rest, they are all adorned with capitals. Hendrick Cooman, who was master mason of Saint Gudila's from 1460 to 1470, probably designed the bays without capitals, and the other bays are most likely the work of his successor, Jan Vandenberg, the builder of the Town Hall, or, to be accurate, of a considerable portion of it, and who also designed the upper church at Anderlecht, where all the columns have capitals. He directed the works at Saint Gudila's till his death in 1485, and the richly sculptured balustrade which surrounds the roof of the nave is attributed to him. The tracery of this feature is in form unique, and more curious than beautiful. It consists of a series of *K*'s, an allusion, perhaps, to the name of the reigning Duke, Karel de Stout (Charles the Bold), or perhaps to Karlekin, as the Flemings called Charles V., but of course in the latter case it cannot be Vandenberg's work.

Though Hendrick Cooman was not so famous an architect as his successor, Jan Vandenberg, he seems to have done very well for himself in his profession, and to have been a man of consideration in the city of Brussels. He was four times a member of the Town Council: in 1448, 1451, 1458 and 1461, and in 1468 he was named burgomaster. There were two burgomasters in Brussels, it should be borne in mind. One represented the patricians and the other the plebeians, and in all probability Hendrick Cooman was second burgomaster. The name of the mason who succeeded Vandenberg should be held in perpetual remembrance. He designed the beautiful porch, much marred by restoration, which gives entrance to the south transept—Jan Vereycken. He occupied the position of master-mason until his death, which took place somewhere about the close of the century, and if he did not actually complete the Church of Saint Gudila, he at all events brought it within measurable distance of completion.

At this time the east end presented a very different appearance to what it does now; the chancel aisles, like the aisles of the nave, being flanked with side chapels—four on the north side, and a like number facing south. They were probably built about the same time as the choir, as the church archives bear witness that one Leefdael, a chatelain of Brussels, who died in 1293, was buried in the Chapel of Saint Peter, the first on the gospel side. All these chapels have disappeared. Those on the left were pulled down to make room for the Sainte Chapelle des Miracles, of which we have already spoken, in 1533; and those on the right, in 1649, when the Lady Chapel was built. This noble structure is of the same form and of the same vast dimensions as the Sacrament Chapel, but the details are less ornate. Here we have the last effort of the Gothic architects of Brussels, an effort not unworthy of their grand traditions.

Whether the interior of Saint Gudila's was ever adorned with a complete scheme of decoration in polychromy is a doubtful question; but when the whitewash was removed, about fifty years ago, some vestiges of mural painting were discovered in the chancel, and we know from the church rolls that in 1543 a considerable sum was paid for illuminating the vault and the niches of the Sainte Chapelle des Miracles.

SAINTE GUDULE—— THE LADY CHAPEL.

Hardly any trace of this work now remains, and the frescoes have long since vanished from the walls of the chancel, but, for all that, the Church of Saint Gudila is still radiant with colour, for it still retains a very considerable number of ancient stained-glass windows, all of which, save Bishop de La Marck's Judgment window, display portraits of the later Sovereigns of Brabant or of other members of the reigning house.

On the clerestory window in the middle of the apse we have the second Duchess of Brabant, Marie de Bourgogne, and her husband, Maximilian of Austria; on the window next to it, on the epistle side, their son Philippe le Beau; further on their daughter Marguerite of Austria, Regent of the Low

Country during the minority of Charles Quint; opposite, the great Emperor himself and his brother Ferdinand; and further on, on the same side, Charles' son Philip II. of Spain. These five windows were painted in 1545.

Charles V. is also represented in the north transept window. He kneels alongside his wife, beneath a vast triumphal arch, and their patron saints are presenting them to the Eternal Father. In the window opposite, in the south transept, we have Charles's sister Marie, with her husband, King Louis of Hungary; they, too, are accompanied by their patron saints, who present them to the Blessed Trinity. Each of these windows was designed and painted in 1538 by Bernard van Orley, and we know, too, what fee he received for the latter—425 florins.

In the second of the four great windows which pierce the north wall of the Sacrament Chapel, Marie and Louis again appear; in the first, another sister of Charles Quint, Catherine, and with her her spouse John II. of Portugal; on the fourth, Charles' brother Ferdinand, and Ferdinand's wife, Anne of Hungary. All of these three windows were painted by Jan Haeck, a famous illuminator of glass, of Antwerp, from the designs of Bernard van Orley; on the third, yet another sister, Éléonore, Queen of Francis I. of France. Here we have another piece of Van Orley's own handiwork. All of the princes whose effigies gleam through these windows are accompanied by their patron saints, and above the portraits are depicted incidents in the legend of the Miraculous Hosts. The first window shows two scenes—the bribery of Jonathan, and Jonathan receiving the stolen ciborium; the second, the piercing of the Hosts, in the synagogue of Brussels; the third, the assassination of Jonathan; and the fourth, Catharine preparing to carry the Hosts to Cologne.

What are we to think of these stupendous windows? The quality of the glass is excellent, the scheme of colour glorious. It would be interesting to know if the cartoons were submitted to Peter van Wyenhoven[34] before they were executed, and if so, what he thought of them. These vast pictures, with their Renaissance accessories and their figures mutilated by the mullions and the Gothic tracery, through which we are constrained to peep at them, should be utterly out of harmony with the architecture and the architectural scheme of ornament which they were designed to complete, but, somehow or other, they are not. In those days there were giants in the land. We pigmies must be content to admire their works, and not presume to imitate them.

All this applies, and in a more marked degree, to the stained glass of the Lady Chapel. The subjects here depicted are, The Presentation of Our Lady, her Espousals, the Annunciation, and the Visitation; and in each case, below, with patron saints, we have the donor or donors of the window:

Ferdinand III. and his wife Eléonore, the Emperor Leopold I., the Archduke Albert of Austria and his wife Isabel of Spain, and, lastly, the Archduke Leopold of Austria. These windows are designed in the style of Rubens, and they were for a long time attributed to him, notwithstanding that one of them bears the signature *T. van Thulden*, legibly written, and the date, A° 1656. This man, we now know, designed all these windows, and we also know that he received 400 florins for his trouble. His colouring is even more glorious than the colouring of Van Orley or of Haeck, and he sinned more boldly than did either of them against the canons of correct taste.

Within the walls of this ancient temple which the Dukes of Brabant raised to the glory of God and in honour of a saint of their own house, endowed for their souls' behoof with gold and broad acres, and richly and lavishly adorned with their own magnificent effigies, many of them found a resting-place. Before the high altar is a white marble slab, bearing this inscription:—Brabantiæ ducum tumulus; and within the vault beneath, lies John II., who died on the seventeenth of October 1312, and alongside of him his duchess, Marguerite of England, daughter of Edward I. Here, too, are the ashes of Catherine of France, the child-wife whom Charles the Bold, aged six, married in 1438, and buried seven years later, and the ashes of her infant nephew, Joachim, the eldest son of Louis XI. then Dauphin, born and died at the Castle of Genappe on the fifteenth of December 1459, and whose little body was escorted to the tomb by dean and chapter and all the crafts' guilds, every man of them bearing three lanterns, an honour reserved for the children of kings. In the same vault sleep Archduke Ernest, grandson of Philippe le Beau, and sometime Governor-General of the Low Country, who died at Brussels in 1596; and at least two scions of the ducal house, whose shields were barred with a bend sinister:—that magnificent prelate Jean de Bourgogne, son of Jean sans Peur and Marguerite Bonzele, a lady of Bruges, whose bones lie in the cathedral there, in the Chapel of the Seven Dolours; and his nephew, Corneille, Lord of Beveren, whom men called Grand Bâtard de Bourgogne: he was the first born of Good Duke Philip's numerous progeny, and strangely enough his mother's name was Marie Corbeau.

In his early days Jean de Bourgogne had followed the profession of arms, and at this time his love affairs were almost as many as those of his half-brother Philip, whom in many respects he resembled. Later on he took orders, and became Provost of Bruges; in 1438, thanks to Philip's influence, he was named Count-Bishop of Cambrai, and as such was a prince of the Empire invested with sovereign rights. This post he held for forty years, and though he seldom visited his episcopal city, and resided for the most part at Brussels—Brussels, it should be borne in mind, was at this time in the diocese of Cambrai—he is described in contemporary documents as a wise and merciful ruler who never failed to do justice to his subjects and was exceedingly charitable to the poor. He died at his country house near Mechlin in 1478, full of years and honours.

Very different was the brief career and tragic end of poor Corneille. He seems to have been a youth of brilliant parts and of a singularly sweet disposition, and to have inherited alike the sterling qualities and the tumultuous passions of his father's race. Of his courage and skill in warfare he gave proof on more than one occasion, and if he had not had a natural aptitude for government, Philip would hardly have named him, young as he was, and in those troublous times, his lieutenant in the duchy of Luxembourg. Endowed with tact, with the charm of address, and, too, with the charm of personal beauty, he knew how to make himself beloved by all with whom he came in contact, too well, sometimes, as more than one woman learned to her cost. He possessed yet a rarer gift, he was able, like his father, to command respect in spite of unworthy actions, and notwithstanding the circumstances of his birth, and the fact that he was Philip's favourite son, he succeeded in winning the goodwill and affection of the Duchess herself, and of the Count of Charolais.

Death came to him in a fearful form and suddenly. He was slain by the men of Ghent at the Battle of Rupelmond in the Pays de Waes on the 16th of June 1452, and he fell flushed with victory, and with the foe in full flight. 'The day and the honour and the glory thereof were Duke Philip's,' says a contemporary writer, 'and yet it was a black day for the house of Burgundy, for Fortune, who is no respecter of persons, directed the pike of some damned disloyal villain into the mouth of Messire Corneille, and being thrust upwards it pierced his skull, and his brain fell through his palate, and so he died. And the good Duke grieved for his bastard, and made great mourning for him, for he loved him much, and so did the Count of Charolais (Charles the Bold), and Messire Anthoine, his brother; and he took Wouter Leenknecht, the leader of the rebels, who had been brought in wounded, and hanged him on a tree, but the death of a hundred thousand rebels would not have assuaged his grief, and thus the day ended. And the body of Messire Corneille was sent to Brussels, where the Duchess gave it most honourable burial in the Church of Saint "Gudile," for she loved him much on account of his good virtues; and Duke Philip founded a daily Mass for the repose of his soul, and ordained that every morning his tomb should be sprinkled with holy water, and that the anniversary of his death should be celebrated solemnly with bells and torches, as is wont to be done at the obits of the princes and princesses founded in this church; and to defray the cost thereof he presented the chapter with 700 golden crowns of 48 gros Flemish.'

The last of the princes of Brabant to be placed in this vault was Louis Philippe, eldest son of King Leopold I. He died on the 16th of June 1834, and when the vault was opened for his interment, some interesting relics were found: on the coffin of Duke John a sword in an enamelled scabbard and a crimson velvet toque embroidered with precious stones; on the coffin of Archduke Ernest, his heart in a silver casket enclosed in a little coffer of oak, and scattered about on the pavement a number of mouldering bones. The crypt needed repair, and these objects were accordingly removed, but they were replaced when the work was done, and there they still remain.

When the Church of Saint Gudila was sacked in 1576, the beautiful fourteenth-century monument which had been originally erected in memory of Duke John II. and his spouse, was utterly wrecked. The present cenotaph of black marble on the gospel side of the high-altar was erected to their memory in 1610 by their descendants, Albert and Isabel, who were themselves laid to rest when their time came in the *Sainte Chapelle des Miracles*. The monument on the opposite side of the chancel with the recumbent effigy of a knight in armour is the monument of the Archduke Ernest. The only inscription which it bears is his motto—— *Soli Deo gloria*. The memorial brasses and marble slabs inscribed with the names of the other princes who are buried in 'the crypt of the Dukes of Brabant' disap peared when the pavement of the choir was renewed in the course of the seventeen hundreds.

The mention of these mighty dead naturally suggests another mausoleum of the Dukes of Brabant, not in Brussels itself, but hard by: the Parish Church of Tervueren, an interesting old building of the twelve, thirteen and fourteen hundreds, in which lie buried the princes of the second dynasty— Duke Anthony, whose bones were brought here from the battlefield of Agincourt; his first wife, Jeanne of Luxembourg, who died at Tervueren on the 12th of August, 1407; and their two sons, poor little hunchbacked Jean, the hapless spouse of Jacqueline, and Philippe de Saint-Pol.

SAINT-PIERRE DE LOUVAIN

The mother church of Louvain, like the mother church of Brussels, owes its origin to Lambert Balderick. They are both collegiate churches; the foundation of each of them dates, if not from the same year, at least from the same decade, and in each case the original building was destroyed by fire within a century of its erection. Thus far the two churches resemble one another, and here the resemblance ends.

When Lambert founded the Church of Saint Gudila, Brussels was already a place of some importance, and probably it was on this account that he chose to retain the lordship of the rising town in his own hands, and to endow his new chapter with lands beyond its limits. Thus the canons of

Saint Gudila's had no shred of civil authority over the inhabitants of Brussels; the only jurisdiction which they possessed was a purely spiritual one; also, though Saint Gudila's was for many years the only parish church in the city, and even later on, when other churches were made parochial, it still held the first place, for some reason or other it was certainly not the church which the burghers most favoured, nor the one most intimately connected with their spiritual life.

It was otherwise in the case of Saint Peter's. When Saint Peter's was first built Louvain consisted of a fortress and a few farmhouses; the site of the new church was further up stream, in the centre of a tract of vacant land, for the most part forest and marsh, and it was on this swampy waste—the domain with which Lambert had dowered his new foundation—that the future capital of Brabant gradually grew up.

Of the nature of the ties by which the men of Louvain were bound to the Church of Saint Peter, of the duties thereby entailed, and their correlative rights and privileges, of how the former were presently evaded, and the latter to the end maintained in all their pristine vigour, of these things we have already spoken; and as we have already seen in a previous chapter, the old collegiate church was so completely identified with the city that proof that a man was *un homme de Saint Pierre* was held to be sufficient proof that he was a burgher and patrician of Louvain: without any further investigation he was at once admitted to all the rights of citizenship.

It is not to be wondered at, then, that the Louvainers regarded their church with feelings akin to veneration, or that when, in 1373, it was for the second time wrecked by fire, they grieved for it as for a friend, but no man thought of restoring it—not then, nor for many a long day afterwards. Louvain was in the throes of revolution, civil war had been raging almost continuously for more than ten years, and when at last the struggle ended with the triumph of Freedom in 1378, the fortunes of the city were at their lowest ebb. She had lost a third of her population, her commerce was almost destroyed, her staple industry gone, and she was honeycombed with debt.

With things in this plight the men of Louvain were in no position to saddle themselves with such a vast and costly undertaking as the reconstruction of their church. It was not till half a century later that they had the courage even to think of it, and then they made up their minds to act, and to act boldly. It happened thus. The founding of the University in 1421 had heralded, as all men believed, a new era. The issue showed they were not mistaken. Trade at once began to revive, and when the burghers had tasted the first-fruits of the harvest they dreamed that the Golden Age had returned, and forthwith determined to rebuild their church in such fashion that its splendour should dim the sheen of the noblest buildings of Brabant. This must have been somewhere about 1424, certainly not later, for in that year Plysis van Vorst was named 'master-mason of the new Church of Saint Peter.'

Although no document has as yet been discovered which states in so many words that Van Vorst drew up the plans of the new building, it may be safely said that he did so. We know that he was held at Louvain to be the first architect of his day, that the burghers desired that their new church should be second to none in the duchy, that they expressly summoned him from Diest, his native town, to superintend the building operations, and that he continued to do so till his death, which took place some fifteen years later. Van Vorst was a man of humble origin. Starting in life as a mason's labourer, mixing mortar and carrying bricks, he presently became a mason himself, and rapidly rose to the head of his profession; and when, in 1418, the burghers of Diest determined to rebuild their ancient Church of Saint Plysis it was unanimously decided that the work could be put in no better hands than those of 'Meester Van Vorst.' Their confidence was not misplaced: the noble structure which Plysis designed for them, and at which he laboured for twenty years—it was completed by his pupil Matthew de Layens, of whom later on—is undoubtedly one of the most beautiful specimens of Brabant work which has come down to us. To visit Diest were a day well spent, if only for the sake of this grand old building, which is adorned without with ancient statuary, and within with a wealth of stained-glass windows, some as old as the church itself, some of the following century, and some of the sixteen hundreds.

It was doubtless the fame the Diest plans earned for him which decided the Louvainers to commission our mason to rebuild their church, and in the following year to name him City Architect. From this time until his death Van Vorst must have been a busy man. His civic appointment was no sinecure; he had not only to direct and supervise whatever building operations the city fathers had in hand, but also to purchase the building materials, which meant frequent journeys on horseback to the quarries at Afflighem and Roteslaer; the work at Saint Peter's, too, must have occupied much of his time, and we may be sure that he was often at Diest to see after the building operations there. Yet somehow or other, like most busy men, he found time for recreation. At times he seems to have amused himself by making models of divers architectural monuments, for we know that the city magistrates were so delighted with some of these productions that, on the 11th of December, 1434, they voted him a *gratification* of 13 golden florins. Again we learn from the city archives that, on the 29th of May 1425, he took part in the Corpus Christi procession, marching at the head of his guild, and we may be quite sure, though the fact is not recorded, that when the religious ceremonies were over Meester Plysis and his brother masons withdrew to their wonted tavern, and there regaled themselves, not on the every-day malt liquor—though Louvain, even in those days, was famous for its ale—but, as was usual on festive occasions, with a bottle or so of the best Rhenish.

Yet another little intimate scene which some entries in the city records have enabled us to reconstruct. It took place on the 20th of May 1439, when the great architect, for the last time, received the congratulations of his comrades. Less than four months later he went the way of all flesh.

It will be necessary to preface the story with a word of explanation. Louvain, at the time of which we are writing, was without a town hall: the old Town Hall in the Vieux Marché was destroyed during the Civil War, and the actual building in the *Place Saint-Pierre* had not yet been erected; its site was occupied by three or four dwelling-houses which had been ceded by their owners to the Corporation, and it was in this block of tenements that the Town Council met, and that all civic business was transacted. From the first it had been but a make-shift arrangement, the premises were small, and in every way unsuited to the purpose to which they were now put, and early in 1438 it was resolved to enlarge them. Van Vorst prepared the plans, and on the 31st of March in the following year the foundation stone was laid by Jacob Utten Liemingen, a member of one of the oldest patrician families of Louvain, and Franciscus Willemans, a man of the people, each of whom was that year burgomaster. The work was pushed on vigorously, and when on the 20th of May the two burgomasters made an official visit of inspection, they were so well pleased at the progress made that they presented the masons with a *drink gelde* of two golden Peters: all of which is duly noted down in the city accounts. And thus, without much stretch of the imagination, we can picture to ourselves, when their day's work was done, the worthy architect and his admiring comrades cheerfully proceeding with animated countenances to carry out the burgomasters' behest. Amongst them, no doubt, old John Kelderman, destined soon to take his place and to carry on for a brief span Van Vorst's unfinished labours; and young Matthew de Layens, the pupil of promise, who lived long enough to complete them; and, of course, that rollicking, scapegrace son, who bore his father's name and inherited some of his talents, whose skill in sculpture is still attested by the beams in the Town Hall, and whose frolics are duly noted in the account books of the city, as, too, are the fines they cost him. We can see them all seated round a long, narrow table in the snug parlour of some old-world inn, like the Vlissinghe of Bruges, for example; there is wine set before them, both white and red, the best, you may be sure, that money can buy, and on the hearth is an armful of crackling faggots, for the nights are still a bit cold, not a great roaring fire, but just enough to give the room a soul, and to take the chill off the Burgundy. And here we will leave 'Meester Plysis van Vorst' in his high-backed chair at the head of the board with his glass in his hand, and his comrades around him drinking his health at the expense of the taxpayers.

When, about the opening of the fifteen hundreds, or possibly even earlier, the Church of Saint Peter's was at last completed, so far as it ever was completed, for, of course, the outside is still in an unfinished state, had the men of Louvain realised their ambition—had they

St. Peter's Louvain Chapel of St. Charles

made Saint Gudila hang her head? The two churches are so unlike that they hardly admit of comparison, though in those days, of course, they more nearly resembled one another than they do now. We think that on the whole the men of Louvain were satisfied with their achievement, are quite certain that they all maintained that their own church was the more beautiful, and, if an impartial critic had been asked to decide the question, we are by no means sure that he would not have said that the Petermen were right. He would have beheld in Saint Gudila's a vaster church than its rival—though it was not so large then as it is now—a church, from the varied styles in which it was built, more interesting, more picturesque, possessed of a charm that Saint Peter's had not—old age, and, with some of its architectural features, more beautiful than anything to be found at Louvain.

In Saint Peter's, on the other hand, he would have seen a church of uniform and well-digested plan, less vast but of nobler proportions, not the creation of many artists of varied taste and unequal talents, but the crowning achievement of one master mind—a church, too, in all probability, more lavishly and more elaborately adorned, and possessed of a richer garniture: walls glowing with frescoes, windows resplendent with stained glass, stonework illuminated with colour and gold everywhere, a screen and rood unmatched in Christendom, choir stalls of chaste design and perfect workmanship, an eagle lectern, unique, a tabernacle fifty feet high, Matthew de Layens's masterpiece; and what a show of metal work!—iron, copper, brass, exquisitely wrought; what triumphs of the goldsmith's art! what precious stones and costly stuffs! how many glorious pictures by the first craftsmen of the age—Boudts, Metsys, Van der Weyden! And what to-day of all this splendour? Fuit ... nunc nihil. Not a splinter of stained glass, frescoes wiped out, an attenuated remnant of church furniture mutilated and defaced. And for this state of things the legal guardians of Saint Peter's of days gone by—for the most part in the eighteen hundreds—the chapter as long as it lasted, and later on the 'Fabrique' must be largely held responsible, though, of course, not altogether: fanatics of various orders also wrought much mischief. Maybe, too, the church was whitewashed for the first time after the great plague of 1576, and, if this were so, the obliteration of the frescoes, however much we may regret it, can hardly be described as an act of wanton vandalism; but what are we to think of the wiseacres of 1793, who broke up the tomb of Duke Henry the Warrior, a relic of the second church, richly sculptured and gilded, which stood in the midst of the choir, because, as they said, it impeded the circulation of the people, and because the great bell had fallen and made a hole in the pavement, and they wanted some rubbish to fill it up with? or of those highly-intelligent church-wardens, who, a few years later, cast down the altars beneath the rood-screen, the high-altar and the canopied sedilia, all of them ancient and of exquisite design, and who afterwards wantonly broke up the canons' stalls, and about the same time sold the famous eagle lectern, said to have been the most beautiful object of its kind in Europe? Or, again, of those who were responsible in 1879 for the sale to the State for 200,000 francs of the great triptych—a signed picture, and perhaps his masterpiece—which Quentin Metsys painted for the guild chapel of Saint Anne—the chapel beneath the north-west tower, now dedicated to Saint Charles—we give a sketch of it—in 1509, and which, carried off by the French in 1794, had been restored to Saint Peter's twenty years later, and is now in the Brussels gallery, where we shall presently have an opportunity of visiting it.

Amongst the relics of antiquity still to be found in the Church of Saint Peter note:—the Calvary group beneath the chancel arch and the beautiful rood-screen which supports it, it dates from 1440, and is one of the finest in Europe: in the chapel under the north-west tower the font, a beautiful six-foiled basin of copper-gilt supported by slender shafts with their bases resting on lions; and the great crane to which the cover was once suspended, a marvellous piece of ironwork forged by Josse Metsys, Quentin's brother, in 1505: in the north transept a colossal statue more curious than beautiful, called Sedes Sapientiæ; it is the work of one De Bruyn, a woodcarver of Brussels, was painted and gilded by Roel van Velper, a famous illuminator of Louvain, and was presented to the church by the Town Council in 1442: in the ambulatory on the north side Duke Henry's tomb above referred to (the fragments were found in 1835, and later on pieced together and placed in their present position); and further on the tomb of his wife and of his daughter, with their recumbent effigies, Mathilde de Flandres and Marie, wife of Otho IV.; and further still, Matthew de Layens's tabernacle: almost opposite to it, in the sacrament chapel and the chapel adjoining, two authentic pictures by Dierick Boudts—a Last Supper and a Martyrdom scene, of these later on: in a chapel off the north aisle, a Descent from the Cross, attributed to Van der Weyden, perhaps not his, but for all that a beautiful picture: and, in the armourers' chapel, the second off the south aisle, the famous Crom Cruys—an old blackened crucifix rudely carved in wood with the figure of our Lord, almost life-sized and clothed in a long tunic of purple velvet, in a strange and unnatural position:—the right hand, instead of being nailed to the Cross, is detached from it, as though the Christ, reaching forward with a violent effort, had just wrenched out the nail; the arm is still stretched out, but slightly bent from the elbow, and the fingers are hanging down. This weird and mysterious image is perhaps the most interesting object which Saint Peter's contains. It is very old, who shall say how old: certainly older than the present church, for the town archives bear witness that in 1382, when Duke Winceslaus was besieging Louvain, the people, bare-headed and unshod, carried it through the streets in solemn procession, as was their wont when things were going ill with them, singing psalms and litanies, and in all probability we have here a relic of the original building of 1040, if, indeed, it does not go back to a still earlier date. Of its origin we know nothing. No written record nor oral tradition has come down to us concerning it, but from time immemorial the men of Louvain have held the Crom Cruys in the highest veneration, it is intimately associated with some of the most stirring and some of the most tragic episodes in the life of the city, and the unwonted position of the crucified figure has given rise to a host of strange legends. Molanus, Dean of Saint Peter's, who died in 1585, relates one of them, which seems to have been widely credited in his day, and which no doubt had inspired the burghers to carry the cross in procession in times of public calamity. He had been told, he says, that the reason why the right hand was thus outstretched was on account of a miracle—a supplicant, bowed down by some great sorrow, was one day weeping before the crucifix, and our Lord, as a token of His sympathy, had caused the image to reach out its hand. 'But the pastors of our church,' Dean Molanus goes on to say, 'cannot vouch for the truth of the story.' 'Its origin is lost in the night of antiquity, and Bernard van Kessel (sacristan of

Saint Peter's from 1495 to 1530, and by trade a painter and modeller) knows nothing of it, although it is his hobby to note down all the information that he can obtain concerning our church. Maybe the *Crom Cruys* was thus from the beginning.' Possibly, but another explanation suggests itself, which, bearing in mind the blackened and charred appearance of the crucifix, seems to us more probable—the great fire of 1176.

INTERIOR OF MECHLIN CATHEDRAL.

MECHLIN.

In the Cathedral of Mechlin, some twenty minutes by rail from Brussels, we have another typical Brabant church of the fourteen hundreds—not all of it, but a very considerable portion. It is a grand old building, but the interior has suffered much at the hands of enemies and of friends, and whatever may have been the case in former days it is now more impressive without than within, as the accompanying sketches show. Albeit it is well worth visiting, were it only for the sake of the Kelderman tower.

Mechlin is rich in mediæval domestic architecture—richer than any other town in Belgium save, perhaps, Bruges. It contains a host of quaint old burgher houses in stone and brick and timber, notably on the Quai de l'Avoine,[35] and at least three ancient palaces:—the palace of Marguerite of Austria in the *Rue de l'Empereur*, the Hôtel Busleyden in the *Rue des Vaches*, and, most picturesque of all, that mysterious old red brick mansion on a back-water of the Dyle behind Saint Rombold's, in the Rue de l'Ecoutete.[36] The visitor to Brussels must certainly make many journeys to Mechlin.

There are other churches in the neighbourhood of Brussels which date wholly or in part from the period during which the architecture of Brabant attained the heyday of its glory. Several of them are most beautiful, none without some interesting features, all well worth considering; but their name is legion, and it would be hopeless to attempt to describe so many buildings, or to give any adequate account of their numerous historical associations, within the limits of our poor little pocket-book. For Brussels and Louvain were each of them suzerains of a host of smaller towns; not mere village communities called towns, as it were, by courtesy, but regularly organised cities—in miniature, some of them, if you will; some of them of considerable size, and harbouring a very considerable population. Great or small, they were all endowed with municipal institutions, and, too, with all those social, industrial, commercial and religious institutions which throughout the Middle Age were inseparable from civic life in the Netherlands, and most of them, at the time of which we are writing, were prosperous.

Now think of what all this means in the way of bricks and mortar. Each had its market, its Town

MECHLIN CATHEDRAL.

Hall, its Bell Tower, its convents, its guild chapels, its Béguinage, and at least one noble Sanctuary. Some of the civic buildings have disappeared, but the churches, for the most part, remain, and several of the most interesting monuments in Belgium are to be found in these towns off the beaten track, whose very names are hardly known to the average British tourist. Let it, then, here suffice to point out a few of the most noteworthy, and the reader, if he feel so inclined, can visit them at his leisure.

At Lierre, between Mechlin and Antwerp, a little way off the main line, there is a grand old church, designed by Herman De Waghemakere and completed by his son, with a rood-screen by old Anthony Kelderman, marvellously wrought—a very curious and most beautiful example of decadent Gothic work, with groups of statuary peering out from an intricate web of flamboyant ornament, so fragile and so dainty that it might almost be taken for lace. In this church there is some of the most beautiful old stained glass to be found in Belgium—late, of course, but of its kind, perfect; and there are several other objects reminiscent of the Middle Age. In the town, too, there are vestiges of bygone civic splendour—a city hall much modernised, and a bell tower which dates from 1420 or thereabouts.

Thienhoven, or Tirlemont as it is called in French, is a picturesque town on the river Gette, some ten miles beyond Louvain. Here there are three most interesting churches—Notre-Dame du Lac, Second Period, with a choir and transepts and a great square tower at the intersection; Saint Germain, partly Romanesque, partly Transition, and with a nave and aisles of the fourteen hundreds, and the old Church of the Béguinage, which dates from the thirteen hundreds.

Every lover of mediæval art should visit Léau, also on the Gette, about seven miles down stream. It was once a busy place enough, and is now a dead city, and on that account none the less interesting. The Church of Saint Leonard is a noble structure, with two massive Transition towers at the west end; the choir is First Period, the nave and aisles and transepts date from the fourteen hundreds. Matthew de Layens worked here; he built the baptistery and perhaps, too, some of the side chapels, and designed a richly sculptured reredos for the Lady-Altar. The metal work in this church is curious and beautiful, and there is much of it—brass, iron, copper. It is well worth studying. In the sacristy there is some antique silver—chalices, reliquaries, cruets and the like, and there are one or two good pictures.

Or, again, take Aerschot, the little town at the gates of Louvain to which the patricians so often withdrew during their great contest with the plebeians. Here there is a stately parish church, which dates from 1337, and was completed in the following century. An inscription on one of the walls of the choir bears witness to the former fact, and informs us, too, of the architect's name—I. Pickart. Here there are carved oak stalls, a rood screen finely wrought, and, in front of it, a chandelier forged by Quentin Metsys, beneath which lie the bones of his wife, Adelaide van Tuylt. Aerschot is on the high road to Diest, of which town we have already spoken.

The Church of Saint Dymphna, in the little town of Gheel, in the midst of the pine woods and heather of the Campine country, is well worth visiting. It was founded by the Berthouts, lords of Mechlin, somewhere about 1250, and was not finished until the closing years of the fourteen hundreds. It is a large cruciform building with single aisles, well-marked transepts, and an apsidal choir surrounded by side chapels. Undoubtedly a noble structure, but not, from an architectural

De Dijk te Mechelen

point of view, amongst the most beautiful churches of Belgium; it is chiefly interesting on account of its mural paintings and its ancient altar-pieces, carved in wood or sculptured in stone and richly illuminated. The fresco above the chancel arch—a Last Judgment—is particularly fine, both in colour and composition. It was discovered some twelve or thirteen years ago, dates apparently from the close of the fourteen hundreds, and is fairly well preserved; whilst the reredos of the high-altar—a triptych with scenes from the life of Saint Dymphna, sculptured in high relief and sheltered by an elaborate canopy of rich flamboyant work, most delicately carved—is of its kind unique. It dates from the early fifteen hundreds. It would be hard to find in Belgium or elsewhere a more beautiful contemporary specimen of this kind of work. The sculptors of Brabant excelled in work of this kind, and here we have one of their masterpieces; it was designed and carved by an Antwerp man.

In the Church of Our Lady and Saint Martin at Alost, a better known and more accessible place, we have another grand old building. It dates from the close of the fourteen hundreds. It consists of a choir and ambulatory, transepts, and three bays of a nave. It is a typical Brabant church, and, if it were completed, would be one of the largest and most beautiful in Belgium. Some very interesting mural paintings have quite recently been discovered here. Alost is a very prosperous, pushing place, and almost all its beauty has been improved away, but the traveller in search of the picturesque will find something to console him besides Saint Martin's Church: in the market-place there are some ancient municipal buildings which date from the twelve hundreds, and if he look about intelligently he will perhaps find something more.

Our list is already longer than we at first intended, but the reader, if perchance he found out the omission, would assuredly never pardon us if we neglected to add to it Hal, a picturesque little town on the Hainault frontier, but almost at the gates of Brussels, only fifteen minutes by rail from the Gare du Midi. We have spoken of it several times in the course of this story. The Church of our Lady and Saint Martin at Hal, though it is not so vast as its namesake of Alost, is perhaps even more beautiful, and certainly more interesting, for here there is gathered together a larger collection of mediæval art treasures than in any other church in Brabant. It is older, too, than the church of Alost—the foundation stone was laid in 1341, but the whole building was not completed until well on into the fourteen hundreds. It is said to be the best example of Second Period work in Belgium. Of this, however, we are doubtful, though assuredly nothing could well be more lovely than the choir, with its beautiful statuary and its elaborate double triforium, which sweeps like a web of finely-wrought lace across the lower portion of the clerestory windows. This feature is as curious as it is rare, and in plan so complicated that it baffles brief description, and unfortunately we have not been able to obtain a sketch of it. The unknown mason who first imagined this glorious gallery, and then turned the dream into sculptured stone, seems to have had in his mind the ordinary model and the Brabant pattern, and to have been able to effect between them a most happy marriage. The little altars in the ambulatory are nearly all of them old, older, perhaps, than the church itself. They merit careful examination. The Lady chapel is lined with frescoes, which, alas, are much damaged and fast fading away, and there are vestiges of mural painting in other parts of the church.

The south porch is particularly beautiful, with its ancient statuary—Our Lady and Angels—and its great

Notre-Dame de Hal Baptistry Gates.

oak door, strengthened with foliated hinges of wrought-iron. Note, too, the richly-sculptured tabernacle at the north side of the choir; the baptistery gates, of which we give a sketch; the beautiful and ancient furniture which the baptistery itself contains; in the sacristy much wealth in goldsmiths' ware—this the pilgrim will hardly see, unless he be armed with a letter of introduction to 'Monsieur le Doyen'; and lastly, in the Lady chapel, a little image, two feet high—the oldest and most interesting treasure which this treasure-house contains, the nucleus of this rich and varied collection, the treasure which attracted to itself all the other treasures, the magnet which drew hither the gold with which this church was built, from all parts of Europe, the famous Virgin of Hal, nigra sed formosa. True literally: we have here one of the most remarkable and beautiful specimens of early mediæval statuary to be found in Belgium. It dates, at latest, from the closing years of the twelve hundreds.

All kinds of curious legends have been woven round this little block of carved and discoloured wood, and all kinds of quaint and incongruous objects, some of them of great value, crowd the walls of its sumptuous shrine. They are the votive offerings of countless pilgrims who throughout many generations have not ceased to invoke the assistance of Heaven through the prayers of Our Lady of Hal.

THE TOWN HALL OF BRUSSELS

There is only one municipal building in Brussels which dates from the period we are now considering, but that building is perhaps unique. Search where you will you will hardly find a more perfect specimen of civic architecture, and this at least may be said without fear of contradiction: no city can boast a nobler town hall than that which Brussels possesses. Ypres, perhaps, someone will say, or Longfellow's 'quaint old Flemish city,' but the great hall of Ypres was not the place where the Senate met, but a cloth market, and though the Town Hall of Bruges is a gem, for this very reason it cannot compete with the Town Hall of Brussels—as well compare, say, the Sainte Chapelle with Westminster Abbey. Of course it is not perfect. Where on earth will you find perfection either in architecture or anything else? But this much may be justly said, the Town Hall of Brussels approaches nearer to perfection than any other building of its kind in Europe which dates from the same period, even in its present state, for we do not see it now, be it borne in mind, as it was in the heyday of its glory. The army of burgomasters who stand under niches between the first and second storey of the east wing were not there in those days: they are a modern addition of 1863, and take the place of a blind arcade of a very simple character, which was certainly never intended to be peopled with statues. Nor is this all, if we would picture to ourselves the old building as it used to be we must not only subtract, we must add. The original statues, about half as many as there are now, probably somewhat smaller, and certainly more vigorously, and, at the same time, more delicately, carved, were all of them arrayed in vestures of gold, wrought about with divers colours, and in those days, we must not forget, the men of the Low Countries had an eye for colour, and the greatest painters of the age did not think it beneath their dignity to busy themselves with work of this kind.

In the early days the Senate of Brussels had no fixed place of assembly. The city fathers held their meetings sometimes in convents, sometimes in churches, sometimes in private dwellings, sometimes in the open air, and it was not until the year 1300 that they obtained a Town Hall, or rather what did duty for a Town Hall—'a house of stone,' in the Ster Straat, now the Rue de l'Hôtel de Ville, which they had recently purchased from a mercer named Odo, and in this old house of stone—most houses were in those days of timber—justice was administered and all public business transacted for more than a hundred years, until at last, in the fulness of time, the present Town Hall was built.

Very little has come down to us concerning its early history. The foundation stone seems to have been laid towards the close of Duchess Jeanne's long reign, probably about the year 1402, and the building operations must have progressed rapidly, for in the town accounts for the month of October 1405 divers sums are entered for the cost of gilding the summits—weather-cocks, doubtless, or something of the kind—of various roofs and towers, amongst them 'the tower opposite the Maison de l'étoile' of which we give a sketch on page 1; and in 1421 Philippe de Saint-Pol, speaking of the Town Hall in his letter to the Emperor Sigismund anent the trouble with the Germans, calls it 'un édifice très grand et formidable.' At this time the east wing must certainly have been completed, and it was from the gallery over the arcade which skirts this portion of the building that Vander Zype and Saint-Pol himself were wont to address the mob.

The building operations had been interrupted by the revolution, and they were not again resumed until the 4th of March 1444, when the little Count of Charolais (Charles le Téméraire), then only six years old, laid the foundation stone of the tower. Five years later, in 1449, Jan Vandenberg was named *Meester van den Steenwerke van den torre van den Stad Raethuyse op de merct*, at a salary of two saluts a day, for which sum he undertook to prepare the plans, to supervise the work, and to hold himself responsible for its good quality. This is the first time that we find Vandenberg's name mentioned in the city records in connection with the Town Hall. He pushed the work on so vigorously that in less than five years it was done; nor had he any reason to be ashamed of the result of his labour: the steeple which he had raised in so short a time was one of the finest in Christendom, and, despite its fragile and lace-like appearance, one of the most solidly constructed.

The story that Vandenberg on the day of its completion hurled himself headlong from the highest pinnacle, disgusted because he had not set his tower in the centre of the façade, is not only absurd on the face of it, but demonstrably false. In 1431, the date of the alleged suicide, the tower was non-existent, and fifty years after the true date of its completion Vandenberg was still alive; but, for all that, a tragedy did occur on that very spot and on that very day—at least so say the monks of Rouge Cloître, and they are generally to be trusted: no one went out of the world, but someone came into it.

On the day on which Vandenberg gave the finishing touch to his work by setting up in its place that colossal statue of Saint Michael which we still admire—a weather-cock, so delicately adjusted that, notwithstanding its vast bulk, it turns with the slightest breeze—it was arranged seemingly that some sort of ceremony should take place on the top of the tower (where no doubt a platform had been erected), by way of inauguration. Among the little band of intrepid climbers who had determined to be present there was a lady, gentle reader, in delicate health, and when she reached her destination the crisis came, and there, at that dizzy height, three hundred and thirty feet above the Grand' Place, suspended as it were betwixt earth and heaven, with Saint Michael hovering above her head, she in due course became a mother, and doubtless the baby was presently named after the archangel who had presided at its birth.

The west wing of the Town Hall was not completed until 1486. Though it bears a general resemblance to the east wing, and at first sight they seem to be similar, on closer inspection it will be found that the two wings differ considerably, not only in detail, but also in their main outlines. It would be hard to say which is the more beautiful, but, all things considered, the earlier portion seems to be structurally the more perfect. The sculptured capitals of the stately arcade—which extends from one end of the building to the other, broken only by the tower, and which contains no less than sixteen arches—deserve to be examined closely: they are all most delicately carved, and several of them display satirical groups, which are sufficiently quaint. Note also the great oak door studded with nails and supported by foliated hinges, and the sculpture with which it is surrounded: all these things are ancient and exceedingly beautiful. Pass through into the courtyard—a very pleasant place in summer time, with its fountains and foliage—and there, if you are a wise man and believe that sightseeing should be done leisurely, you will rest awhile and perhaps compare the old Gothic work of the fourteen hundreds with the work which was put up after the bombardment of 1695: the architecture, of course, is wholly different, but, for all that, not to be despised.

The interior of the Town Hall of Brussels has been so modernised that very little of the original work remains, or is at all events visible; but the general arrangement, at least so far as concerns the upper storeys, seems to be much the same as it was in days of yore, and from their associations several of the rooms are interesting—notably, on the first floor of the west wing, the Council Chamber, where the great council sat to settle the affairs of the city; on the same floor of the east wing the Throne Room, the Salle Gothique as it is now called, where the Dukes of Brabant used to receive the homage of the burghers and swear to maintain their privileges, and where on more than one occasion the Estates-General assembled; and further on, the Hall of Nations, where the nine nations of Brussels met to discuss their affairs, and where, too, the city magistrates sat in judgment. A great crucifix was affixed to the wall to remind them that justice must be tempered with mercy, and hence it was also called the Hall of Christ.

For the rest, in sculpture, tapestry, pictures, furniture of all kinds and of every description, the Town Hall is very rich. It varies in age and also in quality: a little of it, a very little of it, dates from mediæval times; there is much good work of the sixteen hundreds, more of the succeeding century, but modern things are the most in evidence, and some of them show that there are still craftsmen in Brussels who are not unworthy of the title.

THE TOWN HALL OF LOUVAIN

The Town Hall of Louvain, like the Town Hall of Brussels, dates from the Burgundian period, but, unlike the Town Hall of Brussels, which grew up gradually in a hundred years, it is entirely the work of one man—Matthew de Layens, who not only furnished the plans and supervised the construction, but even himself took part in the manual labour. When old John Kelderman died, in 1445, this man had been named his successor, at an annual salary, note, of 30 florins d'or and sufficient cloth to make him a *robe d'apparat*, or, in other words, a dress suit. Van Vorst's council chamber was now finished, and shortly after De Layens's appointment the men of Louvain determined to pull down the block of houses in front of it, and to erect in their place a worthier structure, and of course it fell to friend Matthew's lot to draw out the plans. His instructions seem to have been to follow the main outline of the Brussels Town Hall, which at this time of course consisted of only the east wing; but the details were to be left to his own initiative, and he was to see to it that the copy surpassed the model.

Early in 1448 Matthew was able to send in his plans, and presently Meester Pauwels, the Duke's architect, came from Brussels to examine them, and in due course pronounced them perfect; whereat great rejoicing, and Pauwels and Matthew withdrew to the sign of the 'Blomendale,' there to discuss two pints of Rhenish and two of Baune at the city's expense. It was the Wednesday in Holy Week, and it is not recorded of these honest fellows that they partook of any solid food. Let us hope, then, that they had good stomachs and strong heads, for, in spite of the Hock and the Burgundy, they were presently constrained to call for more liquor: a deputation of city masons came to pay their respects to the great Brussels architect, and what could good Meester Pauwels do but offer them something to drink; and that something cost the ratepayers two golden Peters.

On the following Thursday week the foundation stone of the new Town Hall was solemnly laid by Myn Here Hendrick van Linten, second burgomaster of Louvain, his patrician colleague being absent at Brussels on business with the Duke, when again the masons were entertained with alcohol, and seven of them were presented with gloves, all of which is duly set down in the city accounts.

It was the custom of Matthew de Layens to carry out in his daily life Saint Paul's precept—'Whatsoever thy hand findeth to do, do it with all thy might,' and his hand found so many things to do. He was a man of such keen interests, such wide sympathies, such varied attainments, that in all probability he hardly knew the meaning of the word leisure. An artist to his finger-tips, not only had he practical knowledge of the technicalities of his own trade, but he excelled in sculpture and wood carving, and could, and did, successfully compete with the best metal workers in the land. He was interested in politics, took an active and energetic part in public life, a charitable man, too: when the plague broke out he proved himself a patient and efficient nurse, and when the Dyle overflowed its banks, and all the low-lying part of the town was flooded, he was among the foremost to render assistance to the victims of the catastrophe; and lastly, an entry in the town accounts reveals him a man of principle. It so happened that urgent professional business, which brooked no delay, called him from home one Sunday. He did not refuse to undertake it, but he absolutely refused to receive any remuneration for his services: he would accept nothing more than the money which he had expended on horse hire. Nor would even this item have appeared in the town accounts if the circumstance in question had taken place a few years later, for he soon began to make a very considerable income of his own, and presently he found a widow with valuable house property in Tirlemont, her native town, and several large estates in various parts of the country. She was neither old nor ill-favoured; he made love to her with all his might, and in due course led her

HÔTEL DE VILLE, LOUVAIN.

to the altar, and henceforth, we may be very sure, he had a horse, if not horses, of his own. This was honest Matthew's second matrimonial experience, and it seems to have been on the whole a successful one. By his first wife he had had no children, but his widow gave him two sons, who both died young, and two daughters, of whose fate we know nothing. She seems, too, to have been fond of him, for when Matthew himself died in 1494 she lost her reason, and to the end of her days never recovered it. Like so many lunatics, she attained a great age, and was still living at Tirlemont under the care of relatives in 1520.

With such a man as architect and master of the works it is not surprising that the new Town Hall was very rapidly built. The exterior was finished in the incredibly short time, for the period, of ten years, and in 1463 the interior was also completed. And had the master-mason succeeded? Did his achievement equal the expectation of his fellow-burghers? Was the municipal palace which he had built for them more splendid than the Brussels Town Hall? The latter, of course, was still unfinished; it still lacked the west wing, and the general aspect of the former was at a short distance much the same as it is now.

These things being borne in mind, we think it may be safely said that honest Matthew's horn was exalted, and that the men of Louvain were happy; and perhaps it was on this account that the Brussels folk determined to enlarge their own Town Hall. And yet one cannot help feeling, as one stands before this fascinating and fantastic structure, with its crowd of statues, its dainty corbels, each one carved with a Bible tale, with its bristling roof, its filigree niches, its pinnacles soaring to heaven like crystallised incense smoke, that it is less the triumph of the mason than the triumph of the sculptor, that architecture has ceased to reign, and that one of her handmaids has usurped her place: for what have we here—bricks and mortar, or an elaborate piece of embroidery? And almost all the civic monuments of Belgium erected subsequently to this Town Hall suggest the same question. Strange that the ecclesiastical monuments of the day, planned as they were by the same men and for the same patrons, present such a different appearance. This is true, not only so far as concerns minor churches and those which are unfinished, but also in the case of completed buildings of the most ambitious character, where even such important features as west fronts, towers, transept ends, are singularly free from superfluous ornament. Take, for example, the north and the south façades of Saint Rombold's at Mechlin,[37] or Saint Gudila's Sacrament Chapel, or the western towers[38] of the same church, or the tower of Saint Gertrude's, Louvain, completed in 1453, and probably the work of De Layens.[39] They are all of them far less exuberant than the great ecclesiastical monuments of Germany or England or France erected at the same time, or even than some of those which date from the preceding century. And if, without, the Brabant churches of this period are comparatively simple, within, their architectural simplicity becomes almost severe, though, of course, accessories—altars, rood-screens, tabernacles and such like, are often exceedingly ornate.

Of this we have a striking example in the choir stalls of Saint Gertrude's. The reader must visit them. Nothing could well be more elaborate, and at the same time more lovely, than this fantastic piece of wood carving. Here we have not only the usual canopied statues set amidst rich flamboyant tracery delicately wrought, but a series of charming bas-reliefs with scenes from the life of Christ. There are eight-and-twenty panels; they are exquisitely carved, and in style and composition distinctly recall the pictures of Quentin Metsys. It is more than likely that he designed them, for they are the work of his nephew, Jan Beyaert, and the tragic fate which befell this man makes them the more interesting.

Jan Beyaert was born at Louvain in 1499. He was the son, or perhaps the grandson, of Launcelot Beyaert, chief scribe to the City Council, and, as such, a man of repute, and in fairly easy circumstances; but sculpture was the family calling, and several of Beyaert's kinsmen had set their mark on the monuments of the city—notably, Launcelot's brother Josse, who was town sculptor of Louvain (1475-1476) when Hubert Stuerbout was town painter, and had worked with him under Matthew de Layens at the Town Hall. The carved brackets which adorned the façades were the outcome of their united efforts. Hubert furnished the designs, and the other two carried them out. Many of these still exist, and they are exceedingly beautiful; but there is no evidence to show which of these stories in stone were sculptured by Josse Beyaert. We are not, however, without proof that he was well skilled in his craft: the bas-reliefs in the treasure room, the bosses and corbels in the salle de mariage, with scenes from the life of Christ, and the numerous pendants from the timber roof of the adjoining chamber, were carved by him alone, and the excellent workmanship shows that he was a sculptor of no mean order.

It was in all probability from his uncle Josse that young Jan Beyaert first learned how to handle the chisel. This youth was a genius, and he must have loved his art, or he could never have produced the exquisite things he did; but, like so many artists, he was a hare-brained, reckless fellow, and quarrelsome, too, in his cups: his name appears more than once in the town accounts in connection with fines for brawling, and in 1523 he was indicted for a graver matter—highway robbery in the Place Saint-Pierre, and with violence. The article stolen was only a hat, but in taking it he had grievously ill-treated the owner, a vry gheselle returning home at night most likely from his tavern. The magistrates, however, dealt gently with this roystering youth, perhaps for old Launcelot's sake, perhaps because they regarded the affair as a mere drunken frolic. At all events, he was quit with a fine of 15 Peters.

The next thing that we know of Meester Jan is that in 1524 he married—a most unfortunate proceeding, as it afterwards turned out, not only for himself but for us. If he had been content to remain single, or if he had not been fascinated by the charms of Catherine Metsys, he might have gone on to the end of the chapter, carving sublime statues and intoxicating himself occasionally, with no worse consequences perhaps than a periodical touch of liver, and maybe now and again a fine for assaulting harmless burghers. As it was, his career was cut short, and it was all his Eve's doing.

For a time, however, things went well: Jan settled down to family life, and showed himself an exemplary husband; and if the grey mare were the better horse, he was probably happy in her leading strings, for she seems to have been a most fascinating and accomplished creature, the beau-ideal of an artist's wife. And well she might be, seeing the blood that ran in her veins; for her father, Josse Metsys, whose acquaintance we have already made, was in his way a genius no less remarkable than his more famous brother Quentin. By trade he was a locksmith, but he by no means confined his talent to the fabrication of articles of iron-mongery, though locks and keys in those days were often works of art. He busied himself with clocks and jewellery, was a cunning worker in all kinds of metal, and late in life began to dabble in brick and mortar, and with such success that when Saint Peter's towers were burnt down he was commissioned to build them up again, in spite of the fact that he was not a professional mason. This was in 1507. He prepared his plans, and magnificent plans they were (you may see them still in the Town Hall, traced by old Josse himself on a large sheet of parchment)—a great central tower 535 feet high, flanked by two smaller towers, each of 430 feet; all three crowned with spires of open work, something in the style of Saint Gertrude's.

In due course the foundations were laid, and Josse supervised the building operations for something like sixteen years, and then things came to a standstill—a dispute, seemingly, with the dean and chapter, who refused to pay him his wages. He appealed to the city magistrates; and they, having vainly essayed to arrange matters, commissioned him to carve for them in stone an exact model of the projected building (August 1524), partly because they thought old Josse had been harshly treated and they knew he was poor, and partly because such a model would be useful to his successor, for he was now a very old man, and Death sat close to him.

The issue proved how wise they were. He died shortly afterwards (May 1530), and his towers are unfinished still; but the master-mason who shall one day complete them will have no excuse if he fail to realise the old locksmith's glorious dream, for he lived long enough to make the model (1529), and along with his plans it is still preserved in the archive chamber of the Town Hall. In all probability, the greater part of it was not carved by Metsys himself, but the work was all done under his supervision; and the man who helped him, it will be interesting to note, was his son-in-law, Jan Beyaert.

It was most likely about this time that Meester Jan set to work on his stalls, for we know that they were the gift of Abbot Peter Was, who ruled Saint Gertrude's from 1527 to 1546. An elaborate work of this kind must have taken a man like Beyaert many years to complete; he died in 1543, and for a considerable period before his death he had ceased to occupy himself with art. He had taken up theology instead, and that was his undoing. It happened thus: Calvinism was now making headway in all the towns of the Netherlands, Catherine embraced the new doctrine, she was a woman of will and of energy, and soon she became the leading spirit of the little band of Protestants at Louvain. Of course she had no difficulty in persuading her husband to join them, and soon the poor artist was converted into a hot Gospeller. Strange irony of fate that the man who had made graven images all his life should end his days an iconoclast. He did not turn his hand against his own work; perhaps he still, in spite of his wife, had a sneaking tenderness for sculpture, but his practice squared with his preaching in the matter of pictures, and one night, toward the close of the year 1542, or early in 1543, he broke into the Church of Saint Pierre, and then into the Church of Saint Jacques, in each of them wrecked several valuable paintings, and afterwards, with the fragments, made a bonfire in the Grand' Place. Presently he was arraigned for heresy and sacrilege, found guilty, and condemned to the stake. Hope, however, seems to have been held out to him that if he would give evidence against his accomplices the sentence would be reconsidered, and at last, under torture, he opened his mouth, and who shall throw a stone at him? How many of us, gentle reader, are of the stuff of which martyrs are made? If he believed that his life would be spared he was bitterly disappointed, but his cowardice gained for him this much—instead of burning him they cut off his head. With all his faults, he was a great artist. Let him rest in peace. As for poor Catherine, who had been arrested along with her husband, hers was a more terrible fate. On the 14th of July 1443 they buried her alive.

Reader, before quitting Saint Gertrude's, go into the chapel, which skirts the north side of the choir, and there, on the north wall, you will find a white marble tablet, engraved with a Latin inscription. We have here the requiem of Abbot Renesse, and one likes to think that he wrote it himself. Read it, and perhaps it will make you forget the discordant notes of poor Beyaert's gruesome dirge.

D. O. M.
Viatorum in terris implorat
suffragium
et eorum in cœlis sperat
Consortium
A. G. BARO DE RENESSE
Sanctæ Gertrudis Abbas
XX obiit 8 Martii 1785
R.I.P.

CHAPTER XVII
Pictures and Painters

In another volume of this series we have already said something concerning the origin and history of mediæval Flemish art. Within the limited space at our disposal anything more than a mere sketch would be impossible, and it would be superfluous and wearisome to repeat in the present handbook, which is in some sense the companion volume to *The Story of Bruges*, what has been there set down on the subject in question. We shall therefore content ourselves by adding here, by way of complement, a few notes (culled for the most part from Mr Weale's published writings) on the mediæval art corporations of the Low Country—those famous guilds of Saint Luke, of Our Lady, of Saint John, within whose ranks were formed all the great Flemish masters of the old national school, and by recounting as briefly as may be what is known of the five most noted Brabant painters of the Middle Age:—Roger van der Weyden, Dierick Boudts, Hugo van der Goes, Quentin Metsys, and Bernard van Orley. Men, all of them, whose names are intimately associated with Brussels or with Louvain.

In the early days the art of painting, like all the other arts and crafts, was cultivated only in the cloister, and to the end of the eleven hundreds it was submitted almost entirely to the control of the religious orders. Not that the monks were the only artists and the only artisans: attached to all the great abbeys, and even to some of the smaller monasteries, and to more than one collegiate church, were vast bodies of lay craftsmen—so vast that their numbers were often reckoned by hundreds, sometimes by thousands, as we have documentary evidence to show: these men lived under the protection of the monks, had received their instruction at their hands, worked for them and with them, on the monastic domain, and also, but under strict regulations, for outsiders as well. Presently a change came, brought about by the rise of the cities: the monastery then ceased to be the only place where art could be cultivated in peace, and a vast immigration of artists to these new havens of refuge was the consequence. The new-comers, too feeble to stand alone, and not at first sufficiently numerous to be able to form distinct corporations, solved the difficulty by affiliating themselves to existing trade companies, sculptors joining hands with masons, and painters with glaziers and saddlers. A few abbeys here and there continued for a while to maintain their art schools and their lay art-workers, but their numbers gradually diminished, and by the close of the twelve hundreds there were no lay craftsmen of any kind outside the city walls. By this time the city artists were sufficiently numerous to be able to combine in distinct corporations. The first institution of this kind of which we have any record was the Guild of Saint Luke at Ghent, which was founded by the art-workers of that city as early as 1337; four years later the painters of Tournai followed their example; the guild of Saint Luke, at Louvain, was founded before 1350, that of Bruges in 1351, of Antwerp in 1382, and by the opening of the fourteen hundreds almost every city in the Netherlands possessed its painters' guild.

In no town where a guild was established was any outside painter suffered to ply his craft for money, and no man could become a member of the local guild unless he were a burgher of the town by right of birth or of purchase. If a youth aspired to become a painter, the first step was to enroll his name as a companion or probationer in the register of the guild of the town in which he intended to practise. He was then required to serve an apprenticeship under some master painter approved by the guild, who was responsible not only for his technical instruction but also for his fidelity to his civil and his religious duties. During this time he lived with his master, and was bound to serve and obey him, and the latter in his turn was bound to thoroughly instruct him in all that concerned his craft. Nor was this all, when he had received his indentures he had to serve as a journeyman under some qualified master-painter, but not necessarily a member of the guild which he himself proposed to join. When the time of his probation had expired—it seems to have varied from town to town—he presented himself before the heads of the guild, and brought with him a picture which he himself had painted. If it came up to the required standard of excellence, and if, after examining him, they were satisfied of his technical knowledge and skill, he solemnly declared that he would obey the rules of the guild, promised before God that his work should be good, honest, genuine, the best of which he was capable, paid the prescribed fees, and, without more ado, was enrolled in the books of the guild as an effective member. But though he was now called a free master, had the right to set up for himself, to vote at the annual election of the chiefs of the guild, and was himself eligible for office, he was still submitted to the control of his association: the Dean and Juries could search his workshop when they would, and without warning, at any hour of the day or night, and if they discovered there any painting materials of inferior quality they had the right not only to seize and confiscate them, but to inflict on their owner some penalty commensurate with

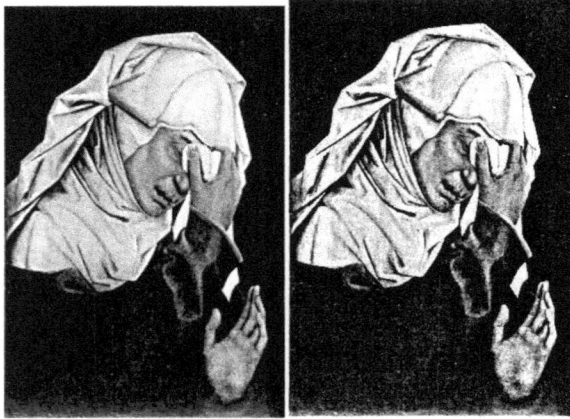

TÊTE DE FEMME EN PLEURS, ATTRIBUTED TO ROGER VAN
DER WEYDEN, BRUSSELS GALLERY.

the offence; and if any dispute arose between a painter and his patron, the matter was brought before the Dean and Juries of the guild, and the city magistrates were bound to enforce their decision.

The art associations of the Low Countries were most powerful during the latter half of the fourteen hundreds, precisely the period when Flemish art attained the zenith of its magnificence. They were united to one another by ties of the closest friendship: members of one guild never had any difficulty in obtaining admission to another, and some painters seem to have belonged to several guilds at the same time. From the middle of the fourteen hundreds onwards, delegates from all the painters' guilds in the Netherlands were wont to meet together every three years in some town or other, where they spent several days discussing topics of common interest, comparing notes, and communicating to one another any new professional discoveries that had been made: hence the remarkable uniformity in the technique of all the Flemish pictures of the period which have come down to us. Such were the institutions which produced some of the greatest painters whom the world has ever seen. They never considered themselves, and were never considered, superior to other craftsmen, but in those days, be it borne in mind, every craftsman was an artist.

ROGER VAN DER WEYDEN

Roger van der Weyden was born at Tournai in the year 1400; he was apprenticed to the Tournai painter, Robert Campin, on the 5th of March 1426, and admitted a free master of the Guild of Saint Luke in that city on the 1st of August 1432.

The above facts are established by local contemporary documents, which are undoubtedly genuine, but though the archives of Tournai have been searched through and through, with a view to finding a possible ancestor for Roger van der Weyden, only this much has as yet been discovered concerning his parentage—that his father's Christian name was *Henry* (*sic*), and that he died before the year 1435. We learn, however, from some entries in the town accounts of Louvain that one *Henrich van der Wyden* was living in that city in 1424, and that he was a sculptor by trade. Was this man Roger's father?

It is not absolutely certain, but there is good reason to believe that before he was a painter Roger himself handled the chisel. This is in itself significant; and though it seems at first sight improbable that a citizen of Louvain should have been the father of a son born at Tournai, when we remember that citizen's calling, and that the sculptors of Tournai were in those days famous throughout Europe, the difficulty disappears. Henrich, we may be very sure, would have made frequent visits to Tournai on account of his professional pursuits; nor is it in the least unlikely that upon one of these occasions he should have been accompanied by his wife, or that during the sojourn there she should have given birth to a son.

Be these things as they may, we know that the great Brussels painter was sometimes called Roger van der Weyden, and sometimes Rogier de la Pasture, and this is in itself prima facie evidence that his family was of Flemish origin. The translation of Flemish names into French or Latin was common enough in the Middle Age, the inverse exceedingly rare.

Roger was married before 1435 to Ysabel Goffart, a lady of Brussels, and it was perhaps on her account that he left his native town: we know that he and his wife were settled in Brussels in 1435. He seems

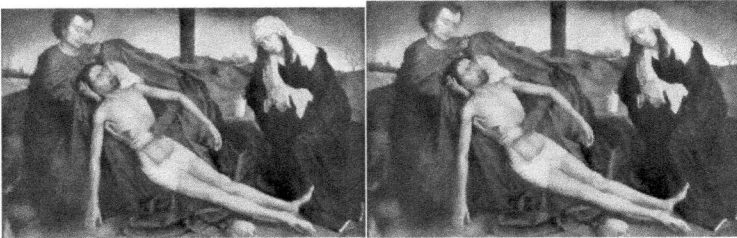

'PIETA' ATTRIBUTED TO ROGER VAN DER WEYDEN,
BRUSSELS GALLERY.

to have rapidly made a reputation, for the following year he was named by the city fathers *Portraiteur de la Ville*. Soon he was busy illuminating the sculptured tomb which Philippe l'Asseuré had erected in memory of Duchess Jeanne in the Carmelite Church, and painting those four panel pictures for the Justice Chamber of the Town Hall, which created so great a sensation, says Albert Dürer, that the whole world came to see them, and which, alas, have long since disappeared.

We know very little of Roger's life between 1436 and 1450, but it is certain that during this time he worked not only for the town of Brussels, but also for various convents and corporations, and for private individuals as well. In 1443 he was commissioned by Willem Edelheere and his wife, Adelaïde Cappuyns, to decorate their oratory in the Church of Saint Peter at Louvain; and the triptych—a 'Descent from the Cross,' with portraits of Edelheere and his wife and their patron saints—which still adorns this chapel, is said to be Roger's work. Indeed, according to M. van Even, the archivist of Louvain, we have here the only painting in Belgium which is certainly Roger's work. Its authenticity, however, is disputed, and it has been much spoiled by restoration.

One at least of Van der Weyden's pictures of this period has come down to us—the 'Descent from the Cross' which he painted in 1440 for the Louvain Confraternity of the *Grand Serment*, and which is now at Madrid. The 'Weeping Woman' (No. 56) of the Brussels Gallery is an ancient copy, or perhaps a study by the master himself, of one of the heads in this picture. The next thing we know of Roger van der Weyden is that in 1450 he made a pilgrimage to Rome for the Jubilee of that year, and we know, too, something of the incidents of this journey. He sojourned, amongst other places, at Ferrara and at Florence, and wherever he went he was welcomed and fêted not only by the members of his own craft, but also by the Sovereigns of the cities he visited. At Ferrara he must have worked for Lionel d'Este, for on his return we find him receiving from that prince 20 golden ducats in part payment for certe depicture executed in his palace there; and at Florence he painted a triptych for Cosmo Medici—the 'Madonna and Child, surrounded by Saints,' now in the Städel Museum at Frankfort.

In each of these cities, then, he must have remained a considerable time. He does not seem to have practised his art in Rome. Perhaps his stay there was a short one, and that his time was fully occupied by sightseeing and devotion. That he fully appreciated the art treasures of the Eternal City there can be no doubt, and we know that he was enraptured with the Lateran pictures of Gentile da Fabriano, whom he pronounced to be the first painter in Italy.

On his return to Brussels, Roger van der Weyden set to work with renewed vigour. We still possess three of the pictures which he painted after his journey to Italy:—the 'Nativity' triptych, with the portrait of Peter Bladelin, now in the Museum at Berlin; the 'Last Judgment,' which Chancellor Rolin ordered for the Hôtel Dieu at Baune (the authenticity of this picture is disputed); and the 'Adoration of the Magi,' in the Pinakothek at Munich. The last two especially show how profoundly the great Brussels painter was influenced by his pilgrimage to Rome: the composition of the Baune picture is almost the same as that of Andrea Orcagna's 'Last Judgment,' and the main outlines of the Munich picture distinctly recall the 'Adoration' of Gentile da Fabriano.

Of the numerous paintings attributed to Roger van der Weyden, probably not more than five or six are of incontestable authenticity. He certainly painted the 'Descent from the Cross' at Madrid, the 'Nativity' at Berlin, the Medici triptych at Frankfort, and the 'Adoration of the Magi' at Munich. These pictures are universally acknowledged to be his work. Of the rest, most are attributed to him merely on account of the similarity of style to the style of the work which is known to be his, and are without signature or other designation.

There is very little doubt, however, that several of these are genuine Van der Weydens—the 'Seven Sacraments' at Antwerp, for example, and the 'Pièta' of the Brussels Gallery; but at the same time, when pictures are unsigned and there is no documentary evidence as to their authorship, it is well-nigh impossible to arrive at absolute certainty. Sometimes a pupil is able to so exactly acquire his master's manner that the greatest experts are thereby deceived. It was so in the case of the famous Sforza picture, formerly in the Zambeccari Collection at Bologna, and now in the Brussels Gallery (No. 31). This beautiful picture—a 'Calvary,' with portraits of Francesco Sforza, his wife Bianca Visconti and their young son Galeazzo— was attributed by some experts to Memling, and it was thus ascribed in the official catalogue of the Brussels Gallery. There were others, no less competent, who were convinced that it was Roger's work; it dated, no doubt, they said, from the time of his sojourn in Italy. Mr. Weale, however, was quite sure that neither of these artists had painted it, and, thanks to his recent research, we now know the true story of the picture. The critics who said that it was in Van der Weyden's style were quite right, but it was not painted by the master himself, but by his pupil, Zanetto Bugatto, of Milan. The Duchess of Milan, it seems, had seen some of Roger's pictures, and was so charmed by them that she requested him to paint her portrait. He, for some reason or other, being unable at the time to leave home, was compelled to decline the commission, and the Duchess sent the young Milanese painter, Zanetto Bugatto, to Brussels in order that he might study with Roger, and thus acquire his style. This was in the year 1460. Bugatto remained in Brussels three years, and on his return to his native town he painted the picture in question.

There is a tradition, which does not seem to be well founded, that Roger van der Weyden was at one time the pupil of John van Eyck. If this were so, he was certainly not much influenced by his master's manner of painting. John delighted in serene immobility, Roger in tragic action. His tall, wan, emaciated figures always live and feel; and though he could, when he would, depict tranquillity, and his portraits are as calm and collected as any of those which were painted by John van Eyck, unlike Van Eyck's, they are almost always ascetic-looking, and very often sad. He seems to have been unable to appreciate the beauty of health and gladness.

Guicciardini says that Memling was Roger's pupil, but there is no documentary evidence to show that such was the case. We know next to nothing of the first days of the great Bruges painter, but his earlier pictures distinctly recall the pictures of Van der Weyden; and if he were not his pupil, he must have certainly studied his work.

Roger van der Weyden died at Brussels on the 18th of June 1464. He left several children. One of them, Peter, followed his father's calling; another, Corneille, after having made his studies at the University of Louvain, became a monk in the Carthusian Priory which the burghers of Brussels had recently founded at Scheut, by Anderlecht.

'THE MARTYRDOM OF SAINT ERASMUS' BY DIERICK BOUDTS, AT SAINT PETER'S, LOUVAIN.

DIERICK BOUDTS

Dierick Boudts was born a few years later than Van der Weyden; the exact date of his birth is unknown, but it cannot have been much before 1420. He was a native of Haarlem, where at this time there was a flourishing school of painters noted for their beautiful landscape backgrounds, and for the care with which they executed their drapery. His father, who was also named Dierick, was one of them, and it was doubtless in his workshop that young Dierick Boudts received his artistic education.

For some reason or other, about the year 1445, he migrated to Louvain, where he soon found a wife in the person of Catherine van der Bruggen, the daughter of a well-to-do burgher family, who presently gave him three girls, who became nuns; two boys, Dierick and Albert, who followed their father's calling, and a large house in the Rue des Récollets—site now occupied by the Jesuit Church—which she inherited at the death of her parents (December 17, 1460). Here Dierick and his family took up their abode, and here it was that he painted his four most famous pictures—'The Last Supper' and 'The Martyrdom of Saint Erasmus' at Saint Peter's, Louvain, and 'The Iniquitous Sentence of Otho' and 'Otho repairing his Injustice' in the Brussels Gallery.

Dierick was commissioned to paint the first two in 1464 by the rich confraternity of the Blessed Sacrament of Louvain, for Saint Peter's, where the brethren of the confraternity had two altars; the pictures were finished in 1468, and the quittance which the artist gave for the money he received for them is still in existence; and note, he signs his name not Dirk nor Thiery, as modern writers often style him, but Dierick Boudts. The Saint Erasmus altar-piece is a triptych; the central panel shows the martyrdom scene, the Gospel wing Saint Jerome and the Epistle wing an abbot, perhaps Saint Bernard. All three panels are still at Saint Peter's. The other altar-piece also had originally wings; on these were painted the First Celebration of the Passover, Elijah fed by Ravens, the Meeting of Abraham and Melchisedek, and the Israelites gathering Manna: the first two are now in the Berlin Gallery, and the others in the Pinakothek at Munich. The subject of the central panel is the Last Supper, and it still adorns the church for which it was painted.

The execution of these important works made Dierick's name famous. Hardly were they completed when the city fathers bestowed on him the honorary title of Portraiteur de la Ville, and commissioned him to paint for the Town Hall a triptych representing the Last Judgment, and four great panel paintings to be hung in the Justice Chamber, for the whole of which they agreed to pay him 500 florins. The triptych was finished in 1472; it has unhappily disappeared. Two years previously he had set to work on the first of the four panels, and shortly afterwards he received a visit from the city magistrates, who were so pleased with what he had done that they made him a present of wine of the value of 96 placken. The next thing we know of Dierick Boudts is that he lost his wife in 1472 or thereabout, and that shortly afterwards he married Elizabeth van Voshem, who was the widow of a rich butcher, and, as we have already seen, the sister-in-law of the glass painter Rombold Kelderman. By this lady he had no offspring, his union with her was not a long one. In the early spring of 1475 he seems to have been in enfeebled health, for on the 18th of April he chose the place in which he wished to be buried—beside his first wife, in the Church of the Récollets, and on the same day he made his will, which is still preserved.

He left to Elisabeth Voshen all his real property, all his outstanding debts, and all his completed pictures; to each of his three daughters a trifling monthly allowance; and to his two sons a silver cup—the only thing, he says, which he himself had inherited from *his* father—the implements of his craft, and all his unfinished pictures, and before the summer was out he had gone the way of all flesh. Only two of the Town Hall paintings were completed. Dierick, indeed, had not had time even to begin the others, and presently the question arose, how much of the 500 florins was due to his executors? Whether there was any dispute about the matter we do not know, but it would seem that such was the case, for three years had elapsed before the account was settled, and at last the city fathers had had recourse to expert advice. We learn from the town accounts of 1478 that the sum of 376 florins 36 placken was in that year paid to Dierick's sons, and that this amount was the value of the pictures as estimated by 'the most notable painter in this land—to wit, he who was born in the city of Ghent, and now resideth in the *Rooden Clooster, in Zuenien*'—without doubt Hugo van der Goes, who had donned the cowl at Rouge Cloître two years before; and we learn, too, from the same source, that this man, during his sojourn in Louvain, lodged at the sign of The Angel, and that the city magistrates offered him a pot of Rhine wine.

The pictures in question were duly hung in the Justice Chamber, and they remained there till 1827, when they were sold to the King of the Netherlands for 10,000 florins. In 1861 they were repurchased by the Belgian Government for 28,000 francs, and placed in the Brussels Gallery, where they still remain (Nos. 3C and 3D).

These two pictures and the pictures above men tioned of Saint Peter's, of Munich, of Berlin, are, of all the works attributed to Dierick Boudts, the only ones whose authenticity is incontestable. Some of the rest are most probably genuine, more, perhaps, than in the case of pictures attributed to Van der Weyden, for Boudts had a peculiar style of his own, which is more distinctive than Roger's.

Several of the pictures formerly attributed to Dierick Boudts are now generally believed to be the work of his son Albert, notably the 'Last Supper,' in the Brussels Gallery (No. 3F). As for Dierick Boudts the younger, no picture painted by him has as yet been identified. His name appears again and again in the town accounts of his native city in connection with fines for brawling, he was born in 1448, and died before 1491, and this is all that we know of him.

HUGO VAN DER GOES

Hugo van der Goes was probably a native of Ghent, and if, as Van Mander says, he was a pupil of John van Eyck, who died in 1441, he must have been born somewhere about the year 1420. Be this as it may, his work bears witness that he was more deeply impressed by the great Bruges master than any other of the Flemish primitives. He was certainly at Ghent in 1465, and henceforth this town was his home until 1476, when, following the example of his brother, the only one of his kinsmen of whom we have any knowledge, he became a monk of Rouge-Cloître, near Brussels.

Why this sudden flight from the world? Grief, suggests Alphonse Wauters,[40] at the loss of a wife. It is a mere conjecture; we do not even know for certain that Hugo was ever married. Van Mander tells how, when he was still a vry gheselle—that is, a bachelor—hence, notes Wauters, it follows that he presently ceased to be such—he painted on a wall, over a chimney-piece in her father's house at Ghent, the portrait of the woman he loved, in the guise of Abigail coming forth to meet David.

'N'y a-t-il pas là un doux souvenir d'un triomphe remporté par l'amour et couronné par l'hymen? L'allégorie me semble évident.' Thus Wauters; and he continues: 'Après avoir aimé avec ardeur et avoir obtenu la main de sa maîtresse, il aura été frappé au cœur par la mort de sa compagne et se sera réfugié dans la solitude pour y vivre de souvenirs et de regrets.' The story as it stands is a pretty one, but one cannot help remembering that David's Abigail was a rich and perhaps an elderly widow, and that immediately after his marriage with her he took a second wife. Moreover, the assumption that Hugo married the lady whose portrait he painted is a wholly gratuitous one; Van Mander does not even as much as hint that such was the case.

But if we have no certain information as to the motives which inspired the great Ghent painter to don the cowl, we have an authentic and detailed account of his life in the cloister, and of the terrible misfortune which there embittered his last days. It was written by a monk of Rouge-Cloître who knew Hugo well, and the manuscript was discovered some fifty years ago by Alphonse Wauters himself. It is a very curious document; and note, the writer makes no mention of Hugo ever having been a married man. And if this had been so, from the nature of his narrative he would have been almost certain to have said something about it.

'In the year of Our Lord 1482 died Brother Hugo, a lay brother professed in this monastery. He was so famous a painter that on this side the mountains, in those days, his like was not to be found. He, and I who write these things, were novices together. At the time of his clothing and during his novitiate, Father Thomas, our prior, allowed him many mundane consolations of a nature to incline him rather to the pomps of this world than to the way of humility and penance; and this was by no means pleasing to some, who said that novices should not be exalted, but, on the contrary, put down. And because he was so excellent a painter, great folk were wont to visit him, and even the most illustrious Archduke Maximilian himself; for they ardently desired to behold his pictures, and Father Thomas allowed him to receive them in the Guest Chamber, and to feast with them there. Some five or six years after his profession it so happened that Brother Hugo made a journey to Cologne along with his brother, Brother Nicholas, an oblate here, and Brother Peter, canon-regular of Trone, then residing in the Jéricho[41] at Brussels, and several others. One night, on the way home, as I learned at the time from Brother Nicholas, our Brother Hugo was seized by a strange mental derangement, which caused him to cry out continually that he was damned and condemned to eternal perdition; and he would fain have laid violent hands on himself, and would certainly have done so had he not been, but with difficulty, restrained by the aid of some who were standing by. And thus the last stage of that journey was not a cheerful one. 'Albeit, having obtained assistance, they presently reached Brussels, and forthwith summoned Father Thomas, who, when he had seen Brother Hugo and had heard all that had taken place, suspected that his malady was similar to that which vexed King Saul, and, calling to mind how that monarch had been soothed by David's harping, he caused not a little music to be played in the presence of our brother, and strove also to divert him by various spectacular performances; but in vain: he kept on crying out that he was a son of perdition, and in this sorry plight they brought him to Rouge Cloître. The kindness and attention with which the choir brethren watched over him by night and by day, anticipating all his wants and always striving to console him, these things God will never forget. But false reports were spread abroad, and by great folk too, that such was not the case.

'As to the nature of the malady with which Brother Hugo was afflicted, opinion was divided. Some said he was mad, others that he was possessed (he had symptoms of each of these troubles), but throughout his illness he never attempted to injure anyone but himself; and this is not the wont of lunatics nor of men possessed by devils, and therefore what it was, I believe, God only knows.

'Now the trouble of our monk painter (*pictoris conversi*) may be regarded from two points of view. Let us say, in the first place, that it was natural—a peculiar form of mania; for there are various kinds of madness produced by various causes—improper food, strong drink, worry, grief, fear, too great an application to books, and, in fine, a natural predisposition to the same. So far as concerns emotions, I know for a certain fact that Brother Hugo was greatly troubled as to how he should finish his pictures, for he had so many orders that it was currently said it would take him full nine years to execute them; and also he very often studied a certain Flemish book. As to wine, I fear he indulged too freely, doubtless on account of his friends.

These things may gradually have produced the malady with which he was afflicted. But, on the other hand, it may have been brought about by the kind providence of God, who desires that no man should perish, but that all should be brought to repentance.

'Now Brother Hugo, on account of his art, had been greatly exalted in our order, and, of a truth, he had become more famous than if he had remained in the world, and, because he was a man like the rest of us, perchance his heart was puffed up on account of the honours bestowed on him, and the divers visits and the homage which he had received; and that God, in order to save his soul, sent him this humiliating infirmity, by which, of a truth, he was greatly abased. He himself, understanding this when he had recovered his senses, humbled himself exceedingly: of his own free will he left our table and meekly took his meals with the other lay brethren.'

How long a time Hugo lived after he had recovered his reason his biographer does not say, nor does he tell us any of the details of his death or of his burial. After again enlarging on his skill in painting, and after some further notes on the origin of madness and a long theological disquisition, he simply says, '*Sepultus est in nostro atrio, sub divo.*' He was buried in our cloister, in the open air.

Though Brother Hugo had been in his lifetime so famous a painter, he was soon forgotten, and Van Mander, who wrote at the beginning of the sixteen hundreds, could not even say when or where he died.

Of his grave, which was probably removed or broken when the Church of Rouge-Cloître was rebuilt during the first half of the fifteen hundreds, no relic remains but the text of a doubtful epitaph—

PICTOR HUGO VAN DER GOES
humatus hic quiescit
Dolet ars, cum similem
sibi modo nescit.

Of all the works of Hugo van der Goes there is only one whose authenticity has as yet been established—

THE WINGS OF THE SAINT ANNE TRIPTYCH BY QUENTIN
METSYS, IN THE BRUSSELS GALLERY.
Shut.

a beautiful triptych which he painted before 1476 for Thomas Portinari, the agent of the Medici family in Bruges, and which Thomas afterwards presented to the Hospital of Santa-Maria-Nuova, at Florence, where it still remains. Amongst the pictures attributed to him with more or less probability, note in the Municipal Gallery of Bruges La Mort de la Sainte Vierge, which, in the opinion of Mr. Weale, is undoubtedly genuine; and in the Musée des Beaux-Arts at Brussels the Sainte Famille (No. 36), which may or may not be his.

QUENTIN METSYS

Quentin Metsys, the son of old Josse Metsys, the metal worker of Louvain, was born in that city in 1466. Like his elder brother, Josse II., whose acquaintance we have already made, he was a man of many parts. By trade, of course, he was a painter, but he by no means confined himself to this craft; he made designs for wrought iron, and carried them out too—witness the exquisite well cover by the great porch of Antwerp Cathedral. He was also an accomplished musician, busied himself with wood engraving, and dabbled, it is said, with some success in Flemish letters.

It was doubtless as his father's assistant that he learned how to forge iron; and there is a romantic story that before he became a painter he was himself a metal worker by profession, and only relinquished this calling for the sake of the woman he loved, whose father would never consent to her marriage with a smith—a most improbable tale, for in the days of Quentin's youth the craftsman who wielded the hammer was quite as good a man as the craftsman who handled the brush.

Molanus asserts that Quentin Metsys was a pupil of Roger van der Weyden—manifestly an error, for the latter died two years before Quentin was born. It is perfectly possible, however, that he was the pupil of Roger's son, Peter van der Weyden. However this may be, he must have completed his apprenticeship before 1491, for at this time he was already inscribed in the Guild of Saint Luke at Antwerp, and seems to have already made for himself a certain reputation, for when we first hear of him at Antwerp he was married and settled in a house of his own in the Rue des Tanneurs. None of his works, however, of this period have come down to us. The earliest of his authentic pictures which we possess—the 'Burial of Christ,' now in the Antwerp Gallery—was not painted till 1508, and the next—the 'Legend of Saint Anne,' now at Brussels (No. 38)—dates from the following year; it is signed on the third panel, 'Quinte Metsys schreef dit, 1509.' These two grand triptyches are undoubtedly his chefs-d'œuvre. The first was painted for the Carpenters' Company of Antwerp, the second for the Confraternity of Saint Anne at Louvain. They are remarkable, like all the earlier works of this painter, for the delicacy of their execution, their elaborate detail, their strange luminous tints. Though Quentin's palette was a rich and varied one, his pictures have not the same mellow glow as the pictures of several of his predecessors—of those of Dierick Boudts, for example; and if his figures are less stiff than theirs, they are also less spiritual. He stands, as it were, at the parting of the ways; his creations, indeed, reflect the sublime beauty of Hubert van Eyck, of Memling, of Roger van der Weyden, but at the same time, they seem to foreshadow the voluptuous splendour of Rubens and of Jacques Jordaens.

Quentin Metsys did not confine himself to sacred subjects. He portrayed also intimate scenes of civil life—merchants in their counting-houses, bankers, money-changers, and so forth. The most famous of

THE WINGS OF THE SAINT ANNE TRIPTYCH BY QUENTIN METSYS, IN THE BRUSSELS GALLERY.
Open.

these works is in the Louvre; it was painted in 1519. In this kind of painting, however, he had many imitators, and most of the tableaux de genre attributed to him are not his. He also excelled in portraiture. One of his best patrons for works of this kind was Peter Œgidius, whose likeness he painted several times. One of these Peter presented to Sir Thomas More, along with a likeness of their friend Erasmus, also Quentin's work, and More acknowledged the gift in a set of Latin verses. 'If future ages,' he said 'retain the least taste for the fine arts, if hateful Mars does not triumph over Minerva, what will not be the price of these pictures in days to come.' They are possibly still in existence. The portraits of Erasmus and Œgidius in the Longford Gallery, near Salisbury, formerly attributed to Holbein, are now generally ascribed to Quentin Metsys, and the portrait of Erasmus at Hampton Court, and that of Œgidius at Antwerp, are now also commonly believed to be his work. 'Si ce ne sont pas les originaux,' notes M. A.-J. Wauters, 'ce sont deux excellentes copies du temps.'[42]

Quentin Metsys was twice married, and he was the father of thirteen children, of whom at least two, John and Corneille, followed his calling, and are represented in the Brussels Gallery. He seems to have been socially inclined, and as he earned a considerable income, and his second wife was rich, notwithstanding his large family he was able to entertain his friends, amongst them Œgidius, Erasmus, More, Albert Dürer, Holbein, Luke Leyden. He was still a comparatively young man when he died at his own house at Antwerp in 1530. They laid him to rest in the cathedral, hard by the great porch, and a hundred years after his death the city erected a sumptuous monument to his memory, which has long since disappeared. He was the last of the Flemish masters who to the end remained faithful to the traditions of the old national school.

BERNARD VAN ORLEY

Everard, Lord of Orley, was a knight of Luxembourg, attached to the Court of Duke John IV. of Brabant, or maybe in the service of his brother, Count Philip of Saint-Pol. Like most of his race and class, his pedigree was in all probability much longer than his purse; at all events, he did not think it beneath him to marry middle-class money. Mistress Barbara, the lady of his choice, was a member of an illustrious burgher family famous in the annals of Brussels: she was the near kinswoman, perhaps the daughter, of Alderman Jan Taye, whose acquaintance we have already made, and she gave her hand to the Lord of Orley somewhere about the year 1425. The issue of this marriage was a son, whom his parents christened Jan, and who, when he had reached man's estate, was enrolled in the lignage called Sleuws—that is, of the Lion—the same lignage, it will be remembered, to which Everard T'Serclaes belonged. In due course he married, and with his mother's wealth and privileges, and his father's name and title, doubtless he was held in high esteem by a large circle of friends; but the lasting fame of the house of Van Orley was built on another foundation: it was the result of Jan's intimacy with a lady, name unknown, who was not his wife, and who in the year 1468 presented him with a son—Valentine van Orley, the father of Bernard van Orley, and the first of a long line of painters who throughout no less than six generations practised their art in Brussels. The last of them was John van Orley, who died in 1735.

The register of the Brussels Guild of Saint Luke has disappeared, and thus it is impossible to say who

THE CENTRAL PANEL OF THE SAINT ANNE TRIPTYCH BY QUENTIN METSYS, IN THE BRUSSELS GALLERY.

was Valentine's master. He probably made a reputation early, for when he was only twenty-two years of age he took to himself a wife, one Marguerite van Pynbroeck. The wedding was celebrated at Saint Gudila's on the 13th of May 1490. In 1512 he seems to have received an important order from Antwerp, for in that year he left Brussels for the city on the Scheldt, and was admitted a free master of the local Guild of Saint Luke; and as he received several apprentices during his sojourn there, he must have remained in Antwerp some years. We find him again in Brussels in 1527, and this is all that is at present known of Valentine van Orley, save that he had several sons who were painters, and several daughters whose husbands followed the same calling.

If any of Valentine's pictures have come down to us, they have not as yet been identified. He must have painted a considerable number in the course of his career, and it is not likely that they have all perished. In the churches and convents of Belgium and in the various public and private collections throughout Europe there are a host of Flemish 'primitives' catalogued inconnu. It may well be that amongst them are some of Valentine's works;

and note, not a few of these anonymous paintings are quite as beautiful as some of the authentic pictures of the greatest masters of the period. Take, for example, in the Brussels Gallery, the strangely pathetic and gloriously coloured Passion scenes of the triptych of Oultremont (No. 537); or the 'Martyrdom of Saint Sebastian' (No. 3E), attributed to Memling and to Dierick Boudts; or the 'Adoration of the Magi' (No. 20), which John van Eyck, Peter Christus and Gerard David are all said to have painted; or the Saint Gudila triptych, *Le Christ pleuré par les saintes femmes* (No. 40), which some very eminent critics ascribe to Bernard van Orley, and in which others equally eminent find no trace of his style; or the 'Virgin and Child' (No. 21), successively given to Hubert van Eyck, Peter Christus, and Quentin Metsys. In a former edition of his catalogue, Monsieur A. J. Wauters wrote against this picture, '*Magnifique ouvrage de l' École de Bruges.*' He would have been on surer ground had he been content with the first two words of this sentence. It is certainly a magnifique ouvrage, and no more and no less can be aptly said of any of the above-mentioned pictures.

But to return to the house of Van Orley. The greatest painter which that house produced—the giant who made pigmies of the rest, was Valentine's second son, Bernard, who, as his parents were only married in the spring of 1490, cannot have been born much before 1493. Of his life before 1515 nothing is certainly known. At this time he was settled in Brussels, and had already made a name, for in 1515 he painted a triptych for the oratory of the Holy Cross in the Church of Saint Walburge at Furnes, for which he received 104 livres parisis (the central panel of this altar-piece is now at Turin); and in 1515 or 1516 he painted the portraits of the children of Duke Philippe le Beau, and also the portrait of his son-in-law, Christian II. of Denmark. These pictures have not come down to us, or at least they have not been identified; but, doubtless, they were all that could be desired, for shortly after their completion Marguerite of Austria, whom Charles Quint on the eve of his departure for Spain had named Regent of the Netherlands, appointed Orley Court painter; and if they were anything like the portrait which he painted two years later of Georges Zelle—now in the Brussels Gallery (No. 42)—they must have been singularly beautiful. This picture is signed and dated 1519.

Orley was now married and living with his wife, Agnes Zeghers, in a house on the Senne, hard by the old Church of Saint Géry; and Zelle, who was town physician and chief medical attendant to the Hospital of Saint John—an institution which was founded in the twelve hundreds, and which still exists—was his friend and near neighbour. Here there is an unsigned picture, dated August 11, 1520—subject, the 'Death of Our Lady'—which, tradition says, is Van Orley's work. The same year that he painted the portrait of Georges Zelle, Orley was commissioned by the Aumoniers of

Antwerp to paint an altar-piece for their chapel in the cathedral there, for which they agreed to pay him 600 florins. This picture is now in the Antwerp Gallery (No. 741 to No. 745)—subject, the 'Resurrection and the Seven Works of Mercy.' It is not signed.

Van Orley was now making a very considerable income, kept good company, and was able to give good dinners. Albert Dürer, who spent a week at Brussels in the summer of 1520, partook of one of them, and thus writes of it in his journal: 'It was such a magnificent spread that I doubt if Master Bernard was quit of it for ten florins. Several great folk were present, whom Bernard had invited to bear me company; amongst others, the Treasurer of Madame Marguerite (Jean de Marnix, Lord of Toulouse), whose portrait I painted, the Town Treasurer (Alderman Jan Busleyden), and the Grand Master of the Palace.'

It was no doubt owing in great measure to 'Madame Marguerite's' patronage that 'Master Bernard' was able to show such lavish hospitality to his friends, for though his official gages—as Bernard himself informs us— was only *un patart par jour qu'est bien petite chose*, sundry valuable privileges were attached to the office of Court painter, and the accounts of Treasurer Marnix bear witness that Madame was constantly giving him orders for pictures for which he was always handsomely paid. Though Marnix describes most of them, hardly any of these paintings have as yet been identified. There can be no doubt, however, that one of them at least has come down to us—'un grand tableau exquis sur la vertu de patience,' which Marguerite commissioned Bernard to paint for her favourite minister, Count Antoine de Lalaing. This great triptych is now in the Brussels Gallery (No. 41); it is described in the official catalogue as La Patience et les Epreuves de Job, and its authenticity is beyond question. It is signed in Latin: 'Bernardus—Dorley—Bruxellanus—Faciebat: A° Dni MCCCCCXXI IIII^a May,' and in Flemish—'ELX SYNE TYT. Orley 1521,' and monogramed with the initials B.V.O. in two places.

This was not the only commission which Bernard executed for his august mistress in 1521: various sums are entered in the treasury accounts for that year as having been paid to him for various pictures, which are there described at length; and then follows this curious item—'Et dix (pièces d'or) des quels ma dicte dame a fait don à mon dit Maître Bernard, outre et par dessus les dits achats d'icelles peintures et marché fait avec luy et ce, en faveur d'aucuns services qu'il a faits à icelle dame, dont elle ne veut pas qu'il soit fait ici mention.' What was the mysterious business of which no mention was to be made?

Maître Bernard had evidently succeeded in winning Madame's confidence, but six years later he thought it worth while to run a serious risk of losing it.

He was imprudent enough to give hospitality to a certain Lutheran preacher, who had been introduced to him by the King of Denmark, and to suffer this divine to hold forth in his house upon no less than four occasions. Protestantism was at this time making headway in the Netherlands, the Regent was straining every nerve to stem the rising tide of heresy, and the most stringent penalties had been decreed not only against the professors of the new teaching, but against all those who should aid or abet them. It is not surprising, then, that presently the poor Court painter found himself in the clutches of Master Nicholas à Montibus, the inquisitor at Louvain. The situation was an alarming one, and doubtless Bernard thanked his stars when the inquisitor pronounced sentence; he was ordered to aller faire amende honorable à Sainte Gudule, and to pay a fine of 200 florins. He did not even lose his situation. When his old friend died two years afterwards, her successor Marie of Hungary retained him in her service, and on the 12th of January 1534, she commissioned him to paint *un beau exquis et puissant tableau de bois de Danemarck pour service sur le grand autel de l' église du couvent de Brou en Bresse*, the church which Marguerite of Austria had built in memory of her husband, Philibert of Savoy, and where her bones lie buried. This picture has come down to us; we know its history, and it is a curious one.

Amongst Marguerite's numerous bequests to the Church of Brou were some beautiful paintings by Bernard van Orley, which Marie was exceedingly loath to part with, and she therefore arranged with her aunt's executors to keep them, and to present to the Church of Brou, by way of compensation, a triptych for the high altar, hence the commission to the Court painter of January 12, 1534; but the beau exquis et puissant tableau, which was the outcome of this arrangement, was not destined to adorn the altar for which it had been ordered. Though Bernard had worked at it eight years, when he died, on the 21st of January 1542, it was still unfinished, and eight years later the canons of Notre-Dame, at Bruges, who were at this time preparing their church for the reception of the relics of Charles the Bold, purchased it from Van Orley's heirs for 286 livres tournois. The three great panels of bois de Danemarck were conveyed to Bruges in as many wagons, and set up behind the high altar in the old Collegiate Church of Notre-Dame, where they still remain, but how much or how little of Van Orley's work is displayed on them is another question: the triptych was completed by the Bruges painter, Marc Geerhaerds, in 1561, and about thirty years later the central panel was entirely repainted and the wings retouched by François Pourbus. This picture has been removed from its original position, and now hangs on the west wall of the south aisle—subject, scenes from the Passion.

Of Bernard van Orley's signed paintings only four have come down to us:—the Job triptych and the Zelle portrait at Brussels, the Holy Family at Stockholm, signed B. v. Orley, but not dated, and an altar-piece at Vienna, showing the death of Saint Thomas and the election of Saint Mathias, and signed Bernardus van Orley, but not dated. This picture is the central panel of a triptych which was formerly in the Church of Notre-Dame du Sablon; the wings are now in the Brussels Gallery (No. 44A). Open, they represent the Incredulity of Saint Thomas and the Martyrdom of Saint Mathias, and shut, the same saints in grisaille, and six kneeling figures, doubtless the donors. From the fact that four small carpenter's tools are painted on the back of each of the shutters, it is likely enough that this triptych was ordered by or for the Carpenters' Guild—a wealthy corporation intimately connected with the Sablon Church. We know nothing of its history.

The portrait of Georges Zelle is without question Van Orley's masterpiece. In colour, composition, technique, this picture is quite perfect. It was his last effort in the old style, and it gives him the right to an honourable place in the ranks of the great masters of the old national school.

Bernard van Orley died on the 21st of January 1542; he was buried in the Church of Saint Géry, and though his tomb disappeared when the church was destroyed, a drawing of it has come down to us. It was emblazoned with the arms of the lords of Orley, without a bend sinister.

From S. Rombold's Malines.

CHAPTER XVIII
Conclusion

The constitution of 1421 continued to be the legal constitution of the city of Brussels until the old order of things was swept away at the close of the seventeen hundreds, save only for a short period—not quite four years—during the reign of Marie of Burgundy. The defeat and death of that stalwart hero, whom men in his lifetime had called the Bold, and afterwards the Rash, was a source of great consolation to all his subjects, for Charles had dreamed dreams of empire, and the people had had to pay for his vain attempts to realise them. The daughter who inherited his throne and his misfortunes was but eighteen years of age, and, with a shattered army and an empty purse, she was wholly dependent on their goodwill.

The times, then, were propitious for asking favours; every commune in the Netherlands was obtaining fresh privileges; and when Marie visited Brussels in the June of 1477 she did not refuse to legalise the result of a successful riot of the year before. But though plebeians could now sit in the College of Aldermen, and the people could now take part in municipal elections, it is worthy of note that the new magistrates were almost all of them members of the old ruling class. Further changes were made in 1480 (this time of a reactionary character), and in the following year the old constitution was once more re-established.

V.—Genealogical Table of the Dukes of Brabant from Philip II. to Philip III.

Philip II. (Philippe l'Asseuré), = Isabel of Portugal

d. 1467 | (3rd wife)

(1) Catherine, daughter = **Charles I.**   = (2) Isabel of
of Charles VII. of   (le Téméraire), | Bourbon
France   d. 1477 | = (3) Margaret of
                 | York (sister
                 | of Edward IV.
                 | of England),

```
                    |      d. 1503
                    
                    |
                    
                    |
                    
Maximilian of Hapsbourg,  =  Marie,
Emperor from 1493,          |  d. 1482
d. 1519                     |
                            
                            |
                            
                            |
                            
                            |
                            
    +----------------------+-+
    |                      |
 **Philip III.**       Marguerite, = Philibert,
 (Philippe le Beau)    Regent of  | Duke of Savoy
                       the Low     | (2nd husband)
                       Country     |
                       from 1517,  |
                       d. 1529     |
                                   
                                   |
                                   
                                   |
                                   
                       Emmanuel Philibert,
                       Duke of Savoy,
                       Regent of the
                       Low Country from 1557
                       to 1559
```

The great struggle between the patricians and the craftsmen was never again to be renewed. The former, now that they had lost their monopoly, dissociated themselves more and more, as time went on, from trade and from municipal affairs, and, becoming more and more chary in admitting to their order outsiders from below, were little by little absorbed in the ranks of the territorial aristocracy. Before two generations had passed away their numbers had become so reduced that there were not twenty-one patricians in Brussels qualified to sit in the College of Aldermen, and under these circumstances Charles V. deprived them of their last political prerogative: in 1532 he decreed that henceforth any nobleman, whether he were a member of a *lignage* or not, should be an eligible candidate for the magistracy. The city was not indeed free from dissensions in the ages which followed, but the strife which divided the people was not the outcome of class hatred, but of differences of opinion in religious matters, and of the impolitic measures taken to restore religious unity by alien rulers, who had no sympathy with the customs and traditions of the Netherlands.

It happened thus: Duchess Marie, who in 1477 had married Maximilian of Hapsburg, son of the Emperor Frederick III., died two years later, leaving two children—Van Orley's friend Marguerite, whose acquaintance we have already made; and Philip, surnamed the Handsome, who, inheriting his mother's domains, ruled them from the time that he attained his majority in 1493 till his death in 1506. Philip had married Juana, the daughter and heiress of Isabel, Queen of Castile, and of Ferdinand, King of Aragon; and the eldest born of this union was the famous Charles Quint.

If old King Ferdinand and Cardinal Ximénez had been allowed to have their way, the Spanish succession would have been settled on Charles's younger brother, and Spain and the Netherlands would perhaps have been spared many years of misery. To this arrangement Charles, naturally enough, objected; and no sooner had he attained his majority than he despatched, 'par devers le roy d'Arragon, pour aucuns grans affaires secretz dont n'est besoin ici faire declaration'—thus it was given out—his tutor, Adrian Boyens. This remarkable man, it will be interesting to note, was the son of a brewer of Utrecht; in his early days he had been curate of the Grand Béguinage at Louvain—a portion of the house which he then occupied is still standing (No. 153 Rue des Moutons)—towards the close of his life he ascended the pontifical throne, under the title of Adrian VI., and at the time of which we are writing he held, along with other preferments, a canon's stall in the old Collegiate Church of Saint Guy at Anderlecht. The ex-curate of Louvain ought certainly not to have been a match for the experienced statesman and diplomatist who at this time held the destinies of Spain in his hands, but, somehow or other, he managed to convince him of the justice of his master's claim: presently, with the approval of his all-powerful minister, Ferdinand consented to acknowledge his eldest grandson as his heir; and when he died, two years afterwards, Charles ascended the throne.

Thus were Spain and the Netherlands united under one sceptre; and the inhabitants of the greater realm were the first to rue it; for Charles, who was a native of Ghent and had been brought up at Mechlin, had little liking for Spain, and took no pains to conceal his sentiments: he refused to speak the Spanish tongue, flouted the aged Cardinal Ximénez (a statesman of whom Spaniards were justly proud, and whom the people regarded as a saint), filled the land with foreign officials, levied illegal taxes, violated the most cherished constitutional rights—in a word, treated his southern domain almost like a conquered country; and when at last the Castilians rebelled, and after a bitter struggle were crushed, he deprived them of their time-honoured liberties.

AT MECHLIN

In the Netherlands the course of events was much the same, but the situation developed later, and only became acute during the reign of his son Philip. Karlekin, as the Flemings called their Sovereign, at all events was one of them; and though the Ghenters experienced his lash when they refused to pay his illegal imposts, and though his 'placards' against heresy were stamped with the cruel rigour of the penal code of the day, they only touched a small minority, and to the end of his reign he remained with the bulk of the people sufficiently popular. Upon the rare occasions when he visited Brussels he was welcomed with *fêtes* and enthusiasm.

Often away from home, he was fortunate in his choice of Regents— Marguerite of Austria, his aunt, and, when she died, his sister, Marie of Hungary. These ladies resided for the most part at Mechlin, in a beautiful Gothic palace, which had formerly been inhabited by Marguerite of York, the widow of Charles the Bold, and which is still standing; and the Court of each of them was rendered brilliant by the artists and scholars who frequented it. They were deservedly loved by their subjects, for they held the reins of government with a gentle hand; and it was in large measure owing to their prudence that when Charles put off his crown, the seventeen provinces of the Netherlands were among the most prosperous in Europe.

When on the 25th of October 1555, leaning on the shoulder of that Prince who was so soon to become the mortal enemy of his race, the Emperor, not old in years but worn out by disease and the weight of a realm on which, as he used to say, the sun never set, bade farewell to the men of Brussels in the great hall of the Coudenberg—we have it on the testimony of an eye-witness—all those who heard him wept. Well might the people weep, if they had only known: they were assisting at the opening scene of a tragedy which lasted a hundred years.

The new Sovereign had been born and bred in Castile, and despite his Flemish ancestry and his Flemish face he was a true Castilian. Of course he knew nothing

BY THE DYLE AT MECHLIN.

of Flemish, and he either could not or would not speak French: he was as much a foreigner in the Low Countries as his father had been in Spain. Like him, he had the instincts and the inclinations of a despot; but whereas Charles delighted to mix with his fellow-men and, when he would, could win their affection, Philip was cold, grave, aloof, and kept even the highest of his Court nobles at arm's length; nor were the Netherlanders sorry when, four years after his inauguration, he bade them farewell. But if they imagined that their Sovereign's fingers were not long enough to reach them from Madrid, in this they were mistaken, as presently they learned to their cost, for it was no vain boast when Philip said that 'everywhere in the vast compass of his dominions he was an absolute King.'

The native aristocracy was indeed represented in the Council of State, but there were foreign councillors as well, and one of them, Cardinal Granvelle, had Philip's ear. It was he who governed the Regent—Marguerite of Parma, a natural daughter of Charles V.—and to all intents and purposes the country was ruled from Madrid. Hence not a little heartburning.

Meanwhile the new doctrine was rapidly making headway. The number of Protestants amongst the working population of the great cities must at this time have been considerable; there were thousands in all classes halting between two opinions, and honest men all over the country, who had no sympathy with the tenets proscribed, were sickened and astounded at the cruel rigour with which Charles's 'placards' were being now enforced, and in the midst of it all, and in spite of the opposition of Granvelle himself, Philip took a step which he ought to have known would be certain to breed trouble: he obtained from Pope Paul IV. a Bull (1562) to increase the number of bishoprics from three to fifteen, and the measure was at once opposed by all sorts and conditions of men:—by the secular clergy, because they believed that the presence of so many bishops amongst them would lessen their prestige; by the monks, who knew they would be shorn of revenue for the endowment of the new Sees; by the nobles, who regarded the great abbeys as the appanage of their younger sons; by the people, who were firmly convinced that this step was only the prelude to further persecution; and opposition was increased tenfold when presently it became known that the proposed metropolitan See of Mechlin was to be confided to Cardinal Granvelle. Philip, however, refused to draw back; but, so threatening was the attitude of the nobles, that at last, at the request of the Regent herself, he consented to Granvelle's resignation (1564), though almost immediately afterwards he gave orders that the edicts against heresy should be enforced with increased rigour. Then, on the 15th of February 1565, came the famous *Compromis des nobles*, and a petition for the redress of grievances, which was presented to the Regent two months later by a deputation of four hundred gentlemen, many of whom were Catholics, with a request that she would transmit it to Philip, and which he in due course refused. '*Ne vous inquiétez pas ce ne sont que des gueux,*' the Lord of Berlaymont had whispered to Marguerite, dismayed at the long line of petitioners who solemnly filed before her in the great hall of the Coudenberg; and that night, at a banquet in the palace of the Lord of Culembourg, now the prison of the Petits Carmes, they made this term of reproach their *signe de ralliement*; they were 'gueux,' they said, 'et fidèles au roi jusqu'à la besace.' They proved it by scattering seditious pamphlets broadcast all over the country, and the following year—the *wonder jaar*, as it was afterwards called—the Calvinist mob began to purge the land of idols. In Flanders alone more than four hundred churches and religious houses were sacked, and what happened at Antwerp is significant—every statue in the cathedral was shattered, save that of the unrepentant thief.

The worst of the trouble was, however, over; order had been restored; Antwerp, where the Protestants were strongest, had opened its gates to the Regent; thanks to her firmness and moderation, the country was being rapidly pacified, and a very general reaction in favour of the government and of the old faith had already set in, when Philip, who, when he heard of the havoc wrought by the Protestants, had sworn by the soul of his father to make them pay for it, despatched to the Netherlands a Spanish army under the command of Alva.

The terrible Duke and his soldiers reached Brussels on the 22nd of August 1567, and sooner than have any share in the horrors she foresaw would ensue, Marguerite laid down her office.

The story of Alva's reign of terror is too well known to need recital here. Suffice it to say that the whole country was declared in a state of siege. In utter violation of those constitutional liberties which Philip had solemnly sworn to respect, he constituted that 'Council of Troubles,' which the people called the 'Council of Blood,' and whose mission it was to judge, or rather to condemn, all those whom the Duke deferred to it. Amongst the innocent victims were Lamoral d'Egmont, a member of Marguerite's Council, and Governor of Flanders and Artois, and his friend and kinsman, Martin de Hornes, Admiral of the Netherlands. They had been the leaders of the opposition against Granvelle, along with William of Nassau, but, unlike him, they were loyal to Philip and loyal to the old faith. Alva, however, thought otherwise, and they died the death of traitors, in the Grand' Place at Brussels, on the 5th of June 1568. It is said that the Spanish soldiers wept when they saw these men led forth to execution, and even Alva himself, though he believed them guilty, was loath to condemn them. 'Your Majesty will understand,' he wrote to Philip, 'the regret I feel at seeing these poor lords brought to such an end, and myself obliged to bring them to it, but I have not shrunk from doing what is for your Majesty's service.... The Countess Egmont's condition fills me with the greatest pity, burthened as she is with a family of eleven children, none old enough to take care of themselves; and she a lady of so distinguished a rank and of so virtuous, truly Catholic and exemplary life. There is no man in the country who does not grieve for her! I cannot but commend her to the good grace of your Majesty, beseeching you to call to mind that, if the Count, her husband, came to trouble at the close of his days, he formerly rendered great services to the State.' Philip granted the Countess d'Egmont an annual pension of 12,000 *livres*, which seems to have been not very regularly paid.

A few years ago a monumental fountain was erected in Brussels in memory of Egmont and Hornes; it stands in the Place du Petit Sablon, hard by the ancient palace, now the Hôtel des ducs d'Arenberg, where poor Lamoral dwelt, and which was originally built by his mother.

But it was not the fierceness of Alva's vengeance, but his oppressive and illegal fiscal measures, which roused the people to rebellion and threw Catholics and Protestants alike into the arms of William of Nassau. At last Philip's eyes were opened, but then it was too late. When he recalled the Duke of Alva in the autumn of 1573 the whole country was in revolt, and the northern provinces were lost for ever to Spain.

Later on, when the Catholic provinces of the South, disgusted at the bigotry and intolerance of William of Orange and his friends, had made terms with the Duke of Parma and returned to Philip's allegiance, and when by their aid the Dutch had been ousted from every town in Brabant and Flanders, save Ostend, and William himself had fallen, struck down

GUILD HALLS IN THE MARKET-PLACE OF BRUSSELS.

by the hand of an assassin, it seemed for a moment that the northern provinces too would soon be constrained to submit to Parma's victorious army; but as Philip had baulked his sister Marguerite, so now did he render of no avail the heroic efforts of her son. He was minded to conquer England. Parma's forces were suddenly withdrawn to second his vain endeavour, and the opportunity lost through the King's infatuation, never again returned (1584). The war dragged on intermittently for more than sixty years, and then at last, by the Treaty of Westphalia, Spain consented to acknowledge the independence of the Dutch Republic.

But to return to Brussels. During the troubled years of Philip's reign Brussels suffered less than most of the other great towns of the Spanish Netherlands; for though she experienced the kindness of Alva and afterwards had to endure the tender mercies of the Gueux, Parma presently re-established order, made her the seat of his government, restored her municipal rights, and thus, little by little, trade and industry revived.

In the days of Duchess Isabel (1598-1633) and her husband Albert of Austria (1598-1621), on whom on his deathbed King Philip had conferred the sovereignty of the Low Countries, Brussels enjoyed unbroken peace and a period of comparative prosperity. They resided for the most part in the old ducal palace, and were greatly beloved by the burghers: they did what they could to make them forget the miseries of Philip's reign. If they had been able to found a dynasty, it is likely enough the land would have been spared many years of trouble; but, dying without offspring, their heritage reverted to Spain, and shared the misfortunes of that once great nation, now in full decadence. From 1635 to 1714 the Spanish Netherlands was the scene of almost uninterrupted warfare; yet, strangely enough, throughout the whole of this period the masons of Brabant went on building, and, stranger still, were able to erect structures not unworthy of their great traditions.

NOTRE-DAME D'HANSWYCK,
MALINES.

At Brussels, for example, the beautiful Gothic Chapel of Our Lady of Deliverance (1649-1653), the Renaissance Chapel of the Brigitine Nuns (of about the same date), the Chapel of Saint Anne (1655), the Church of the Béguinage (1657), of the Riches Claires (1665-1671), of Notre-Dame de Bon Secours (1668-1673), the Guild Halls in the Grand' Place—no less than seventeen of them, all erected after the bombardment of 1695.

Brussels, of course, was now the capital, and probably too at this time the richest town in the Spanish Netherlands; but cities which had not these advantages somehow or other managed to produce grand buildings. At Louvain we have the Church of Saint Michael (1650-1666), the College of the Holy Trinity (1657), the College of the Holy Ghost (1720); and at Mechlin, the Church of Saint Peter (1677) and the Church of Our Lady of

Hanswyck (1670). These strange rococo creations assuredly cannot compete with the buildings of the fourteen and fifteen hundreds, but they have a certain fantastic charm of their own; they are at least picturesque, and, curiously enough, they bear no trace of the lean years which produced them. Wherefore?

SAINTS PIERRE ET PAUL, MALINES.

The industry, the thrift, the business qualities of the burghers, who still through their representatives in the Estates of Brabant administered the finances of the realm; their inborn love of the beautiful; their traditional skill in creating it; the survival of the mediæval craft guilds and of the mediæval faith: in these things we probably have the answer to the riddle.

The Treaty of Rastatt at the close of the War of the Spanish Succession gave Brabant and the other provinces of the Spanish Netherlands to the Emperor Charles VI., a descendant, in the direct line, of Duke Philip the Handsome, and the domination of the Austrian Hapsburgs continued, save for an interval of four years, till the end of the century. On the whole, the change was for the better. After the long years of excitement the nation needed repose, and under their new rulers the Belgian Estates, as they were now called, vegetated in obscure tranquillity. The opening years of Charles's reign were not, however, without trouble. He was ill represented by his first governor, the Marquis de Prié, who seems to have made no attempt to win the people's confidence. An Italian by birth, and a man of utterly unsympathetic character, avaricious, violent, cold, his impolitic and vexatious fiscal measures irritated the whole country, and the craftsmen of Brussels resisted them.

LA PORTE DE HAL, BRUSSELS.

As time went on the agitation increased, and at last the mob got out of hand, broke into the Chancellery where the Estates of Brabant were sitting, and wrecked the houses of several of the Regent's partisans; and when order was once more restored, De Prié, like a second Alva, thought only of vengeance.

Having treacherously obtained possession of the persons of five of his principal opponents, four of them were condemned to exile, and the fifth to death. This man was François Anneessens, Dean of the Nation of Saint Nicholas, and by trade a turner of chairs; he was seventy-three years of age, a good man and a good citizen, known and esteemed by the whole town. It was said that he had fomented sedition, but in reality he died for defending the traditional rights of his order. His head was struck off in the Grand' Place on the fifth of February 1719. He was the last of the old Brussels guildsmen to give his life for liberty.

The time-honoured civic institutions of Belgium were not destined to survive much longer; they were soon to be swept away by the backwash of the French Revolution—to bring their years to an end, as it were a tale that is told.

VI.—Genealogical Table of the Dukes of Brabant from Philip III. to
Francis

```
Philip III.   = Jeanne (La Folle), daughter of
(Philippe le Beau),  |  Ferdinand of Arragon and
       d. 1506  |  Isabel of Castile

                 |
    +-------------+----------+---------------------+
    |             |          |
    |             |          |
Marguerite = Charles II.   = Isabel      Marie, = Louis,   Ferdinand I.,
van Gheest | (Karlekin),  | of Portugal  Regent  King of   Emperor.
of         | Duke of      |              of the  Hungary   d. 1564
Audenarde  | Brabant      |               Low                |
           | (1506-1555), |              Country              |
           | King of Spain|               from                |
           | (1517-1557), |              1530-1555            |
           | Emperor      |                        |
           | (1519-1556), |                        |
```

```
   | d. 1558      |                              |

   |          +----------------------+       +---------------+

   |                     |                          |

+-------+          +-----------+----------+     +------+------+

   |                 |         |        |         |

   |                 |         |        |         |

Marguerite, = Octavius      Anne, = **Philip IV.** = Elizabeth,  Marie =
Maximilian II.,  Charles,

Regent of  | Farnese,   daughter | (II. of  | daughter of     | Emperor,
d. 1590

the Low    | Duke of  Maximilian | Spain)   | Henry II.,      | d. 1576
   |

Country    | Parma       II. | d. 1598   | of France       |              |

from 1559  |          (4th wife) |        | (3rd wife)      |              |

to 1567    |                 |         |          |                  |

   |                 |         |          |              +--+

   |                 |         |          |                  |

   |                 |         |          |                  |

   Alexander,             Philip III.    Isabel, Regent  =  **Albert**,
Ferdinand II.,

   Prince of             of Spain,     of the Spanish      Duke of
Emperor,

   Parma, Regent        d. 1621      Netherlands       Brabant from   d.
1637

   of the Low         |           from 1621,     1598,            |

   Country from       |             d. 1633      d. 1621          |

   1578 to 1596       |                                           |

             +---------+---------+          +------------------------+

             |         |         |          |

             |         |         |          |

         **Philip V.**      Marie Anne = Ferdinand III.,
```

```
(of Brabant),              |  d. 1658
IV. (of Spain),            |
  d. 1644                  |
      |                    |
      |                    |
Charles III.          Leopold I.,
(of Brabant),         Emperor,
II. (of Spain),         d. 1705
  d. 1700                 |

                      Charles IV.
                      of Brabant, Emperor,
                        d. 1741
                          |
                          |
                      Marie Therese,
                        d. 1780
                          |
                          |
  +-----------+-------------+-----------+
  |           |             |
  |           |             |
Joseph,   Leopold,   Marie Caroline = Ferdinand I. of
d. 1790   d. 1792          | Sicily
    |                      |
    |                      |
  Francis,          Marie-Amélie = Louis-Philippe
  inaugurated              | of France
  at Brussels              |
```

1794, and left |

immediately afterwards |

     Louise = Leopold I.,

       | King of the Belgians

       |

     Leopold II., of Belgium

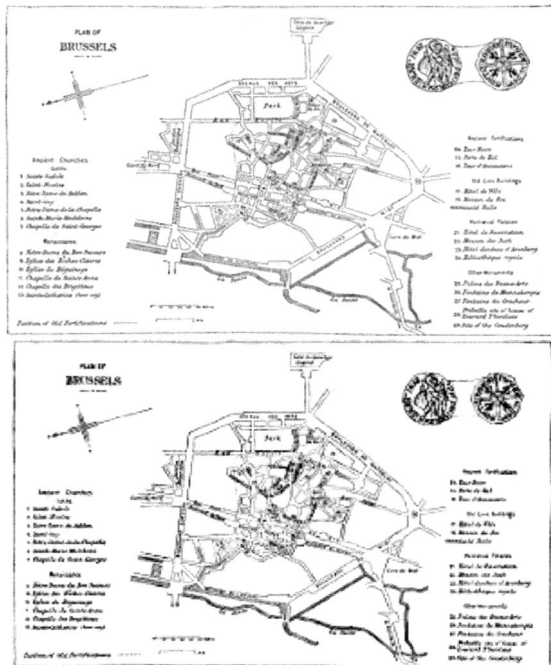

J. M. Dent & Co., London
Banks and Bain, London

Plan of Brussels

Notes

1 l'Ancien Régime, livre 1er, ch. i. § 1.

2 The reigning sovereign of Belgium, King Leopold II., is a descendant of Régnier au Long Col. (*See* Genealogical Table VI.)

3 *Anselme, Gesta episcop. Leod., Mon. Germ. Hist. Script.*, t. vii. p. 225.

4 Histoire de Belgique, vol. i. ch. iii. p. 57 (Brussels, 1902).

5 Lettres de Gerbert, ed. J. Havet, No. 50, p. 47 (Paris, 1889).

6 See *The Story of Bruges*, ch. iii.

7 The old Cloth Hall of Louvain, for example.

8 Guillaume Cornelius of Antwerp. *See* Thomas de Cantimpré (a native of Brussels, born in 1201), *Bonum universale de apibus*, p. 433 (Duaci, 1605). 'Il importe de remarquer toutefois,' notes Pirenne (vol. i. p. 353), 'que ce Cornelius était hérétique, mais, même dans l'église orthodoxe, des prédications analogues à celles de Lambert le Bègue (*see* 'Story of Brussels.' p 233) et l'ardent mysticisme des premières béguines (*see* pp. 228 and 233) devaient agir fortement sur le peuple.'

9 *See* Divæus Annales, 1262.

10 Within, that is, the first line of ramparts. For their circuit, *see* map (dotted line). The outer ramparts were not constructed till some fifty years later (1357-1359): during the reign of Duke Winceslaus. No vestige of them remains but the Porte de Hal. Their site is now occupied by the Outer Boulevards (*see* map).

11 *Chron. Brabant*, t. iii. p. 47.

12 The Castle of Heverlé is still standing; part of it dates from Coutherele's time, but the greater portion was erected in the course of the fifteen hundreds. It is a grand old building, picturesquely situated on the banks of the Dyle, in the midst of a beautiful and well-wooded park. It is one of the country seats of the Duc d'Arenberg, who kindly allows strangers to visit it.

13 A portion of this building, now called La Tour d'Anneessens, is still standing. It is situated in a garden behind a tavern called à la vue de Steenporte, at the entrance to the rue Steenporte, on the left hand side of the way (*see* map). It is not visible from the street, but the landlord is always glad to allow his customers to visit it.

14 T'Serclaes' house was at the end of what was then an impasse, called the Eetengat, now the rue de Berlaimont (*see* map).

15 *See* p. 315.

16 The ducal banner, which displayed on one side the Lion of Brabant and on the other Our Lady, was laid up in the Abbey of Afflighem, hard by Alost. This great benedictine house was the richest and most privileged in the Duchy. Its abbot had the right to wear episcopal robes, and he took precedence of all other ecclesiastics in the Estates of Brabant. Founded in 1080, it was demolished by the French revolutionists towards the close of the seventeen hundreds. Some vestiges of the church and cloistral buildings still remain.

17 *See* p. 299.

18 *See* Genealogical Table IV.

19 *See* p. 289.

20 Chronique du Duc Philippe, chap. lv.

21 De Dynter, c. 161.

22 These men seem to have been near kinsmen of Nicholas de Swaef.

23 *See* De Dynter.

24 *See* page 305.

25 Or Feudal party, as distinguished from the Kabiljauws or Town party, broadly speaking. 'Il n'est guère plus aisé' says Pirenne (Vol. II. p. 165), 'de comprendre l'acharnement qu'elles manifestèrent l'une contre l'autre pendant quatre-vingts ans, (1347-1427) que de découvrir l'origine des appellations par quoi elles se désignèrent. S'il est vrai que les Kabiljauws représentèrent surtout la politique urbaine et les intérêts de la bourgeoisie marchande, il ne l'est pas moins qu'ils ne les représentèrent pas uniquement. On trouve parmi eux de nombreux barons, de même que l'on constate dans le parti des Hoeks, plus spécialement nobiliaire, la présence de plu sieurs villes.

26 This cathedral no longer exists. It was destroyed by the revolutionists in 1793.

27 Until 1349: in that year Charles IV. recognised the principality as a fief of the Duchy of Brabant.

28 See Revue de l'Art Chrétien, 3me livraison—Mai 1902, p. 244.

29 See *Histoire de Belgique*, vol. i. p. 337.

30 See p. 206.

31 De Imitatione Christi, lib. i. cap. i. 3.

32 Since writing this la Commission royale des monuments has intervened, and the proposed act of Vandalism will not be perpetrated.

33 It was made a parish church in 1210. Previous to this date it was a chapel of ease to Saint Gudule's.

34 *See* page 206.

35 For illustrations see pp. 7, 40, 85, 211, 364 and 375.

36 *See* illustrations on pp. 307 and 361.

37 *See* p. 303.

38 *See* p. 271.

39 *See* p. 57.

40 Hugues van der Goes sa vie, et ses œuvres, par Alphonse Wauters, Archiviste de la ville de Bruxelles, etc. (Bruxelles, 1872.)

41 A monastery which formerly stood at the corner of the Marché aux Grains and the Rue de Flandre. The modern *Rue de Jéricho* takes its name from this monastery.

42 La Peinture Flamande, par A.-J. Wauters. (Bruxelles.)

Milton Keynes UK
Ingram Content Group UK Ltd.
UKHW042144281024
450365UK00010B/588

9 789362 923981